The Sound of One Voice

EUGENE FORSEY AND HIS LETTERS TO THE PRESS

In true democratic fashion the great Canadian academic and constitutional aficionado Eugene Forsey chose to air his heartfelt opinions in the broadest of public forums, the letters-to-the-editor page. His foremost concern was the survival and success of Canada as a unified nation, but the demise of the English language, litter, and the misguided aesthetics of government agencies in the placing of public statuary did not escape his at times acerbic pen.

Selecting from some eight hundred letters written over sixty years, Hodgetts weaves together a remarkably full picture of this patriot, whose debates in the press ranged from the role of the governor general, the senate, the judiciary, and the rule of law, to his last battle over the Meech Lake Accord. In answering the question of why such a prominent public figure would attach himself to this particular genre, *The Sound of One Voice* broaches the greater meaning of the letter to the editor, a much neglected area in the literature of democratic politics.

The author's light touch – belying his solid scholarship – combined with the wit and erudition of Forsey's letters, makes for immensely pleasurable reading. Friends made through the press will be delighted to read this collection; those who missed his public voice by a generation will get a veritable crash course in Canada's central national issues.

J.E. HODGETTS is Professor Emeritus at the University of Toronto, President Emeritus at Victoria University, and a Skelton-Clark Visiting Fellow at Queen's University.

The Sound of One Voice

EUGENE FORSEY AND HIS LETTERS TO THE PRESS

Hi Heather
Sorry this is a
late birthday (1999)
but not forgotten
[illegible]
June 21/00

J.E. Hodgetts

UNIVERSITY OF TORONTO PRESS
Toronto Buffalo London

Toronto Buffalo London

Printed in Canada

ISBN 0-8020-7804-4 (paper)
ISBN 0-8020-0755-4 (cloth)

Printed on acid-free paper

Canadian Cataloguing in Publication Data

Forsey, Eugene A. (Eugene Alfred), 1904–1991
The sound of one voice : Eugene Forsey and his letters to the press

Includes bibliographical references and index.
ISBN 0-8020-0755-4 (bound) ISBN 0-8020-7804-4 (pbk.)

1. Forsey, Eugene A. (Eugene Alfred), 1904–1991 – Correspondence. 2. Legislators – Canada – Correspondence. 3. Letters to the editor – Canada. I. Hodgetts, J.E., 1917– . II. Title.

FC601.F67A4 2000 971.06'092 C99-932447-0
F1034.3.F67A4 2000

Every effort has been made to obtain permission to reproduce the letters that appear in this book. Any errors or omissions brought to our attention will be corrected in future printings.

University of Toronto Press acknowledges the financial assistance to its publishing program of the Canada Council for the Arts and the Ontario Arts Council.

This book has been published with the help of a grant from the Humanities and Social Sciences Federation of Canada, using funds provided by the Social Sciences and Humanities Research Council of Canada.

University of Toronto Press acknowledges the financial support for its publishing activities of the Government of Canada through the Book Publishing Industry Development Program (BPIDP).

Canada

Contents

Acknowledgments

My greatest debt is, of course, to the author of the eight hundred or so letters that make up a substantial portion of this book. When R.I.K. Davidson of the University of Toronto Press suggested to Forsey in 1979 that he should undertake such a compilation of his letters himself, Forsey replied: 'I'd rather be sentenced to penal servitude ... Some blighted editor would want to change every second word and he'd want a mass of information about every person or event touched on. My first ancestor in Newfoundland lived to be a hundred. I couldn't do this job if I lived to be two hundred.' This observation did not reach me until after I was well launched; otherwise I might also have had second thoughts about this undertaking, which was first put to me by John Matheson (known among other attributes as the originator of the Canadian flag).

Fortunately, help came from so many quarters that I was encouraged to soldier on in the face of Forsey's dire predictions, thereby acquiring debts that require extended acknowledgment. I began with the enthusiastic support of Eugene Forsey's daughters, Margaret and Helen. I am especially grateful to Helen Forsey who, in the course of preparing a biography of her father, has generously shared revealing tidbits from his personal correspondence which I have shamelessly pirated. At the outset, too, Professor Peter Neary, who had intended to produce a compilation of Forsey's letters but was obliged to abandon the project, graciously ceded the field to me and turned over some of his preliminary findings.

A hint from Jeffrey Simpson of the *Globe and Mail*, pointing out the underground, follow-up correspondence that Forsey was wont to carry on with journalists after he had pilloried them in published letters, led me to poll his 'victims' for anecdotal addenda. All of this information proved invaluable for Part One, 'Forsey Meets the Press.' A journalistic contingent from the *Globe and Mail*, Forsey's primary outlet, whose comments were most helpful, includes Senator Richard J. Doyle, A. Roy Megarry, Donn Downey, and Jack Kapica (a one-time letters' editor himself and author of *Shocked and Appalled: A Hundred Years of Letters to the Globe and Mail*, a unique and most useful volume). John Kalbfleisch of the *Montreal Gazette* put me on to a network of journalists who had been with the *Gazette* (Forsey's third most popular outlet), and the *Journal* and *Citizen* of Ottawa: my thanks to Tim Creery, Charles King, Christopher Young, and John Grace. Robert Fulford most generously shared his recollections of his days at *Saturday Night* and more generally his views on the letter to the editor. Douglas Fisher, proving that his early training as librarian and archivist has never deserted him, hand-delivered a thick bundle of material, replete with wily musings on the strategic use of letters to the press during elections, which must be saved for another day.

Response from academic colleagues, when asked to share their reminiscences of Forsey, were equally forthcoming. Several of them were associates of Forsey during the years he taught at Carleton University: Paul Fox, Peyton Lyon, David Farr, Michael Oliver. Professor John Wilson provided recollections both academic and personal covering Forsey's brief period at the University of Waterloo. Equally helpful were Professors Peter Russell and James Mallory, who shared with Forsey an expertise on matters constitutional; thanks, also, to Ramsay Cook and the late Kenneth McNaught for their personal reminiscences. I am particularly indebted to Dr Frank MacKinnon, one of Forsey's students in political science at McGill in the 1930s, who shared a treasure trove of letters and memoranda that Forsey had showered on him throughout a half-century of shared interests.

G.C. Eglington, legal adviser to the Joint Select Committee of the Senate and House of Commons on Regulations and Other Statutory Instruments when Forsey was a member and co-chairman, provided illuminating insight into Forsey's compulsive letter-writing habits, especially when ensconced in Mr Eglington's law office. I must also thank one of the front-line letter-writing activists, Mr C.N.R. Stewart, who may by now be closing in on Forsey's record and who has shared with me his astute observations on the process.

For the tracking down of the Forsey letters, I am greatly indebted to Amanda Valpy, librarian at the *Globe and Mail*, who provided me with microfiche copies of Forseyana references, prior to the Infoglobe indexing which began only in November 1977. The starting point of this expedition was, of course, the Forsey Papers in the National Archives of Canada. I join the legion of other users of this fine institution in thanking the staff for facilitating my access to, and use of, the Forsey Papers. My special thanks to William Ambrose, volunteer research assistant, who deployed his stamp-collecting expertise in assiduously tracking down in over 350 microfilm reels the elusive records of the *Ottawa Journal* from 1950 until its demise in 1980; in addition, he scouted every issue of the *Montreal Gazette* for the decade of the 1930s when Forsey's letter-writing was taking off.

I am especially indebted to Professor C.E.S. Franks for his invaluable comments on a preliminary draft, and to Diane Mew whose editing skills over the years have rescued my prose from egregious literary blunders. The editorial staff of the University of Toronto Press, as usual, have been unfailingly generous with advice and encouragement, though all of the above are held blameless for such blemishes that may still remain.

A final vote of thanks goes to Queen's University and my old Department of Political Studies for successive renewals of a Visiting Skelton-Clark Fellowship that provided me with the physical facilities and collegial support so essential to the completion of this project.

Permission to publish the letters selected for this work has been sought and generously given, not only by the administrators of the Forsey Papers themselves but also by his many correspondents and fellow writers of missives to the press. If I have, perchance, overlooked any such contributor, I trust my sins of omission will be granted absolution.

Had Forsey not foresworn the task of compiling this collection of his letters to the press, I am sure he would have joined with me in dedicating his work to all those letter-writers who share with him the belief that 'even one voice, shouting a good case loud enough and long enough, may produce some effect.'

J.E.H.
August 1999

The Sound of One Voice

EUGENE FORSEY AND HIS LETTERS TO THE PRESS

Introduction

It is said that a man can be known by the company he keeps. In Eugene Forsey's case it might also be true to say that a man can be known by the letters he writes. This collection of Forsey's letters to the press was not undertaken with such a specific biographical objective, since one would be more likely to find clues to his life and character in his private correspondence, which is not included here. Nevertheless, as I tracked down the many hundreds of letters which Forsey addressed to the press, it became apparent that his favourite mode of communicating with the public also illuminated the intellectual enthusiasms which he passionately pursued in the public press, all the while seeing himself as an exceedingly private person living 'a life on the fringe.'

Forsey's assembled papers provide ample evidence that in his devotion to the epistolary art he was a twentieth-century throwback to the great letter-writers of Victorian and earlier times. His letters to the press appear to be a natural extension to the public domain of the prolific private correspondence he conducted throughout his life with an extraordinarily wide network of family, friends, colleagues, passing acquaintances, and major public figures. Yet Forsey's lifelong dedication to the public letter is cause for speculation about the compulsion that would drive a person to favour this form of communication when singularly blessed with access to so many other venues from which to pronounce on the world around him. For years he was an academic with a powerful platform from which to address (and dress down) captive student audiences. For nearly three decades he was director of research for the Canadian Congress of Labour (later the Canadian Labour Congress) and a prime spokesman for the interests of organized labour. Although he made four attempts, he was never able to win a seat in the elective assembly of a local, provincial, or federal authority. However, during the decade of the 1970s he was an appointed member of the Senate of Canada, where his active and vocal participation in no way diminished his correspondence with the press. With growing acclaim as an informed and entertaining speaker, Forsey also had access to a wide variety of public platforms offered by academic groups and the banquet circuits of Canadian clubs, service clubs, church groups, and local historical associations. He was equally popular (and available) for radio talks and, later, television appearances. Surely, few if any other contributors to the letters columns of the press could lay claim to such an array of alternative modes of communication – which only deepens the mystery of motivation.

As will become clear, although his letters were often launched with that element of impish gamesmanship that motivates the professional letter-to-the-editor writer – one who proudly notches his gun (or trusty typewriter, in Forsey's case) and keeps score after each published submission – this was clearly not the major compulsion driving Forsey. His reaction was so automatic, with such Pavlovian ardour, that even when an offending newspaper had no letters column available, he could not resist firing off a heated letter to the editor.

Pursuit of the answer to the mystery of motivation leads to a consideration of the place of the 'letter to the editor' from the perspective both of the sender and of the recipient newspaper. In short, the letter to the editor joins its chief exploiter as the focus of the first chapter of this book. In tracing the association of Forsey, the letter-writer, with the press, it is clear that the 'Editor' addressed is more often than not a columnist, a reporter, or another letter-writer. It is also clear that the relationship between the press and Forsey was symbiotic. Forsey needed the press but the press needed Forsey even more; indeed, the press might be said at times to have feasted off Forsey's contributions, treating him almost as an unpaid columnist, while promoting his credentials as an, if not *the*, expert on Canadian constitutional matters.

Chapter 2 provides a decade-by-decade census of Forsey's letters over a period of close to sixty years, dating back to his student days at McGill and covering a host of newspapers of which the *Globe and Mail*, from the 1970s on, became the favoured recipient. Forsey himself claimed to have no idea how many letters he had written but one can safely say that the approximately eight hundred identified in our census as published is a conservative assessment of his total output. Without the temerity to claim complete and total coverage of all published letters, in their sheer number and the variety of recipient journals, Forsey's output is surely unchallenged. Also unparalleled is his high acceptance rate in a competition for publication that is notoriously fierce. Attesting to his fame as letter-writer is the accolade vouchsafed to no other: the four cartoons of himself in the *Globe and Mail*, three of which, with the kind permission of that newspaper, have been reproduced at appropriate places in this book.

The census of the letters chronicles by decades landmarks in Forsey's career and serves to preface the presentation in Part Two of a selection of Forsey's letters, grouped in accordance with the major themes addressed. These themes begin on the lighter side with Forsey appearing as Literary Guardian, to be followed by Forsey the Civic Censor and Moral Arbiter. Then, as a result of increasing public appearances, there appear the corrective and self-exculpatory letters: 'You've Got Me Wrong.' Many of these were, in a sense, self-induced because of Forsey's rapid-fire delivery, peppered with colourful *bon mots*, and the inability to resist hyperbolic overkill.

A substantial number of letters were signed in Forsey's capacity as director of research for the Canadian Congress of Labour. These have not been given a separate grouping because the approach to the topics dealt with differed in no way from his views both before and after his formal association with the labour movement. Indeed, one gets the impression that his colleagues in the CCL sometimes thought he misspent his time chasing constitutional exotica. However that may be, Forsey, ever the independent, was always more comfortable speaking on his own account, even though he might be signing a letter in one of his many official capacities.

Finally, and dominating the selection in terms of their number and the importance of the themes addressed, are the letters he wrote in his capacity as a 'Constitutional Authority' – a title which he publicly disclaimed but privately took very seriously and which was nonetheless deserved for all that it was media-conferred. Under this rubric there are issues associated with the institutions of government: the role and status of the governor general in respect of the conventions relating to the operation of a system of responsible parliamentary–cabinet government; his views on the Senate of Canada, much the most debated of our governmental institutions; the functions of the judiciary in upholding the rule of law and interpreting the constitution with its relatively new Charter of Rights and Freedoms. Ranging beyond these specific institutions, and bringing to a fitting climax this assemblage of letters, are those letters addressed to the very foundations of Canada: the symbols of nationhood, the ever-present threat of Quebec's separation from the union, and the equally perennial problem of amending the Canadian constitution to meet the challenges of the approaching millennium.

This book was initially undertaken with the thought that reproduction of Forsey's views on this last overarching theme, as found in his letters, might contribute to the ongoing debate over the future of Canada. However, the richness, variety, and humour of Forsey's offerings on a number of other themes irresistibly led to a broadening of the original focus so as to produce a more rounded picture of the letter-writer. Moreover, the letter to the editor – a singularly unexamined subject – acquired a status of its own, affording as it did an opportunity to explore the relationship of citizen to press and the response of the press to the implicit assumption that it has an important role to play in a democracy by providing access for a wide range of opinion from the attentive public of readers. In this respect, with Eugene

Forsey being perhaps the chief exploiter of this access, one could scarcely find a better model for such an inquiry.

There are those who, during the course of our ongoing debate over Canada's future, have sadly asked: 'Where is Forsey when we need him most?' Despite the passage of years, such is the enduring nature of the debate over the future of Canada that readers may still find enlightenment and inspiration in this selection of Forsey's letters on this encompassing theme, which preoccupied him throughout his active life. It is fitting that this collection concludes with the last letter Forsey wrote, two weeks before his death. It is a passionate and eloquent plea to preserve Canada as more than a mere blob on the map. Should the resurrection of his words through this assemblage of his letters to the press inspire and instil in others the dedicated loyalty to civic virtue and a fair dominion from sea to sea, epitomized by Eugene Forsey, the 'sound of one voice' will still continue to be heard throughout the land.

PART ONE: FORSEY MEETS THE PRESS

CHAPTER ONE

Forsey's Letters to the Editor

The letters-to-the-editor columns have been described by Norman Webster, formerly editor-in-chief of the *Globe and Mail*, as the newspapers' 'prime editorial real estate' for correspondent readers.[1] In this light, the letter to the editor appears to support one of the principles endorsed by the Canadian Newspapers Publishers Association: 'Access. The newspaper is a forum for the expression in its columns of disparate and conflicting views. It should give expression to the interests of minorities as well as majorities, and of the less powerful elements in society.' Endorsing this principle, the Royal Commission on Newspapers, reporting in 1981, concluded: 'good newspapers are essential to the democratic process in a free society. That is at the root of the special kind of social responsibility which makes the newspapers more than a business.'[2]

From a business rather than a social perspective, a lively letters page may serve as a gauge of readers' attraction to, even approval of, the newsgathering choices of reporters and, more importantly, their reaction to the positions taken on issues which anonymous editors and columnists with bylines have chosen to highlight. Richard Doyle, reflecting on his years as editor of the *Globe and Mail*, claimed that 'the letters department produced not only the *Globe*'s best writing but the most interesting and best informed correspondence in all the wide countryside. Or so it seemed in the uncertain world of newspapering where the daily battle cry was "Don't assume a god-damned thing."'[3]

One seasoned newsman, Robert Fulford, injects a note of caution when viewing this essentially rosy picture of a serendipitous relationship. The 'real estate,' he suggests, is too valuable to be left to the free-wheeling mercies of the reader. It requires careful nurturing and watchful editorial control. After all, the letters page is a perfect illustration of the biblical adage that many are summoned but few are chosen. And in the choosing lies the discretionary control which the editorial staff exerts in shaping the contents, the *weltanschauung*, so to speak, of the entire newspaper. Careful editing, in Fulford's view, is the secret to successful letters columns.

> An element of cunning is involved: the editor gets to know after a while what letters will provide more letters, possibly better ones. The editor also realizes that there are a few correspondents (Forsey above all others, in my lifetime) whose contributions are more valuable than those of paid employees. The editor takes good care of these people, not necessarily running all of their letters but certainly responding to anything they send. What the editor wants most, of course, is not balance but an interesting feature; fairness has only a little to do with it, I think.

Recollecting his own practice while editor of *Saturday Night*, Fulford claimed he 'emphasized negative letters. I reasoned that the original article had aired the view of the contributor and now the other side (or several other sides) should be heard. Over the years I began to realize that not everyone was pleased with this ... People in the advertising department thought that advertisers would assume it contained all the letters received and therefore demonstrated that readers didn't like the magazine.'[4]

From the viewpoint of both press and letter-writer, the letters page might be likened to question period in the legislature, which is used primarily by the opposition to call the government to account for alleged misdeeds or failures to act. The backbencher shares with the letter-writer the same problem of access: for the legislator, getting a place on the order paper and, in the writer's case, surviving editorial screening. Both letter and question period also share the same tendency to stress a reactive, critical approach rather than a forum for initiating or proposing action. There is more than a hint of subversion for both: potential discomfiture of the government in the one instance and the satisfaction of the 'Gotcha!' response for the writer. C.N.R. Stewart, one of the most assiduous practitioners of the letter format, captures this note when he speaks of himself as one of the 'Front Street Irregulars,' representing Everyman.[5]

In some respects, the letters column offers its users more than the question period affords members of the legislature: not only does it offer the opportunity to hold editors, columnists, and reporters to account, but it also provides a platform from which to engage in dialogue with other letter-writers. In this latter respect, the letters column ideally may be said to contribute to the objectives of participatory democracy. Still a far cry from the Athenian forum, it may be said, but for those who manage to gain access, a not insignificant contribution to the process of alerting and educating those members of the public deemed to be attentive because of their newspaper-reading habits.

Contemporary critics of parliamentary government bemoan the failure of legislatures to serve as formulators of policy and as critics and checks on overweening executives. The call for broader forms of popular participation, embraced in the notion of participatory democracy, became a rallying cry in the late 1960s and 1970s, as the governing structures not only of the nation but also of such venerable institutions as universities and professional guilds like those dominating medicine, came under attack. An updated version of participatory democracy, to accord with the envisaged miracles of personal intercommunication to be wrought by electronic technology, has now emerged in the form of a communitarian movement. The thought is that the state should facilitate debate outside the traditional legislative venues by harnessing the new technology to create interactive forums to carry on a continuing public dialogue over the values that should guide public policy into the next millennium.

The idea that the internet might become a surrogate for the Athenean forum may, at this stage, be relevant only for those amongst the 'chattering class' who possess and are comfortable with using the new technology. Even without looking this far forward, the new technology may already be making an impact on the letters page. Our Front Street Irregular, C.N.R. Stewart, who is so low-tech that he claims to deliver his letters to the press by bicycle, has analysed his acceptance rate in light of the recent advent of e-mail. Assuming that perhaps not more than one out of ten offerings will be selected, there would seem to be a decided advantage in getting one's submission in early. Stewart found that his acceptance rate had declined significantly since e-mail had been introduced. Was his 'snail-mail' the cause, he plaintively asks, or was it because he 'just couldn't cut the mustard anymore?'[6]

Why Forsey Wrote Letters

Eugene Forsey would have shared Stewart's concern and, as a techno-peasant, would have found it difficult to participate on the websites envisaged by the communitarian movement. Even the telephone was, for him, an instrument to be avoided if at all possible. However, in the only published declaration of his reasons for writing letters to the press, Forsey clearly endorsed the more traditionalist notion of participatory democracy and, not incidentally, provided the inspiration for the main title of this study. In the conclusion to a letter-cum-article in the *Ottawa Journal* on 2 January 1974 ('When Forsey Writes Letters He Can Cause a Lot of Rows'), Forsey declared: 'Perhaps letters to the editor may be a useful form of participatory democracy. Perhaps even one voice, shouting a good case loud enough and long enough, may produce some effect, even on ideas, policies and governments which seem impregnable.'

In his memoirs Forsey observed that he caught the writing bug, during his period at Oxford as a Rhodes scholar, from his exposure to the godfather of the genre, *The Times* of London.[7] Even before this period, however, Forsey had begun his career as a writer of letters to the press when as an undergraduate he favoured the *McGill Daily* with his offerings. In the 1930s, as a lecturer at McGill, he honed his letter-writing skills primarily in the *Montreal Gazette*, largely on economic and social issues. However, it was the grand battle in 1943 with the renowned editor of the *Winnipeg Free Press*, John W. Dafoe, that 'blooded' Forsey as a constitutional authority and set up the widening circle of his epistolary contributions.

Forsey's persistance in using the letters page of the daily newspaper is surprising. He was surely not driven by the motives that correspondent C.N.R. Stewart only half-facetiously attributed to himself in November 1993: 'I just have to see my name in the paper,' he wrote, 'and the only other easy (I've never been given to over-exertion) way is to die which seems a little extreme and what can you do for an encore?' Forsey's distinguished career might have been thought to be cause for a drying-up of his letters to the press. Yet such was not the case, for the use of alternative platforms for airing his views created the need to produce letters to offset misinterpretations of his utterances in these other forums. Indeed, one of the most impressive aspects of Forsey's overall contribution to public discourse was what economists would term the 'multiplier effect' which Forsey's performance in one theatre had on other venues from which he made pronouncements.

Whether as research director, university teacher, senator, or just plain constitutional expert, Eugene Forsey was always good copy for the press and a readily available mother-lode of information to be mined mercilessly by inquiring reporters whenever a constitutional crisis surfaced. Family members describe the ambivalence of Forsey under such pressure: on the one hand the feeling of being burdened, almost abused, by the pressing inquiries of journalists; on the other hand the sense of public obligation amounting almost to a duty to respond to each and every request. Forsey expressed it best himself in a round-robin Christmas letter to friends, shortly before his death: 'My bad temper keeps me spluttering to the newspapers over the nonsense that so often appears in them. Also, a ridiculously large number of people regard me as some sort of constitutional maid-of-all-work, and whenever anything goes wrong in the body politic expect me to kiss the place and make it well.' (Was Forsey perhaps aware of a letter written by 'Victorian' to *The Times* who wrote: 'To have a letter in your columns is frequently felt to be the duty of the distinguished; it is even the ambition of the obscure'?)[8]

Two clues to Forsey's conception of letter-writing as an inescapable public obligation have surfaced in his papers. Typed on the back of a program for a seminar on labour relations at Princeton University in June 1948 is the following:

> Ryerson's quotation from Macaulay: 'No misrepresentation should be allowed to pass unrefuted. When a silly letter makes its appearance in the corner of a provincial newspaper, it will not do to say "What stuff!" We must remember that such statements, constantly reiterated and seldom answered, will assuredly be believed!'[9]

Perhaps more revealing, because it was written at the height of Forsey's unsuccessful battle to retain his teaching position at McGill, was this lament to his mother, in a letter dated 21 January 1940:

> Very few of us [obviously referring to the professoriate] will stand up and defend ourselves or take the part we should in guiding public opinion. Then also there is this poisonous Canadian tradition that no one (except fools and knaves) should ever write to the paper. So the Hepburns and the Drews and the rest of the clowns, boors, ignoramuses, scallawags and noodles go on their way rejoicing, and rule the country.[10]

Clearly, these were the convictions that motivated Forsey throughout his life, leading him to make himself available to all requests, no matter the consequences for his increasingly fragile health. Forsey's private and public correspondence at the height of the Meech Lake debates, for example, testifies to the passionate commitment that energized him, even as it threatened to overwhelm his frail physique. He even summoned his own press conference to supplement his letters and other public appearances to present his case against the accord – although, to authenticate his action, he had nothing more to draw on than his personal reputation as *the* constitutional expert, conferred by the press itself as a result of his letters. Perhaps it was with remorse for the impositions of his journalistic brethren that Christopher Young, in the *Montreal Gazette* of 22 February 1991, concluded his obituary on Forsey with these words: 'He was not the type to rest in peace, but may he rest where no reporters call.'

In the late 1930s, when Forsey was becoming addicted to the letter-to-the-editor form of communicating, the genre was certainly not as well developed in Canada as in England, and newspapers varied widely in the space and importance they attributed to correspondence. In 1971, contributing to the debate on the report of a select committee of the Senate on the mass media, Forsey commented:

> There is only partial reference to this in the report, but one change that has come over at least some of the newspapers in this country in the last 30 to 40 years ... is the extra prominence given to, and enhanced quality of, the letters to the editor. Here I certainly cannot speak impartially, because perhaps my sole title to eminence now is that I am an ardent writer of letters to the editor. Indeed, a year or so ago, when I was teaching at Carleton University, the chairman of the department discovered that the younger members of the department had absolutely no idea who I was until, after thinking about it, they exclaimed, 'Oh, he is the chap who writes letters to *The Globe and Mail*.' [Letters in Canada, Forsey continued, have] now begun to assume something of the salutary function of letters of the better kind to the *London Times* ... But we do have good letters here, and if they have assumed an extra importance it is a good thing they have, because as a result of letters to the editor, there are some very useful contributions made to public discussion today.[11]

Forsey's observation that the letter to the editor had received little attention in the committee's report could also apply to the royal commission study of the press chaired by Tom Kent some ten years later. Indeed, apart from Jack Kapica's compilation of letters to the *Globe and Mail*, there appears to be only one scholarly examination of the Canadian genre, a useful chapter in Richard V. Ericson, et al., *Negotiating Control: A Study of News Sources*, and a brief study by the University of Alberta's Institute of Law Research and Reform, *Defamation: Fair Comment and Letters to the Editor.*[12]

In his introduction to his collection of letters, Kapica places Forsey among 'the genuine recidivists – those who continuously hone their quills while contemplating the editor's jugular.' The motives of such letter-writers he finds difficult to explain. He suggests they usually evolve from responsibilities as a designated spokesman for some group or other and then 'their talents quickly transcend the merely functional purpose of writing.'[13] But Forsey did not need the incentive of being an official spokesman for labour to encourage his letter-writing: he was well launched before 1941 when he assumed office at the Canadian Congress of Labour. Indeed, I think it can be argued that Forsey, ever the independent maverick, was never completely comfortable acting as a spokesman for anybody but himself.

Under whatever auspices he wrote, Forsey's love of argument and powerful command of the written and spoken word gave a sparkle and spice to his letters, whatever the subject matter. Letters' editors always maintained that they could recognize 'a Forsey' before they reached the signature.

The authors of *Negotiating Control* categorized letters to the editor according to the purpose served: 'To raise an issue; offer additional input to ongoing story; remedy imbalance; correct facts, or to simply amuse.'[14] Forsey's letters were sufficiently varied to serve all these objectives, although the majority fell in the corrective/instructive category, even as they often provided amusement. Essentially, Forsey used letters not to propose but to dispose. Therein lay their strength and attractiveness for publication. His colourful, often astringent, phrases were well adapted to demolition rather than construction, to conservation rather than innovation. Forsey's command of the facts and his oft-stated assertion that he had never been caught out in error amounted to what an old colleague called an obsession. This obsession did not match that of Dickens's Mr Gadgrind, who proclaimed: 'Teach these boys and girls nothing but Facts ... In this life we want nothing but Facts, sir; nothing but Facts!' Nevertheless, when coupled with his phenomenal total recall capacity (boldly illustrated in his memoirs by his production of the serial number of the beloved bicycle he took to Oxford some sixty years before!) and his ability to deploy the facts, liberally laced with apt quotations from the classics, Forsey was a formidable protagonist in any battle of letters.[15] In short, his mastery of the 'Gotcha!' technique made him immensely popular with all but his victims – and even they were grudgingly disposed to acknowledge they had been bested by a master.

One of Forsey's oldest colleagues, the late Donald Creighton, has captured the essence of the Forsey style and manner in his introduction to a collection of Forsey's occasional papers, entitled *Freedom and Order*. Forsey's historical method, Creighton contended, was characterized by 'thoroughness, exactitude and trenchancy.' The other weapons in his intellectual armoury were 'his epigrammatic wit and controversial skill,' while 'irony, satire, comic exaggeration, and a copious knowledge of the rich vocabulary of denigration, were all brought into play.'[16]

Forsey's standard approach when combating an anonymous editor, identifiable journalist, or other letter-writer was to show them woefully wanting in their version of the facts, purveyors of 'constitutional fairy tales' of which he was quick to disabuse them by deploying a formidable array of the real facts. Someone has coined the expression 'Infoslam' to characterize this form of debate, and clearly Forsey was a master of the technique. Of course, it could boomerang on a less knowledgeable exponent. But Forsey was seldom challenged and, if he was, nearly always had the last word.

Indeed, so famous and feared had Forsey's reputation for factual accuracy become among the journalistic fraternity that Donn Downey confessed towards the end of a three-column résumé of Forsey's career at the time of his death that 'This obituary was shown to Mr. Forsey before his death and he wrote back that it was accurate but for "a few minor points." He then listed several pages of corrections, most of which are incorporated in the story.' This astonishing concession to Forsey's obsession with getting the facts right was granted to only one other person while still alive, the proprietor of the newspaper, but with obviously different motives and with completely different result – return of the draft obituary without comment![17]

There is a danger, to be sure, in depending on superior command of the facts to overwhelm one's opponent. It is one thing to claim victory in a debate by proving you are the only true purveyor of the facts. But Forsey sometimes took the unwarranted step of assuming that because his facts were correct and his opponent's were wrong, then the only acceptable conclusion to be drawn was his own. In the great debate with Forsey, precipitated by the late Donald Smiley over the propriety of invoking the War Measures Act during the October Crisis of 1970 in Quebec, both proponents were guilty of taking that extra step of assuming their own totally opposed conclusions were the only acceptable ones – a particularly dangerous assumption when the 'real facts' were (and remain?) much less certain than the ones with which Forsey customarily did battle.

The colourful words, the apt quotations which stood ready at Forsey's command and made press and public so receptive to his letters, posed a more obvious challenge to Forsey than the most unlikely chance that he might be caught out in a dispute over facts. Anyone who ever witnessed the crisply assertive and colourfully pungent Forsey on a platform or on television would be able to conjure up the same persona from his letters. Their charm and instant attraction, to be found in his memoirs as well, derive from the sense that we are hearing the man speaking. But the spoken word, especially when the speaker prefers the off-the-cuff spontaneity of sketchy notes rather than a stodgy reading from prepared script, can lead to misunderstanding and consequent challenges. As Forsey's reputation as a public performer spread, many of his letters were devoted to what he regarded as inaccurate reporting of his remarks, misrepresentation of his political philosophy (the accusation, for example, that he was a communist), or misinterpretation of an aside that he had been unable to resist.

Curiously, for such a meticulous wordsmith, Forsey seemed to have lacked sensitivity to the power of words to cause personal affront and, perhaps more importantly, the possibility that excessively coloured wordplay could undermine the very case for which he was arguing. One of his close associates, commenting on this proclivity, claimed that 'he sometimes acknowledged a lack of restraint and told me more than once that the reason he did not drink was not principle but fear that he would not be able to exercise self-restraint.'[18] Might it be also possible that this inconsistency sprang from the differences between the public persona, as expressed through the letters to the press, and a private persona to be found in his personal dealings, one on one? The many replies solicited for the purposes of this study from journalists, colleagues, and acquaintances who had occasion to be touched by Forsey's critiques are virtually unanimous in confirming this dichotomy. Even those most seriously impaled by Forsey's public pen invariably concluded with the saving assessment: 'but ... what a kind and unassuming person he was.'

One might speculate that for the exceedingly private person that made up one side of Forsey, the letter to the editor presented the opportunity to distance himself from his targeted opponent, just as with the speaker's platform or debate in Parliament where the speaker is separated from his opponents. Thus distanced, Forsey was relieved of any inhibitions he might otherwise have had, enabling him to endulge the linguistic hyperbole that ornamented his public utterances. Setting aside Forsey's early and unsuccessful forays as a political candidate in the 1940s, there seem to be no instances where Forsey took to the streets demonstrating for a cause – although he made an exception when he embarked on the campaign trail for Pierre Trudeau in 1972. The word was his sword and his verbal engagements, however passionately professed, always preserved that distance between his private person and the waspish, sometimes angry, public instructor and civic censor revealed in his letters.

In an introspective letter of 20 November 1951 to Arthur Meighen, perhaps the man he most admired in public life, Forsey revealed a self-awareness, worthy of Hamlet. Expressing relief after his unsuccessful adventures in electoral politics – the last two ventures as a CCF candidate against George Drew – he writes: 'I am really glad I am out of politics. It leaves me much freer to call nonsense by its right name.' Then, in a remarkably perceptive appraisal, he continues, 'My tragedy, if that's not too strong a word, is that I'm too radical to be a good Conservative and too conservative to be a good radical. I am also too academic to be a good trade unionist, and too good a trade unionist to be a good academic man; too partisan to be independent, and too independent to be a good party man.'[19] With such a view of himself, it is no surprise that Forsey selected as the title for his memoirs, *A Life on the Fringe*.

Relations with the Editor

Generally speaking, for English-language newspapers, 'the editor' is rather like 'the corporation' in business, an abstract personality. In some of the French-language newspapers, such as *Le Devoir,* the signed editorial affords letter-writers the opportunity to engage in a personal debate rather than taking on the opinionated anonymous collective 'editor' in the English press. Where the letter-writer has a bone to pick with an editorial, the tradition in the French press (possibly a European tradition as opposed to a British tradition?) affords the semblance of a head-to-head debate. This was a situation in which Forsey revelled, for he always denounced letter-writing opponents for hiding behind pseudonyms. (In his memoirs he writes of his delight in unmasking one opponent who, in his duelling with Forsey in the *Montreal Gazette* during the 1930s and 1940s, had adopted some seventeen aliases.[20])

In earlier days of more personalized journalism, even in the

English-language press, little care was taken to preserve the notion of editorial anonymity. In perhaps his most dramatic epistolary encounter with an editor, Forsey crossed swords with the redoubtable John W. Dafoe of the *Winnipeg Free Press* in 1943. Ostensibly, the controversy arose from Dafoe's review of Forsey's recently published doctoral dissertation, *The Royal Power of Dissolution in the British Commonwealth.* A large portion of the book was devoted to the King–Byng dispute of 1926 wherein Governor General Byng had refused Mackenzie King's request for a dissolution of Parliament but subsequently had been obliged to grant it to King's successor as prime minister, Arthur Meighen. The central constitutional issue involved competing views of the role of the representative of the Crown in Canada, particularly whether, in addition to the purely ornamental, symbolic powers of the governor general, there was also a discretionary or reserve power to act independently of the advice of the first minister.

What is of interest here is why, with his front-page headlines blazoning the allied breakthrough in the North African campaign, Dafoe elected to devote five full columns of virulent prose to his review. Forty years after the event, not unfairly, Forsey described the articles, 'un-signed but unmistakeably his [i.e. Dafoe's]' as 'nicely compounded of outright mendacity, gross distortion, and sheer Billingsgate.'[21] Forsey's immediate reaction (letter of 22 May 1943), given the provocation, was comparatively mild, beginning as follows:

> Your review ... is compounded of about equal parts of misrepresentation and abuse. Anything in it which bears any resemblance to argument is already answered in the book itself. Of the abuse, I need only say that most of it would form a very suitable description of the review. Of the misrepresentation, I think your readers are entitled to a few of the more glaring examples. [There then followed four enumerated detailed paragraphs.]

Dafoe kept the pot boiling by appending an 'Ed. Note' in which he wrote dismissively:

> We are quite prepared to leave the points at issue between us – not only those upon which he thinks he can put up some form of argument but also the more serious censures which he finds it advisable to duck – to the judgment of our readers and the public. That judgment, we are confident, will be that as an objective study in history Mr Forsey's magnum opus has no claims to respect; as a partisan diatribe designed to support pre-determined conclusions it doubtless has attractions for those who share his hopes and hatreds.

Despite this provocation, at the time Forsey was initially inclined to avoid getting into 'this mug's game,' in which the editor would inevitably have the last word. Finally, however, he decided to respond, encouraged from the right by Arthur Meighen and from the left by Tommy Douglas to 'let Dafoe have it with both barrels.' Dafoe accorded three full columns of the 12 June 1943 issue to Forsey's fifteen-point reply and an additional full column to a second Forsey letter responding to related matters arising out of Dafoe's 3 June article on the policies of the CCF party. However, in lieu of a reply couched as an appended 'Ed. Note,' Dafoe once again used three dense columns of his editorial page to respond to 'Excitable Letter-Writer' and, as Forsey anticipated, to declare closure in no uncertain terms:

> The Free Press is through with Mr Forsey as the supposed impartial student of constitutional matters. It is not interested in Mr Forsey, the partisan advocate adept in all the tricks of one-sided argument. This is how he stands revealed to the public by his own words; and this is how he will be regarded in the future when he addresses the public through the columns of journals, which take him at a slight percentage of his valuation, or by some pretentious volume conceived and produced in the style and manners of the work to which the Free Press has given an unnecessary measure of attention.

Dafoe may have concluded that he had won this particular battle but Forsey never relinquished the view that no genuine student of the constitution (including the eminent political scientist R. MacGregor Dawson) had ever disproved his facts and that subsequent political events involving the governor general confirmed his interpretation of the reserve power vested in the office. In the event, the Dafoe–Forsey exchange set off the process by which Forsey became popularly known through his succeeding letters as *the* constitutional expert with whom one tangled at one's peril and to whom it was likely the last word would invariably belong.

The peculiar gloves-off character of this exchange was never to be repeated. That it should have arisen over such an apparently abstruse constitutional issue is to be explained by the editor's personal agenda as well as by his style, which was, according to one biographer, honed by his work as a political reporter – 'the art of writing political invective, an art he continued to practice for the rest of his life.'[22] Dafoe's personal agenda was his partisan support of the Liberal party and his unwavering loyalty to Mackenzie King, its leader, and particularly his antagonism to that symbol of colonialism and empire, the governor general. Forsey's sin was to have written a book apparently defending the symbol and vesting the office with more than Walter Bagehot's 'dignified' functions. Moreover, the other main participant in the King–Byng dispute, Arthur Meighen, was Forsey's personal hero but Dafoe's sworn political foe. To top it all, Forsey was an active member of the CCF party with which Dafoe carried on a vicious vendetta, apparently viewing it as the entering wedge of the Red Menace.

Since Forsey always fretted that Dafoe took advantage of his editor's office to have the final word, perhaps here we may give Forsey his closing assessment of Dafoe, carried in a 1958 letter to Murray Donnelly, who had announced his intentions to undertake a biography of Dafoe. Commenting that he did not envy him the task, Forsey was reminded of Goldsmith's lines on Burke:

> Who, born for the universe, narrowed his mind,
> And to party gave up what was meant for mankind.

'I have often said,' Forsey continued, 'that on anything which did not touch the vital interests of the Liberal party, he was a great man; but that on anything that did touch the vital interests of the Liberal party, he was just an ordinary, common or garden liar and crank.'[23]

The editorial prerogative of having the last word by attaching the 'Ed. Note' to a correspondent's communiqué is now much less used than formerly. David Hayes in his insider's history of the *Globe and Mail*,[24] describes how in the 1960s, under the editorship of Richard Doyle, these so-called shirt-tails were banished, on the principle enunciated by a later editor, Norman Webster, that letter-writers should 'occupy the space in their own way' and editors should refrain from 'adding those cute quips to the bottom of letters which make the editor out to be so much more clever than his correspondent.'[25]

While Forsey's letters were completely relieved of this instant reply technique in the *Globe and Mail*, there was still the ultimate option open to the editor – namely, that of refusing to publish at all. In Forsey's case, it was an option seldom exercised. In the study undertaken by the authors of *Negotiating Control*, a section devoted to an analysis of the intake of letters to the editor and the policies applied in the selection for publication on the letters page of a national newspaper (the *Globe and Mail*) reveals that, of an average annual intake of sixteen thousand letters, roughly one out of eight to ten submissions is accepted for publication.[26] During the heat of the debate over the Meech Lake Accord, Forsey felt that his offerings were suffering from a high rate of rejection. But this sense of injustice must have been fuelled by his experience over half a century during which the newspaper fraternity – the *Globe* in particular – had welcomed and published a very high percentage of his letters. The small number of draft letters in his papers at the National Archives for which no published versions could be found testifies to a batting record with the press which towered above the norm for lesser literary lights.

Nor was Forsey one to take a rejection lightly, as instanced by his exchange with Ken Lefoli, editor of *Maclean's* magazine, in

May–June 1964 over a letter he had written about an article proposing an elected Senate.[27] To the editor's comment that 'your passionate defence of the status quo adds to the discussion but does not illuminate it in any way,' Forsey responded: 'I trust this means you are going to publish my letter in spite of your inability to see that it doesn't illuminate it in any way.' (The record reveals that Lefoli stood firm on his rejection.)

A more acerbic exchange with an editor of *Maclean's* occurred in April 1959 in which Forsey, at his vitriolic best, opened a letter with: 'Of all the empty-pated smart-alec productions I have ever seen, your editorial on the Newfoundland strike is about the worst.' To which Ralph Allen replied: 'I suppose the only way I can answer your series of rhetorical questions is to ask whether you have read our editorial?'[28] Equally forthright was Oakley Dalgleish's rejection of a Forsey offering to the *Globe and Mail* on 9 December 1957 of two dense pages criticizing an editorial that attributed inflation to wage increases brought about by the undue power of trade unions. This letter was signed in his capacity of director of research of the Canadian Congress of Labour. 'Your letter dealing with our editorial,' wrote Dalgleish, 'has been passed along to me. You may feel our statements merit two pages of examination. I do not. I have in front of me every month a balance sheet, which is all I need in support of the editorial.'[29]

Such outright rejections, however, were few and far between. Much more normal were the letters such as that from I. Norman Smith, editor of the *Ottawa Journal*, apologizing for cutting a very long piece on the two nations concept which had been published on 16 September 1967; or yet another on 6 June 1968, expressing regret that the timing of the letter made it inappropriate for publication on election day, softening the blow with the reminder that the paper had been glad to publish an earlier one.[30]

In another instance, involving a letter to the *Montreal Gazette* concerned with a decision of the board of governors of McGill University, Forsey expresses his gratitude to the editor for withholding publication because he had based his letter on what proved to be inaccurate reporting of the facts. His thank-you letter closed with a typical Forsey flourish: ' It just goes to show how unwise it is to trust newspapers – except, of course, the *Gazette*.'[31]

Forsey kept a close eye on editorial tampering with his submissions, often comparing his own drafts with the published version. A typical instance was his response in the *Globe and Mail* in 1978 to René Lévesque's article on a 'true confederation.' Despite the commanding placement of a long letter which was given the fetching title 'Lévesque's article same old "misleading advertising,"' Forsey's marginal lamentations over the omitted passages in the original draft, although very much in character, seem somewhat out of proportion to the damage done.[32]

Forsey occasionally responded warmly to a polite editorial suggestion for clarification, as in the following exchange with Philip Jackman, assistant features editor of the *Globe*. 'Sorry for not contacting you earlier about your piece,' wrote Jackman. 'One of our editors has gone through it and reduced its length a bit. As the piece deals with such a complex subject, perhaps you would look at the enclosed edited version and let me know what changes are needed. P.S. I have marked one paragraph that I have trouble understanding. Perhaps some rewording is needed.'

Instead of bridling at such editorial intervention, Forsey replied: 'Thank you very much for the enormous trouble you took with my piece on Quebec and the Constitution. The changes in the revised version that I think are necessary are so numerous, and in some instances so complicated, that I think I must produce a revised version, keeping it within the limit of words you have set ... I don't wonder you had trouble understanding the paragraph you marked ... I shall send you my revised version as soon as I can. I should be able to get it done tomorrow.'[33]

Forsey was similarly gracious in dealing with B.K. Sandwell, editor of *Saturday Night*, when responding to editorial suggestions for amending a letter. 'Can't see my way clear to sacrifice the fourth and fifth paragraph of my letter, but I have redrafted it so that it is now even shorter than it would have been if I had left them out ... I shall conclude this outrageously long letter by saying that, if you feel the changes I have made from my first letter are such that you cannot possibly print the new draft, that is perfectly all right with me. I am only grateful for having been forced to squeeze out some water.' In this instance, Forsey's amended version does not appear to have been published.[34]

By no means all of Forsey's relations with the editor were of an adverserial nature. In his correspondence, one finds numerous instances of his desire to be helpful by contributing notes, letters, and memoranda, none of which he expected to be published. He was particularly close to Gratton O'Leary and I. Norman Smith, editors of the *Ottawa Journal*, often favouring them with such personal communiqués. Even Dalgleish's abrupt put-down from the editor's desk of the *Globe and Mail* in 1957 did not prevent Forsey from writing a letter two years later congratulating him for a recent editorial and enclosing for his edification two sample copies of petitions for disallowance.[35]

Editors also occasionally reproduced a Forsey letter as an editorial in its own right. One such unusual occasion occurred on 9 March 1982 when, under the heading 'Why the bells ring,' the *Globe*'s lead editorial reproduced and wholeheartedly endorsed one of Forsey's letters dealing with the niceties of parliamentary procedure. Such preferred treatment was also exemplified, usually by the *Globe*, by occasionally placing Forsey's name in the heading over his letter, as in '10-headed monstrosity target of Forsey' (24 January 1980) or 'Professor unduly alarmed about Quebec, says Forsey' (4 February 1982), or 'Mum's the word for some ranks, Forsey insists' (18 May 1982).

Possibly the best illustration of the high regard with which Forsey's contributions were viewed from the editor's desk was provided by A. Roy Megarry, then publisher of the *Globe and Mail*, in 1985. Responding positively to a request from Forsey for an original cartoon of himself by Franklin, Megarry wrote:

> You have frequently been a source of information, knowledge and humour for The Globe and Mail staff and readers.

> Consequently, it is nice to be able to do something for you for a change.
>
> I am so pleased that you have noticed the improvement in the editorial content of The Globe and Mail. We have all been working hard – and investing a lot of money – to achieve these improvements. It is a great source of satisfaction to know that someone as knowledgeable – and critical – as you has observed and approved of the changes. You have many admirers at the paper.[36]

The strongest testimony to the extraordinary influence on editors of Forsey's letter-writing occurred at the time when he was about to step down from the Senate, having reached the obligatory retirement age of seventy-five at the end of May 1979. Feelers were put out from both the *Ottawa Journal* and the *Montreal Gazette* inquiring as to his interest in becoming a regular columnist. John W. Grace, then editor of the *Journal* and a near neighbour of Forsey's, was the first to raise the subject. Recalling their conversation on the way home from work and being reminded of Forsey's imminent retirement from the Senate, Grace accordingly wished 'to put before you the proposition that the *Journal* would be a congenial forum for you when you are a private citizen. Perhaps others have already extended such an invitation.' Grace's feeler closed: 'It's time you began being paid for your journalistic contributions.'

Forsey replied on 16 November: 'No other newspaper or periodical has even thought of approaching me, and I am immensely pleased that the *Journal,* for which I have such a high respect ever since the days of P.D. Ross, and of course perhaps especially during the regime of my old and valued friend, Grattan O'Leary, should have thought of me. I need hardly add that my pleasure is increased by the fact that the invitation has come from you.' Despite these protestations, because of his long association with the labour movement, Forsey thought it would be 'unbecoming of me' to accept as long as the *Journal*'s dispute with the Typographical Union remained unresolved. The letter closed in typical Forsey fashion: 'I have been saying that once I was out of the Senate I should enjoy a peaceful existence "the world forgetting, by the world forgot." I am flattered that at least one person thinks the second part of the quotation may not apply.'[37] The next decade was, in fact, to reveal Forsey the letter-writer at his prolific best, far from a forgotten man, right in the midst of the madding crowd, but not as a columnist.

The folding of the *Journal* in 1980 precluded a renewal of Grace's invitation. Forsey presumably must have responded favourably to a later and similar invitation from John Kalbfleisch, at the time deputy editorial page editor of the *Montreal Gazette*, for in a letter to Forsey on 31 May 1979 he wrote: 'I'm delighted that the idea of contributing from time to time to our Background page appeals to you ... Social affairs and the constitution are two obvious areas I expect would interest you. But I would hate to think we would automatically not be interested in your views on any subject.'[38]

The implication that Forsey's stint as a senator had disrupted his journalistic forays is, of course, disproved by the unceasing, indeed, increasing flood of his letters to the press over the decade of the 1970s. However, few of these found their way to the *Gazette*, a clear indication that Forsey never did take up the invitation to become a regular contributor. Nonetheless, it is interesting to imagine how Forsey would have fared as a regular columnist. Surely, his forte was the letter, fired off extemporaneously in the heat of the moment. At least this is the impression provided by Brian Eglington, a close associate of Forsey. 'He used to read the G&M at breakfast and on the bus on his way into the city,' wrote Eglington. 'In his later years his morning routine was fairly leisurely and he would often arrive at his office (with me from his retirement from the Senate until 1986 and then grace and favour in the Centre Block and the Victoria Building) all steamed up, ready to type out a letter he had already formulated in his mind on the bus.'[39]

A commitment to a regular column would have required a different sort of energy and might well have exposed him to the same critical letters with which he had bombarded more than one generation of editors and columnists. While he was fond of paraphrasing Harry Truman – 'if you can't stand the cold stay out of the refrigerator' – one could not be at all certain that Forsey would have been any more capable of suffering the slings and arrows of critics than purportedly he was in confronting hecklers in the early days of his unsuccessful attempts to win elective office for the CCF.[40] The letter format shielded Forsey from his adversaries and usually left him in control of the situation – essential to a successful deploying of the 'Infoslam' technique.

However, there is no need to speculate about Forsey's probable performance as a regular columnist or commentator because he himself modestly disclaimed such ambitions to Douglas Fisher, a long-time practitioner and exemplar. In a commemorative piece, 'A Rare Jewel in Politics,' for the *Ottawa Sun* on 22 February 1991, Fisher revealed how Forsey had responded in 1979 to Fisher's published suggestion that retirement from the Senate should provide the occasion for a newspaper or network to take Forsey on as political columnist or commentator. 'I couldn't do a regular column, or a regular broadcast, to save my neck. How you chaps manage it is, for me, one of the mysteries which are quite insoluble. Every day, and in every way, I know less and less!'[41]

Relations with Journalists

Reporters assigned to cover Forsey's numerous public appearances often found themselves targets for his corrosive corrections. A sampling of such letters has been brought together under the heading 'You've Got Me Wrong!' and no more will be said here about such adversarial relationships, other than that they reflect Forsey's passion for getting things right, especially where his own words or ideas were involved. His strictures on hapless reporters also reflected the dyspeptic view he claimed to have acquired in teaching students at Carleton University's School of Journalism: 'They were a pretty mouldy lot,' he informed his fellow senators, 'and their capacity to write English ... was something that threw me almost in despair.'[42]

Forsey could engage directly the journalists with bylines, who were not shielded by a cloak of anonymity. It is not altogether clear, however, whether the regular columnist is as free to prolong a debate initiated by a letter-writer as the editor would be. As Jeffrey Simpson, among other journalists, has revealed, Forsey was wont to supplement his public debates with private letters.[43]

Geoffrey Stevens, when he was the *Globe and Mail*'s Ottawa correspondent, deployed one method of striking back at Forsey in a playful column posing as a mock letter addressed to Forsey, headed 'But If You Were Editor, Senator, to Whom Would You Write Letters?' (17 December 1977). There are also a very few instances where columnists such as Douglas Fisher or Peter Newman have used their columns to debate points with Forsey, although as often as not the response took the form of a *mea culpa*, as instanced by a Forsey–Fisher exchange in the *Toronto Telegram*, 15 January 1964.

> Tely columnist Douglas Fisher, MP (7 January) says that Claude Ryan 'has been a strong proponent of the separatist swing in Quebec, which he sees as a justification that Quebec should have an unusual sovereignty. Mr Ryan has been heralding the end of Confederation as we know it.'
>
> I have read scores of Mr Ryan's articles in Le Devoir. Not one of them has contained a single syllable which would justify Mr Fisher's assertions. He might as well have accused the Pope of being an Orangeman.
>
> I should be vastly surprised if Mr Fisher could find in any of Mr Ryan's articles anything which comes even as near support of separatism as some official pronouncements of the party of which Mr Fisher is deputy House leader [NDP].

As promised in an appended editorial note, Fisher's column of 18 January appeared under the heading, 'A Sincere Apology to Monsieur Ryan,' in which he acknowledged both Ryan's own demurer in *Le Devoir* and the correctness of Forsey's complaint. 'I wronged Mr Ryan,' he wrote. For which open acknowledgment of a mistake, Forsey, in typical fashion, immediately sent him a congratulatory note. It was also typical of Forsey's concern for the reputation of his associates that he had sent a long letter of apology to Ryan on 9 January just after Fisher's comments had first been published.[44]

Such open responses to Forsey's critiques were rare, however, and one must turn to Forsey's private correspondence with columnists to obtain a clearer picture of this relationship. On the whole, it can be characterized as a guarded respectfulness. Guarded, in the sense expressed by one seasoned newsperson, that particularly if the issue concerned a constitutional matter, one would be wise to wait until Forsey pronounced before committing oneself to print.

Nor was this attitude of cautious reserve limited to journalists. R. MacGregor Dawson, for example, reportedly claimed that he found it unthinkable to publish his textbook on *Government in Canada*, upon which generations of political science students had been brought up, without having Forsey's critical scan. Indeed, in its sixth edition, Norman Ward, who was responsible for the revision, made reference to this dependency in what must be a unique vote of thanks: 'This is the first edition ... not directly touched by Eugene Forsey, a remarkable circumstance that deserves special mention. Dr Forsey's influence is here, of course, for his clear (and freely expressed) opinions affected all its predecessors. This revision is the poorer for the want of his hand. But it does leave us free to dedicate the book to him.'[45]

In what was probably a mock expression of the journalist's similar fear of being skewered by a Forsey correction, a communication from John Fraser, when he served in the European Bureau of the *Globe and Mail*, nicely portrays the *angst* experienced on receipt of a Forsey letter and the relief on finding one's sin not as serious as one thought. Dated 24 January 1985, Fraser wrote:

> I received your letter yesterday and you will appreciate that I had to wait a full 15 minutes before I could summon up the courage to open it. While thus composing myself for the expected laceration,

I fortified my sagging spirit with a stiff sherry and thought, 'Well, whatever the mistake, if it was *very* bad, he would have written the editor, not me.' ...

In any event the mistake got me that complimentary first line of your letter, and on such succinct approbation I can float around for hours on Cloud Nine.[46]

That this direct correspondence with a journalist was neither unique nor a product of a temperament sweetened by advancing years is revealed in a letter from Jean-Pierre Fournier, Tribune de la presse in the House of Commons. Responding to a letter in which Forsey pointed out an error in an article dealing with the constitution in the 7 October 1964 issue of *Le Devoir*, Fournier wrote: 'La vigilance des gens de votre savoir, croyez-le, facilite considérablement la tâche des journalistes et les incite à cet esprit de recherche et à cette précision qui fut si misérablement défault dans notre presse.'[47]

With old 'familiars' in the press, a lighter note was struck, as in this exchange between Forsey and Blair Fraser of *Maclean's* in September 1955:

Dear Blair:

I've caught Homer nodding again.

You speak of Alexander Mackenzie being a pillar of Scots Presbyterian rectitude, or words to that effect (I haven't your article before me at the moment). Actually, he was a Baptist. See his Life, by Buckingham and Rose, p.55.

Dear Gene:

Thanks for your note of September 20th.

Would you consider accepting a small bribe to discontinue your subscription to Maclean's? Or, alternatively, maybe I could send a copy of my pieces to you so that you could catch the mistakes before publication instead of after![48]

Even with journalists who had tangled often and seriously with Forsey, there was an old-fashioned courtesy and generosity that is a touching reminder of a more civil form of discourse among fiercely opinionated individuals. One remarkable illustration is found in this exchange between Forsey and Bruce Hutchison, long associated with Forsey's *bête noire*, the *Winnipeg Free Press*. Forsey wrote on 13 February 1946:

> Dear Mr Hutchison:
>
> I have said some hard things about some of your writings in the past. I hope, therefore, that you will believe in the genuineness of what follows.
>
> I have been meaning for some time to write and say how much I enjoyed your article on cocktail parties, which appeared in the Journal here last October, and which is one of the most powerful pieces of writing I have seen in some time.
>
> I should like also to say how much I enjoyed a more recent article of yours, reprinted in the Montreal Gazette: 'The devil and Gen. Chisholm.' If it is not an impertinence to say so, I should call it both wise and witty. It is quite the best thing on the Chisholm affair that I have seen.
>
> Don't bother to answer this.

Hutchison, disregarding Forsey's last admonition, replied on 15 February:

> Dear Mr Forsey:
>
> Coming from one whom I know to be in honest disagreement with many of my views, your recent letter struck me as a very handsome thing and I thank you for it. I am particularly happy to find you in agreement with me in the Chisholm matter because I have been widely attacked in letters from people on the Left who imagine that anyone who disagrees with General Chisholm must be a fascist, – a very curious paradox when the General's theories seem to me to be the starting point of the whole Hitler philosophy.
>
> There are, of course, many matters in which I find myself in agreement with the CCF, as I have often said to my good friend M.J. [Coldwell]. One of them is the Japanese situation in British

Columbia where I have said as much as I could to denounce the racialists and to approve the policy of your party. You will have noted, I imagine, the line the Free Press has taken on this issue and I think you will approve it. I think you will approve also our demand for a bill of rights and I cannot imagine why M.J., who first suggested it in Parliament, never pursued it.

I hope that we may meet sometime in the East and repeat my appreciation of your most kindly letter.[49]

Unquestionably, the most remarkable illustration of the civility that prevailed, even in the midst of the most partisan differences, was provided in an exchange between Forsey and George Drew. It occurred shortly after Forsey's second electoral defeat by Drew, in the course of which bitter words had been spoken, including the charge that Forsey was a communist. In this context, Forsey is found writing to Drew on 23 November 1949 complimenting him on his speech in the House of Commons. Drew was criticizing the St Laurent government for its failure to make public, as the law required, the report on the flour-milling industry by the combines commissioner, G.A. McGregor.

Dear Mr Drew,

As a constituent, I should like to offer my congratulations on the reply you made ... to Mr Garson's [minister of justice] suggestion that, as long as we have elections every few years, Governments may break the law as they please. The glaring contradiction between this notion and the basic principles of parliamentary government is manifest to anyone with an elementary acquaintance with those principles. But, your reply is, I think, a classic ... it couldn't be improved upon.

As I told a member of your party not long ago, some of the recent performances of this Government ... make me feel that I owe you an apology for having felt that on certain matters you exaggerated during the election ...

Ministers seem never to have heard of the Rule of Law. Add to that the whittling away of rights by what my friend Mr Meighen calls 'asinine decisions' of the Speaker, and you have a nasty and ominous situation. Much of it, notably Mr Garson's curious theory of plebiscitary democracy, is the flowering of seeds assiduously sown by Mr King ...

I have said some hard things about you in past campaigns, and meant them. If I am ever a candidate again, which I think is unlikely, no doubt I shall again express, with equal vigour, my disagreement with your policies. But I hope I can give credit where credit is due ...

Do not bother to answer. Keep your letters for people who vote for you!

Notwithstanding Forsey's last injunction, Drew responded on 25 November, closing with:

> I do want to thank you for writing to me as you did. You speak of the vigor with which you have spoken of my policies. I wonder if we have not both spoken rather vigorously – perhaps too vigorously – about what we regard as the personal attitude of each other to matters of policy ... On looking back over the things to which each might object most strongly in what the other has said, I am inclined to think we will both find that they relate to motives which have been attributed to the other, rather than to those points of view which strictly can be regarded as statements of policy. We may not even agree on this. In any event, I was glad to get your letter.[50]

Most correspondent journalists, like Fraser, Hutchison, and, in rather different circumstances, George Drew, accepted Forsey's critiques with as much good grace as they could muster. Few were tempted to persist with the correspondence until the withers of the disputed issue had been thoroughly wrung, at least to Forsey's satisfaction. In the Forsey Papers there is an illuminating correspondence with Roland Bird, who wrote for *The Economist*. On 16 July 1965 Forsey had written offering an extended critique of one of Bird's pieces, to which Bird replied in kind. This reply drew from Forsey six dense single-spaced pages dealing with major and minor matters. In a two-page reply to this missive, Bird wrote this perceptive closure to the correspondence:

> You belong to the photographic school of accuracy. This is entirely admirable and responsible in its attitude to facts, but it is not a conclusive attitude to truth, nor is it a method that a journalist should adopt.
>
> The arts of journalism are to interest, to depict, to persuade, and to assert – always within the limits of what is intellectually honest and also, since he has to make a living, without boring the heads off his readers.
>
> We are mismatched because we work from different sets of rules. I respect yours, indeed; but I would despair of persuading you to think well of mine.[51]

A similar assessment, not from a journalist but from an admiring though critical reader, reached Forsey some two months later. In August 1965, at the annual Couchiching Conference on Public Affairs, Forsey, a regular and popular contributor to its proceedings over the years, gave a speech on the problems of Canadian federalism which was widely reproduced in the press. Amongst the many congratulatory comments received by Forsey was a personal letter from P.J.T. Ohearn of Halifax commenting on and debating some of Forsey's arguments, concluding in part:

> Otherwise, allowing for the fact that I do not share your emotional attachment to things British, one way or the other, I find myself agreeing with you on point after point. It was only when I came to the end that I noted, with some amusement, that you are consistently devoted to the concrete and the particular and mistrustful of the abstract and the general. This is both a philosophical trap, of the kind that Russell tried to solve in *Principia Mathematica* with the Theory of Types, and, you will forgive me, a practical miscalculation. A unitary society does not need to discuss general principles with any profundity – it takes them for

> granted as the substance of its unity. A pluralistic society is bound to discuss them because its nature brings them into collision ... The equality of citizens in French and English, the rights of parents to educate their children free of tax penalties are in issue in Canada because we are pluralistic.[52]

There is no indication of a formal reply from Forsey but on the margins beside the second-to-last sentence Forsey has scrawled 'It didn't in 1865' and against the final sentence 'Aha!' It is interesting, however, that he made no marginal comments beside his critic's references to his devotion to 'the concrete and the particular' and his mistrust of 'the abstract and the general.' Undoubtedly, Roland Bird and P.J.T. Ohearn fairly captured a dogged Forsey mind-set that forced generations of editors, journalists, and competing readers reluctantly to cede the field of verbal combat to Forsey, exasperated and exhausted by his relentless command of the 'concrete and the particular' and by his devotion to the 'photographic school of accuracy.'

Forsey's letter-writing relationship with the press is fittingly brought to a close with his 25 January 1987 communiqué to A. Roy Megarry, then managing editor of the *Globe and Mail*. The slight signs of pique are surely forgivable when one realizes that over the forty-five intervening years since Forsey's first letter had appeared in the *Globe*, more than three hundred others had been published. This letter is reproduced here in its original hand-written form.[53]

711-315 Holmwood Avenue,
Ottawa, K1S 2R2,
January 25, 1987.

Dear Mr. Megarry,

This morning, at 8.30, I received a telephone call which surprised me.

It purported to come from the *Globe and Mail*.

The voice was rather faint, "like horns of elfland, faintly blowing."

But it asked if I had written a letter to the *Globe and Mail*.

I said "yes".

Then came something that sounded like "the publisher has to know if its authentic".

I said, "Why? Didn't I sign it?"

"Oh! yes. But it has to be authenticated."

I said: "Well! This is most extraordinary. This has never happened to me before."

"Have you ever written a letter to the *Globe and Mail* before?"

"Yes, hundreds of them."

"Have they been published?"

"Yes."

I then asked if this was a new rule.

"Oh! no. It's always done."

"Well, its never been done to me before."

Your office here confirms that this *is* the rule.

I realize now that I should have asked the lady to authenticate *herself* by telling me what the letter was about. It is possible that someone has been playing games with my name.

and sending in some preposterous document, e.g., whooping it up for the Rhinoceros Party.

So I shall be more careful in future. I do not think quickly on the telephone, and surprise had deprived me of such wits as that instrument ordinarily leaves me.

The whole business may have the salutary effect of stopping me from bothering the paper with letters. A very lively contemporary describes himself as "in the prime of my senility." He has kindly given me permission to apply the phrase to myself. Perhaps your staff has decided that he has hit the nail on the head. My handwriting may well lead you to the same conclusion.

Yours sincerely,
Eugene Forsey

I am enclosing a typed copy, lest the tremors of my handwriting prove too exasperating.

E.A.F.

National Archives of Canada

CHAPTER TWO

A Census of Forsey Letters

Pursuing Forsey letters to the press, written over a period of six decades, is akin to collecting postage stamps: one strives for completion of the set knowing full well that there will always be elusive rarities that evade capture. The Forsey sightings listed here, and from which the selections grouped by theme have been made, must be viewed in that light. A search of the Forsey Papers in the National Archives was restricted to those boxes labelled 'Letters to the Editor,' which contained originals and clippings for some but by no means all of the originals. A check of the newspapers confirmed that virtually all of the originals were indeed published but also turned up many for which there were no original copies. Fortunately for the collector, the main recipient of Forsey's letters, the *Globe and Mail*, has preserved a microfiche 'morgue' of Forseyana, rendered complete since November 1977 with the introduction of Infoglobe. The same cannot be said for other newspapers, particularly the second most favoured recipient, the *Ottawa Journal*, which died in 1980.

Contributing to the collector's problems is Forsey's growing reputation throughout the country as a popular speaker who invariably attracted journalistic coverage that Forsey often deemed so inaccurate as to require a correcting letter in the local press. Since these were scattered virtually in every sizable newspaper across Canada, it is probable that this census has picked up only the most salient of these corrective missives. Adding to the likelihood of substantial underestimation in the census is the thinness of the records when Forsey was at McGill, as a student in the 1920s, and as an instructor in the 1930s.

Excluded from the census are the lengthy pieces, which are treated as articles written 'By Eugene Forsey.' Since a number of Forsey's letters were as long as his articles, I sought without success to obtain the newspaper fraternity's criteria for making the distinction. Was the governing consideration that the piece had been solicited, commissioned, or paid for? Perhaps the reason for the evasiveness of the replies I received to this question is to be found in Senator Richard Doyle's account of one experience he had in dealing with Forsey.

> On only one occasion did I approach him on the use of his letters. If memory serves, the item at hand was a rousing piece on the War Measures Act – a crisis that produced very heavy traffic in our letters department. The conversation went like this:
>
> Doyle: We have your excellent letter on the crisis. We would like to display it as an article instead of using it as a letter.
>
> Forsey: It is a letter not an article. But it is not for me to say how you use it.
>
> Doyle: If it is used as an article we will pay you for it. As you know we do not pay for letters. If we used it as an article, we would hope to have exclusive use.
>
> Forsey: I have already sent the letter to several other papers and I would not want to tell them how they should use it or they should not use it. Not at all. It is a letter.
>
> Doyle: Thank you, Mr Forsey.[1]

'I might say,' concluded Doyle, 'that I never again tried to haggle with him – the only writer I know whose best stuff always came free – leaving us to rush it into print before other beneficiaries could scoop us.'

With these exclusions and reservations noted, the number of letters confirmed as published ranges around the eight hundred mark. Nearly half the total, 375, were published in the *Globe and Mail*, two-thirds of these in the 1970s and 1980s. If the *Ottawa Journal* had survived beyond 1980, it might well have rivalled the *Globe;* even so, with about 150 letters over four decades, beginning in the 1940s, it was a distant runner-up. Despite the fact that Forsey's contributions to the *Montreal Gazette* became fewer and more desultory after his departure from McGill in 1941, with 73 letters it holds third place, ahead of the *Ottawa Citizen,* for which only 53 confirmed sightings were found. The *Citizen* compensated somewhat by accepting or commissioning full-scale articles from Forsey, together with generous extracts from public speeches and presentations to various parliamentary commissions and task forces. For the most part, where longer pieces identified as 'by Eugene Forsey' appeared in the *Citizen* and in the features page of most of the other main recipients of his letters, they have not been included in this census.

Once the four main recipients have been accounted for, the number of letters directed to other dailies drops off significantly. Only *Le Devoir* with 15 entries and the *Toronto Star* with 12, show double digits, leaving the *Winnipeg Free Press* trailing with 8 published sightings and none of the others showing more than 4. From west to east, within Canada, the tally for the remainder runs as follows: *Victoria Daily Times,* 1; *Vancouver Sun,* 3; *Vancouver Province,* 1; *Edmonton Sun,* 1; *Calgary Herald,* 2; *Regina Leader Post,* 1; *London Free Press,* 2; *Toronto Telegram,* 3; *Toronto Sun,* 1; *Financial Post,* 2; *Kingston Whig-Standard,* 1; *Ottawa Sun,* 1; *McGill Daily,* 2; *Montreal Star,* 5; *Le Soleil,* 1; *La Presse,* 1; *Quebec Chronicle Herald,* 1; *Saint John Citizen,* 1; *Halifax Chronicle Herald,* 2; *Cape Breton Post,* 1; *Charlottetown Guardian,* 1; *St John's Evening Telegram,* 1. The eastward path of the letters fittingly crossed the Atlantic, where the *Manchester Guardian Weekly,* 1; *The Economist,* 3; and *The Times,* 1, topped off the list of occasional entries.

The census is completed with Forsey's offerings to the *Canadian Forum,* at least 12; *Saturday Night,* 22; and *Maclean's,* 3. For the first two, the letters comprised a minor part of his contributions, which were conveyed much more in articles that have here been excluded from the count. Also excluded are the occasional letters addressed to more learned journals such as the *Canadian Bar Review* and the *Canadian Journal of Economics and Political Science.*

The bare-bones census covers six decades of letter-writing that embraced a broad spectrum of subjects which attracted Forsey's encyclopaedic mind and his trusty typewriter. In Part Two, selected letters have been assembled around what appear to be the central, recurrent themes that engaged Forsey over the years. Before turning to this exercise, it may be useful to take a decade-by-decade look at the letters, observing along the way the specific circumstances that triggered the letters and how their number and content related to Forsey's own richly endowed career paths.

The Early Decades, 1920–40

In the 1920s and 1930s, Forsey's location and dominant career interest governed both the choice of newspaper and the subject matter addressed. As a university student in the 1920s, the *McGill Daily* became his earliest proving ground (although a pencilled draft of a letter to the *New York Outlook* in 1923, dealing with naval warfare, is early evidence of more venturesome ambitions whose success it has been unable to trace).[2] The topics addressed were primarily economic and social issues and the treatment was long, serious, leaning to numbered paragraphs, and replete with statistical overkill that was to characterize many of his offerings in subsequent years. Since the Forsey Papers contain so few records of his letters to the *McGill Daily* and no additional search was made, only two of his early letters have been numbered in this census.

During the years of his untenured academic career at McGill in the 1930s, the *Montreal Gazette* became his primary outlet, with occasional sorties in the *McGill Daily*, and regular monthly offerings (mostly by way of short articles rather than letters) to the *Canadian Forum*. His dialogues with the *Gazette* were dominated by the social and economic consequences to the workingman of the Great Depression and the gathering premonitions of a second great war. They began in 1937 with six letters, followed in 1938 with four, only one in 1938, and a rash of eight in 1939. In the *Forum*, not only were these subjects addressed but Forsey entered into the heated controversy among left-wing forces arising out of suspected communist infiltration of the socialists' positions. His strident opposition to the Padlock Law imposed in 1937 by the Duplessis government would, in its support for civil liberties and the rule of law, strike a theme he was to uphold with passion throughout his life. At the time, however, his civil libertarian position could be and was misconstrued as a defence of communists, which the Padlock Act had presumably been introduced to eradicate. On this account, during the 1940s he was obliged to use his letters to fight off allegations of communist leanings and set the record straight.

Forsey's anti-establishment position on all such matters derived from his exposure while at Oxford to socialist thought. Back home it was reinforced by his association with people such as F.R. Scott and Frank Underhill in the formation in 1930 of the League for Social Reconstruction and by his less secular adherence to the Christian socialism of the Social Gospel movement. Closely related was the emergence of the CCF party in 1932 for which Forsey, as Quebec provincial president, undertook the first of his four unsuccessful electoral ventures, running as a candidate for the City of Montreal Council in 1940.

The gloomy 1930s were not all dead serious; it was in the *Canadian Forum* of the period that flashes of Forsey's satirical, witty prose and samples of his puckish doggerel verse first bubbled to the surface, applied to subjects as varied as honorary degrees for tycoons ('Pecuniary Degrees'), to a poem based on a quotation from economist Wladimer Woytinsky, discussing French statistics in 'The Social Consequences of the Economic Depression.'[3]

Woytinsky's statement, 'It is extremely probable that during the depression, taxpayers were inclined to be unduly pessimistic when making their returns,' was embellished as follows by Forsey to the tune of 'The Wearing of the Green':

When a millionaire does not declare the whole of what he earns
Some call it tax evasion, and their wrath against him burns.

But a kindlier phrase the man himself from Prof. Woytinsky learns
It's 'unduly pessimistic when making his returns.'

The plutocrat is weary. For greater ease he yearns.
Hence you find him pessimistic when making his returns.
He would not defraud the government. Deception low he spurns.
But he can be pessimistic when making his returns.
There are times when he in foreign climes a better chance discerns
Of being pessimistic when making his returns.
So don't be hard upon him if in Nassau he sojourns
Where he's safely pessimistic when making his returns.
In Canada the habit sometimes spreads to large concerns;
They too get pessimistic when making their returns.
With concealed reserve the textile magnate all his woes adjourns
That's how he is pessimistic when making his returns.
Then let's drink to great Woytinsky, let us crown his brow with ferns,
Nor to him be pessimistic when making these returns.

That these were anonymous contributions is interesting, in view of Forsey's professed disdain for letter-writing opponents in the *Gazette* who took such refuge. In a contribution to the *Forum* in May 1939, for example, Forsey struck at his anonymous critic:

> The quotations ... are from the gifted pen of Montreal's leading writer of anonymous letters to the press: 'Student,' alias 'Antonius,' 'Enquirer,' 'Democrat,' 'S,' 'Conservative,' 'One Voter,' 'Soyons Sages,' 'Soyons Raisonables,' and possibly some other things. But the Gazette in one of its editorials quoted approvingly from one of those letters; and it apparently submits replies to 'Student' to his scrutiny before printing them. (At any rate, one such reply [by Forsey], dated March 11, and printed March 13, was answered by 'Student' in a letter dated March 12).[4]

While close family members, as he later admitted in his memoirs, would have wished he emulate 'Student's' anonymity, if not abandon the practice of writing to the newspapers altogether ('Everybody knows that people that write letters to the paper are crazy'), he was later to sign such efforts quite shamelessly and repeat them in Senate speeches and convocation addresses – particularly his (sung) versions of the national anthem.[5]

The tally of confirmed 'sightings' of Forsey letters during the 1930s is twenty-three, nineteen of which were in the *Montreal Gazette*, one formal letter (but numerous other signed and unsigned contributions) in the *Canadian Forum*, a stray entry registered in 1938 in the *Saint John Citizen*, at least one letter to the *McGill Daily*, and a very early entry in the *Montreal Star* on 23 October 1933.

The letter to the *McGill Daily*, dealing with a speech delivered at the university by the Duke di Rignano on Italy and the modern world, was used by Forsey to provide satirical comment (by way of comparison with fascist legislation) on collective agreement legislation pending before the Quebec legislature. Enclosing a copy of this letter to his mother, he wrote, 'Leacock, who is a Fascist himself, will probably want to bite me, but I can't see that he can do anything. Hemmeon [head of the department], for the first time in my experience, burst forth unrestrainedly in my praise. So have several colleagues and students.'[6]

Such contretemps had emerged almost from the moment Forsey became a lecturer in the Department of Economics and Political Science in 1929. As early as 20 October 1933, Sir Arthur Currie, the principal of McGill, received an anxious letter from no less a personage than Premier Taschereau, enclosing and commenting on newspaper clippings that reported Forsey's latest utterances. 'I have been advised,' the premier wrote, 'that several good families of Quebec hesitate to send their boys to McGill on account of the spirit which seems to prevail among some professors.' The letter closed: 'May I be permitted to express my surprise that in these hard times the great McGill University should lend a helping hand to socialism!' The following day, the much-beseiged principal responded with a two-page, single-spaced apologia that demonstrated, as he put it himself, 'I am between the devil and the deep sea. If I dismiss Mr. Forsey, which I shall likely do, it will be heralded from one end of Canada to the other that McGill dismisses its professors because of their political views, that we are a class university, one in which freedom of speech is not tolerated.' On the other hand, Sir Arthur ruminated,

> The very press which criticizes Forsey are the very ones who demand the right to say what they please in their editorial columns, and I cannot see why, as a matter of principle, editorial writers should have more freedom than university professors ... But ... I assure you, my dear Premier, that you do not condemn Mr Forsey's views any more severely than I do. But it is a wrong thing to indicate that McGill is a socialist institution ... two men out of four hundred and fifty [the other was F.R. Scott] do not make the University a socialist university ... What I shall do with Mr Forsey I am unable to state this morning, but the matter cannot be allowed to rest where it is.

Rest it did, however, for another eight years, despite the pervasive view, as expressed by his senior colleague, Stephen Leacock, that 'Mr Forsey's opinions are mistaken and silly' and that 'if he were an open agitating communist, I would want him fired not only from McGill but from Canada.' Since there was no reason to assume the worst, Leacock's genuine concern for academic freedom and the adverse impact on the public image of McGill, views he shared with the principal, dictated that nothing be done.

What may have been the cause of the final fraying of the thread by which the sword so long suspended over Forsey's head at last fell in 1941 was the rumour that circulated in such high quarters as the Red Cross Group of the Women Associates of McGill, late in 1940. Gossip associated him with a publication attributed to the Young Communist League, and once again forced a furious Forsey to his own defence. But the accumulation of grievances against him could no longer be denied. Even the direct appeal of an eminent Montreal lawyer and one-time secretary of state in R.B. Bennett's 1930s cabinet, the Honourable Charles H. Cahan, to McGill's chancellor, Sir Edward Beatty, was of no avail. In a remarkable endorsement, coming from a man who preferred to be known as a 'continuing Conservative' rather than a Progressive Conservative, Cahan defended Forsey's 'radical tendencies,' being personally disposed, as he put it, 'to think that radical thought in youthful minds best serves to stimulate study and enquiry and leads to the building of better foundations for our social and economic life.' To his final plea – 'Is there any way in which those of us, who have confidence in Forsey's personal character and intellectual qualifications, can exercise any influence on his behalf?' – came there answer none.[7]

His painful parting from McGill in 1941 was somewhat assuaged by a one-year interregnum in 1941–2 as a Guggenheim Fellow at Harvard. He then became director of research for the Canadian Congress of Labour, an association he was to retain for twenty-seven years, setting him on a new career path which placed him in Ottawa. In view of his emerging preoccupations, this was a serendipitous location and one which he was to maintain for the rest of his life.

The 1940s

At this time, many of Forsey's letters were written and signed under his new official capacity as spokesman and defender of trade unionists. But there was no change in the positions he had already assumed in his 1930s contributions to the *Montreal Gazette* or the *Canadian Forum*. He now had preferred access as regular contributor to the publications of organized labour, such as *Canadian Unionist*, *Labour Research*, *Canadian Labour*, and continued his regular contributions to the *Forum* on similar themes. The first offerings to the *Globe and Mail* were labour-oriented and in fact were used by Wellington Jeffers in his Report on Business columns in 1943 and 1944. Toronto *Saturday Night*, then a weekly journal, also became a recipient of Forsey's critiques of what he considered to be its anti-labour biases, under its editor, B.K. Sandwell.

Apart from the letters related to his position in the labour movement (roughly one-third of the fifty-three confirmed sightings), the decade of the 1940s witnessed Forsey's emergence in the role for which he became much more celebrated, that of authority on the constitution and the governing institutions it sustained. It is passing strange that this reputation should have begun in the pages of the *Winnipeg Free Press* with J.W. Dafoe's critical review in 1943 of Forsey's doctoral dissertation, just published under the title of *The Royal Power of Dissolution in the Commonwealth*. These exchanges not only established Forsey as the sharp-tongued, indefatigable debater, always battling for the last word, but also set out views of the constitution and its attendant practices and precedents. He would repeat these views over and over again down the years in letters, articles, and memoranda, unrevised and unrepented – and, it must be added, with growing reluctance by others to question the Forsey interpretation. These constitutional themes spread out from the *Free Press* and found their way into his other newspapers of choice, the closer to hand *Ottawa Journal* now among them, picking up where his offerings to the *Montreal Gazette* began to dwindle. *Saturday Night* featured a series of Forsey articles on constitutional themes, as did the *Toronto Evening Telegram*. Interestingly, the *Globe* was yet to become an outlet for Forsey's instructive constitutional commentary.

The whimsical treatment of side themes, which I have characterized as Forsey the defender of the English language, and Forsey the civic censor, also began to expand upon his 1930s effusions in the *Forum*. He was to maintain a steady correspondence throughout the decades with the two Ottawa papers, the *Citizen* tending to get his civic censorship letters, while his more serious offerings were reserved for the *Journal*. *Saturday Night* also shared these lighter offerings, along with his constitutional utterances in both letter and article format.

Forsey's unsuccessful ventures into electoral politics came in the 1940s. They were important for the letters that Forsey felt obliged to write in response to the accusation of communist leanings, often dredged up from the battles he had had to fight in the 1930s. Some of these were voiced by powerful opponents: a Tory cabinet minister, George Dunbar, in an Ontario by-election and George Drew campaigning for a federal seat. These are reproduced below under the theme 'You've Got Me Wrong!' and account for four of the ten letters to the *Globe* and a flurry of letters to the *Montreal Gazette* which still remained, by far, Forsey's favoured client.

The 1950s

Confirmed sightings of Forsey letters, at seventy-seven, remain about the same as for the previous period. The *Ottawa Journal*, with one-third of the total (twenty-three entries located), now completely displaced the *Montreal Gazette*, for which only two entries could be found. The *Globe and Mail* begins to reveal Forsey's growing interest in this outlet, but at nineteen letters and one article, still lags behind the *Journal*. The *Ottawa Citizen* and *Saturday Night* run distant thirds, each with eleven letters found. His other contributions were more widespread than formerly, and extended to the *Toronto Star*, the *Rural Cooperator*, the *Western Producer, Western Star* (Corner Brook, Newfoundland), the *Evening Telegram* (St John's, Newfoundland), the *Letter Review* (Fort Erie, Ontario), the *Sudbury Daily Star*, the *Canadian Forum, Maclean's, Le Devoir*, and a near miss in the United States with the *Atlantic Monthly* in 1955.

Clearly, the highlight of the decade was his letter to the *Ottawa Journal*, on 31 May 1956, in which his criticisms of Mr Speaker Beaudoin's rulings on the pipeline debate nearly, but to his subsequently expressed regret, never did bring him before the bar of the House to answer for his alleged denigration of the honour of the House and its standard bearer.[8] The number of letters addressing labour issues and signed in his capacity as director of research for the Canadian Labour Congress declined in relation to his other offerings as concerned citizen (his censorial role) and, most importantly, as defender of Canada with all its insignia of nationhood and British constitutional heritage.

This last theme was to become Forsey's prime preoccupation in succeeding decades, as Quebec's Quiet Revolution of the 1960s presaged the threat of separatism emerging out of the two nations doctrine and variations on that theme which threatened, in Forsey's view, the integrity of Canada. The erosion began in 1951, with the appointment of a home-grown governor general. In the letters' column of *Saturday Night* Forsey criticized this move because he concluded it would undermine the concept of an office standing above the play of partisan politics. He was to reiterate this same concern years later, in 1984, when criticizing then Governor General Edward Schreyer's alleged 'musings' about his prospects of re-entering politics after leaving the vice-regal office. These were also the years in which Forsey mounted his first attacks on the attempts to drop 'Dominion' from Canada's title, along with the other 'funny work with names,' particularly the attempt to eliminate 'Royal' from Royal Mail and other such instances of what he branded as 'the relentless pressure of creeping republicanism.'

Pausing on the threshhold of the 1960s to sum up the tone and substance of Forsey's letter output over three decades, one is impressed by the limited number of references to what one might assume to have been the major policy issues of the day, associated with postwar adjustments in the late 1940s and 1950s. As official spokesman for organized labour, he directed a few letters against opponents of price control, unemployment insurance, and the alleged adverse impact on organized labour of such programs. However, the policy issues arising from the introduction of universal pensions, medicare, and social welfare projects were pretty well overlooked in Forsey's letters, even though it is clear from his self-described philosophical stance as a 'Sir John A. Macdonald Conservative' that he was an ardent proponent. By and large, he was content to use his letters to snipe at those like the doctors who dragged their feet on medicare. His serious concerns were and remained focused on

Canada and the preservation of a strong central government for a single nation, with all the attendant symbols of independence consistent with the preservation of a monarchical tradition. Due process, whether in the application of the law, the operations of Canada's parliamentary institutions, or the working of its constitution, was, and would remain, the dominating theme. Given Forsey's insistence on the importance of *process,* it is not surprising that he was fond of quoting from St Paul: 'Let all things be done decently and in order,' and from the order for the solemnization of marriage in the Anglican prayer book: 'It is not by any to be taken in hand lightly, or thoughtlessly, but reverently, discreetly, soberly, and in the fear of God.'

The 1960s

This decade witnessed Forsey's full flowering as letter-writer, his offering of some sixty-two letters to the *Globe and Mail* alone nearly equalling his total output in the previous decade. The *Journal* continued to place a close second, with fifty-six identified published letters, while its Ottawa competitor, the *Citizen,* entertained only nine. Reflecting the mounting attention to constitutional matters and the place of Quebec in confederation, eight submissions in French to *Le Devoir* appeared, equalling his contributions to the *Canadian Forum.* The remaining thirteen were widely scattered, from the *Victoria Daily Times, Vancouver Sun, Regina Leader-Post,* and *Winnipeg Free Press* in the west, to the *Halifax Chronicle-Herald* and the *St John's Evening Telegram* in the east. The *Toronto Star* and *Toronto Telegram, Maclean's,* the *United Church Observer* and the *Montreal Star* were among that number. There were failures, as well: a 15 July 1967 letter to the *New York Times* was not accepted, nor was a communication with *The Economist* in May 1964 (although he was to have better luck with this magazine during the 1970s).

The doubling of Forsey's output of letters and the variety of subjects tackled reflected the eventful 1960s, both for Forsey and for the country he loved, as it moved to celebrate its centennial.

On the academic front, Forsey was elected to the presidency of the Canadian Political Science Association in 1961–2. His presidential address, unusually well covered by a press that normally pays scant attention to annual gatherings of 'The Learneds,' was on the topic 'Canada: One Nation or Two?' – a passionate fixation with Forsey until his very last letter to the press, two weeks before his death in February 1991.

The award of the Skelton-Clark Visiting Fellowship at Queen's University for the year 1962–3 enabled him to return to work on Canada's constitution which he had begun two decades before while on his Guggenheim Fellowship at Harvard. Although poor health prevented him from completing the magnum opus he had in mind (and which remained unfinished at his death), important segments of his study surfaced in a series of articles, originally for the *Hamilton Spectator* but widely copied by other newspapers such as the *Ottawa Journal*.[9] These articles were as learned as those he submitted from time to time to such journals as the *Canadian Bar Review* and the *Canadian Journal of Economics and Political Science*. Much of their content was also to appear in the numerous memoranda Forsey presented over the years at the behest of parliamentary committees and task forces. Although many of his letters on similar constitutional themes are scarcely distinguishable from such articles either in terms of length or seriousness of topic (Forsey always appeared to be excused from the usual editorial space constraints applying to regular letter-writers), for this census the pieces clearly intended as articles 'By Eugene Forsey' have not been counted.

Additional evidence of Forsey's recognition by the scholarly community came in the award of honorary degrees, beginning with the University of New Brunswick in 1962. In light of his dismissal in 1941, there was a certain irony when McGill bestowed an honorary doctorate in 1966. Given the accusations of radicalism that led to Forsey's dismissal twenty-five years before, it was interesting that the *Ottawa Journal*'s coverage of his address stressed the conservative elements of Forsey's 'Lay Sermon': 'hold fast that which is good,' and 'look before you leap' (6 June).

There was further irony in Forsey's ensuing letter ('Two-Part Text,' 11 June) in which he sought to restore the balance:

> Thank you for your kind words about my McGill convocation address (June 6).
>
> It will perhaps mitigate the surprise and pleasure (or displeasure) of your readers if I venture to add:
>
> (1) that my text had two parts, of which the first was 'Prove all things,' and
>
> (2) that I said also that it was part of the function of university people to be radical, to go to the roots of things.

Other recognitions of Forsey's academic merits came with his appointment in 1966 to the board of governors and subsequent elevation to chancellor of Trent University and his election to the Royal Society of Canada in 1967, followed in 1968 by his appointment as an officer in the Order of Canada (upgraded to companion in 1989).

Only the first of these honours, his association with Trent University, provided an occasion for letters to the press. These were triggered by an editorial based on a critical article on Trent University in the *Globe and Mail* on 30 January 1973. Forsey was joined by three other governors in offering an eloquent defence of the university in the *Ottawa Journal* (6 February 1973). Challenged in a subsequent letter by Matthew Robins of Carleton University, the governors, again led by Forsey, responded in kind on 3 March:

> May we, the 'venerable guardians of Trent,' have space to deploy our wheel chairs into line to respond to the broadside delivered by Mr Matthew Robins from under the stirring banner 'Challenge to the Governors of Trent'?
>
> Mr Robins' purple prose, or perhaps our council mentality, makes it a little difficult to establish exactly what is his point of outrage.
>
> He seems to claim that (a) academic faculty members of English, Scottish or French nationality hired during the sixties

> are 'European rejects' who 'would be fighting for jobs in high schools' except for the protection of tenure, and (b) that in comparison most American faculty members are much more qualified and have performed much better since coming to Canada. 'They can hustle with their Canadian counterparts. They don't need tenure.' Canadian faculty as a whole he ignores, except that he seems to equate our venerable 'generation of Canadian academics' with the 'deadwood academics junior in terms of years.'
>
> Obviously we can raise our quavering voices only for Trent ... As an example, Trent was established in the early sixties, therefore according to Mr Robins it should be swamped by 'European rejects' hired in panic. In fact, the Trent faculty membership whose citizenship is French, English or Scottish – and of whom we are extremely proud – comprise less than one sixth of the total faculty. It would be most interesting to have Mr Robins identify the 'rejects' of whom he speaks so knowledgeably.
>
> Tenure, as such, is an extremely complex subject and is under review in Trent, as in every other university.
>
> So also is the 'publish or perish' thesis which Mr Robins seems to espouse so fulsomely. There is considerable heart-searching going on all over the academic world as to where lies the professor's major responsibility – research in his chosen field, or the imparting of knowledge to his students. Neither of these complex and complicated problems is capable of solution in the correspondence columns of the press ... Meanwhile, back to the 'Geritol'!

The 1960s were eventful for Forsey on other fronts as well. At the end of the decade he retired from the Canadian Labour Congress, still burdened by his vast research project on a history of the labour movement in Canada. This was an undertaking which he had begun after relinquishing his position of director of research and one which he carried with him into retirement, clinging like an albatross round his neck until its final publication a decade and a half later.

Paradoxically, in 1961 Forsey parted company with the political party which he had helped to found and which held itself out to be most supportive of the social causes he espoused. The break occurred formally shortly after the founding convention that transformed the CCF into the New Democratic Party. The convention had agreed, against Forsey's strident objections, to adopt a resolution favouring the two nations concept. To Forsey, it was blatantly nonsensical 'to form a new national political party' and begin 'by acknowledging that there was no nation to form it in.' Dogmatically principled to the end, Forsey dropped his membership with no other result, he said, than a stone sunk 'into a barrel of warm tar.'[10] The *Ottawa Journal* felt otherwise, however, for in an editorial on 20 October 1961 it commented:

> Without Dr Eugene Forsey the New Democratic Party will be duller than it might have been. And it has less hope of keeping its feet on the ground without his honed logic to puncture utopian balloons.
>
> Democracy is a lifeless thing without critics. It will do Canada no harm to have Dr Forsey without political ties, free to be a thorn in the side of all parties ...
>
> Dr Forsey's capacity for articulate indignation, which rose to noble heights during the pipeline debate and the imposition of closure in the Commons, is too valuable to be considered the property of any one party.

The *Journal* editorial accurately forecast Forsey's total engagement in what he himself described prophetically in 1990 as 'a battle that has now lasted almost thirty years and seems likely to last the rest of my life, and perhaps beyond.'[11] While the question of Quebec's place in Canada was prominent in Forsey's battle to preserve a single nation state, there was also the associated issue of finding a method for domesticating the process – in other words, for amending the British North America Act so that it would no longer be necessary to depend on the United Kingdom Parliament. The long-held desire to bring the constitution home took on a special urgency with the approach of Canada's one hundredth birthday. From 1960 on, it produced formal proposals enshrined in what came to be known as the Fulton-Favreau formula. An associated move to address the question of the bilingual character of Canada was taken up by a royal commission on bilingualism and biculturalism. The rising tide of French-Canadian separatism led to additional attempts at reconciliation, such as the Banff Conference on National Unity in 1964 and the Ontario Advisory Committee on Confederation, 1965–7. Forsey participated in both as a sort of devil's advocate, drawing on his immense historical and constitutional knowledge to correct myth-makers – the purveyors of 'constitutional fairy tales' – who, in his view, did no service to Canada by allowing emotions to override facts.

A fair proportion of Forsey's letters to the press during the 1960s mirrored his involvement in these issues of national unity, preservation of a strong central government presence in the face of provincial demands for more powers, constitutional amendment, language reform, and the place of Quebec in all of these.

The 1970s

This decade marked the ascendancy of the *Globe and Mail* as the preferred recipient of Forsey's letters, with 115 of the total of 238 published offerings located there. The *Ottawa Journal* held distant second place with 60 letters and the *Citizen* with 13 brought up the rear. The remaining 50 or so were scattered thinly across Canada from the *Vancouver Sun* to the *Charlottetown Guardian*. Abroad, Forsey managed to gain acceptance by the *Manchester Guardian Weekly* and *The Economist*. Reflecting the accumulating concern over the Quebec question, linguistic rights, and the hardy perennial of constitutional reform, *Le Devoir*, *Le Soleil* and *La Presse* carried Forsey letters in French. Offerings to his old standby, the *Canadian Forum*, tapered off, and his other weekly favourite, *Saturday Night*, seems to have been abandoned.

In October 1968 a tiff with the *Ottawa Journal* for publishing pictures of the queen against her express wishes had induced Forsey to cancel his subscription (announced by letter); the rift was soon closed, however, for by 1972 he was back with 5 letters. The year 1978 appears to represent the high-water mark for Forsey's letter-writing: at least 53 letters were published, of which 25 appeared in the *Globe* and 17 in the *Journal*, to go along with four major articles, one each in the *Globe*, the *Montreal Gazette*, *Le Devoir*, and *Le Soleil*.

With his appointment in October 1970 to the Senate of Canada, one might have expected that having this advantageous podium from which to express his views would have reduced his reliance on letters to the press. The actual increase in output during this decade of Senate service discounts this assumption. Indeed, not only did his colourful speeches in the Senate provide fodder for the press in the form of published generous extracts, but often a Forsey letter was required to correct what he contended was an inaccurate rendering or interpretation of his words. A sampling of such letters is to be found in the chapter 'You've Got Me Wrong!'

The 1970s witnessed an intensification of the debates over the future of Canada and the place of Quebec within it. Just as Forsey entered his freshman year in the Senate, the October Crisis of 1970 precipitated the invoking of the War Measures Act and the mustering in Quebec of federal forces to deal with suspected insurrection. Civil libertarian that he was, Forsey nevertheless joined majority public opinion in siding with the forces upholding 'peace, order and good government.' Five years later, when others with the presumably superior vision of sober hindsight contended that Forsey had abandoned his principles in defending the action, he responded unrevised and unrepentant to the needling of the late Donald Smiley in an exchange reproduced under the theme of 'The Judiciary and the Rule of Law.'

This violent opening to the decade was followed by the election in 1976 of the Parti Québécois, which was dedicated to a separatist platform and a resolute opposition to what it viewed as useless tinkering with constitutional amendment procedures when nothing else would serve but a new deal for the Quebec nation. This position had been firmed up when a formula for patriating and amending the constitution, the Victoria Charter of

1971, was unanimously approved, only to be rejected shortly thereafter by Quebec and the Liberal government of Robert Bourassa. In November 1976 the Parti Québécois, led by René Lévesque, formed a new government dedicated to separatism, championed under the conveniently amorphous rallying cry of sovereignty association. One of its first steps was to build on the language measures of the previous Liberal government which had sought to assuage burgeoning Quebec nationalism by protecting and expanding the use of the French language not only in education but also in everyday commercial transactions. All these matters swirling about the province of Quebec precipitated a storm of letters from Forsey, who fiercely contested the separatists' constitutional and linguistic propositions with historical facts and constitutional arguments.

Throughout the 1970s and, as the endless debate continued, into the 1980s, Forsey's letters were permeated by two convictions. First and foremost was his belief in the absolute necessity of maintaining a strong central government to give meaning and authority to the country called Canada. Calls for changes in such institutions as the Senate, or for reallocation of the constitutional powers conferred on the national government, required careful and critical scrutiny lest they become excuses for power grabs on the part of 'provincial warlords,' not all of whom were to be found in the province of Quebec.

In doing battle with the special claims of Quebec, Forsey was often obliged to express his other conviction that his opposition was not to be construed as anti-francophone prejudice: as he liked to remind his readers, he was fluently bilingual and for years had attended and even conducted services in French in a United Church that served the Ottawa francophone community. Despite this declared empathy for the French fact in Canada, Forsey never permitted emotional considerations to override what he often described as 'fairy tales' that derived from sheer ignorance or misbegotten soft-heartedness or soft-headedness. His fact-driven letters were constantly deployed in the service of enlightenment that alone could save Canada from such divisive ideas as 'two nations' and 'sovereignty association.'

The 1980s

Forsey's voice was silenced in the Senate by his retirement in 1979, but this in no way reduced his impact on the important constitutional manoeuvrings with which the 1980s opened and closed. Although his letters were no longer signed from 'The Senate,' it was hard to break the habit of referring to him as Senator Forsey. One newspaperman greeting him thus on the Sparks Street Mall recalls Forsey's peppery response: 'Don't call me "Senator" ... I'm not a senator any more. The Americans keep their titles for life, but we do not.'[12]

Much grist to Forsey's letter-writing mill was provided by the build-up to the patriation of the Canadian constitution that resulted in the Canada Constitution Act of 1982. The inclusion of a Charter of Rights and Freedoms, along with the complex amendment procedures that affected such federal institutions as the Senate, provided just the sort of subjects to which Forsey's encyclopaedic recall of all known precedents could be aptly applied. The threat by Prime Minister Pierre Trudeau to make the constitutional transfer, unilaterally if necessary, added an extra dimension to the debate and won for Forsey in 1981 a letter in *The Times* of London instructing members of the British Parliament on the legal niceties of the situation.

In the aftermath of Quebec's refusal to accept the new made-in-Canada constitution, the stage was set for three years of struggle over the Meech Lake Accord which then Prime Minister Brian Mulroney promoted in an effort to reconcile Quebec and 'bring it back into the family.' Throughout this campaign Forsey waged a vigorous attack against the accord by letters and articles in the press, presentations to sundry committees and, less publicly, by serving as a sort of *eminence gris* to the advisers of Clyde Wells, premier of Newfoundland. Had he lived to see its successor, the Charlottetown Agreement, there is little doubt that he would have contested it as vigorously as he did Meech Lake, if one can judge from the final letter he wrote to the press in February 1991.

Forsey's epistolary engagement with these events is covered

in the theme sections that follow, particularly 'Quebec,' and 'Forsey's Last Stand: The Meech Lake Accord and Its Aftermath.'

The total of 186 verified published letters to the press during the 1980s showed a decline. No doubt the demise in 1980 of his second most favoured outlet, the *Ottawa Journal*, helps to explain this reduced output. Moreover, serious health problems that culminated in 1988 with triple-bypass heart surgery and a resultant trifling output of just seven letters for that year, surely contributed to the decline. Possibly another signal of diminished energies was to be found in Forsey's concentration on the *Globe and Mail* as the prime beneficiary of his epistles (155 out of 186). Finally, since many of Forsey's letters in earlier times had been corrective responses to mis-reporting of his utterances on other platforms, a decline in such public appearances (including his formal presentations in the Senate) may have occasioned the reduction in his offerings to journals other than the *Globe*.

The overloaded constitutional agenda, as noted, provided the occasions for the production of the bulk of Forsey's letters. But, there was still time for whimsical defences of various causes, not the least of which was the defence of English usage and a continuation of his vendetta against policies he regarded as aberrant or ill-conceived, such as proposals to join the Organization of American States. As in previous decades, Forsey continued to reiterate home truths about appropriate constitutional procedures: correcting prime minister and journalists alike on the appropriate procedures to follow when a minority government received a vote of no confidence in the legislature; when it was proper to call a fresh election; what to do when an election failed to produce a clear winner; and statements on other lesser constitutional matters which anyone else but Forsey would have deemed more suitable for Trivial Pursuits.

Forsey had abandoned his party affiliation with the left in 1961 when he resigned from the newly formed New Democratic Party on a matter of principle. At the close of the decade, Pierre Trudeau's stout espousal of a united Canada and a strong central government in opposition to the rising tide of Quebec nationalism and separatist sentiment induced Forsey to throw in his lot with the Liberal party. However, when he was appointed to the Senate in 1970, as he makes clear in his memoirs, he was not regarded by party members as truly one of them and, indeed, voted in the Senate very much as the independent he always was. In 1982, no longer in the Senate but still a watchful guardian of civil liberties, Forsey broke his always frail loyalty to the Liberal party, resigning on matters of principle having to do with the government's failure to deal satisfactorily with the findings of the royal commission investigating the Royal Canadian Mounted Police, and arbitrary decisions affecting railway services made without consulting Parliament.

These matters raised questions about the executive's exercise of discretionary powers conferred by Parliament to which Forsey, as co-chairman of the Joint Committee on Statutory Instruments throughout the 1970s, had given his undivided attention and had waged constant combat with the Department of Justice. Forsey construed these actions by a Liberal government to run so contrary to two basic tenets of liberalism – the sovereignty of Parliament and the rule of law – that he could no longer support the party. Since he had joined in the first instance largely because of his belief in Pierre Trudeau's vision of a strong one-nation Canada, his withdrawal from the party did not affect his capacity to join forces with Trudeau when, subsequently, both entered the fray to seek the defeat of the Meech Lake Accord.

The Last Months in the 1990s

Even at the end of his life the flow of Forsey's letters to the editor continued undiminished. His output in 1990 of twenty letters to the *Globe* (plus several that went unpublished much to his chagrin) is remarkable considering his declining health and the exhaustion that attended the task of seeing his volume of memoirs through the press. Virtually all of these letters were emotion laden, dealing as they did with his lifelong battle to preserve intact the Canada he loved. There is a frenetic quality to his attacks on the Meech Lake Accord and the aftermath of its rejection, as if he anticipated the silencing of his voice through the only medium which his diminished physical strength permitted. It was the *Vancouver Sun* that became the recipient of what appears to be his last letter, published on 25 January 1991, directed to disarming the 'knife at the throat' argument presented to the Campeau-Belanger Commission in Quebec by a long-term verbal sparring partner, Professor Leon Dion. 'Sovereignty association won't work,' the letter was headed.

This was an argument that was to be enlarged on by Forsey's final effort ('it seems it is about all I can do'), an essay which he completed at the behest of friends on 7 February 1991, and which appeared posthumously in the *Toronto Star* on 21 February under the heading, 'Canada is more than a splash on the map.' The letters found for the closing themes, 'True Patriot Love' and 'Keeping the Faith,' have been chosen as a fitting epitaph for the doughty guardian of a Canada which he considered to be true to the legacy of the Founding Fathers.

PART TWO: FORSEY'S ABIDING CONCERNS

From the census of Forsey's letters, we proceed to a sampling of his output, assembled in accordance with the themes with which he was most consistently preoccupied. The topics addressed ranged from the ridiculous to the sublime, from the apparently frivolous to the weightiest matters of state. Forsey devoted the same energy and passionate attention to detail to every subject because at that moment each carried equal weight in his scheme of things. For this reason, it seems appropriate to include a sample of his letters on some of the lighter themes with which he sought not only to amuse but to instruct and censure his fellow citizens. The themes are arranged in ascending order of weightiness, the transition from the lighter notes to more serious concerns occurring when Forsey is obliged to tackle those who dared differ with him, misinterpreted him, or stooped to smear his good name.

The lighter themes begin with 'En Garde! For the English Language.' Forsey's own command of the language, his sense of the dangers of its misuse, and the inveterate teacher within him all combined to make his forays on this theme more than amusing diversions. Their relevance became particularly striking when he began to parse the vocabulary of the separatists/sovereignists.

With increasing acerbic wit but still on a relatively light note, there follow examples of Forsey as 'Moral Arbiter and Civic Censor.' Again, despite the deftness of the rapier touch, there was usually a serious undertone of the engaged citizen, concerned as much about the plight of flooded Florentine merchants as about the dangers of crossing Ottawa streets. His outbursts against the aesthetic judgment of those responsible for selecting and placing statuary in public places irritated many of the cognescenti, who were prone to equate him with the amateur who proclaimed not to know much about art but to know what he (dis)liked. Even in this subjective realm of taste, however, Forsey revealed a grasp of aesthetics which drew respect for, if not agreement with, his views.

The third group of letters, headed 'You've Got Me Wrong!' become more serious because they represent his constant concern to keep the record straight, whether it be a misquoting of his words or, more importantly, a defence against personal attacks. In addition, scattered throughout all the theme sections are letters which, in asserting 'you've got it wrong,' proclaimed Forsey's passion for getting the facts right.

Beginning with chapter 6, the letters present Forsey's serious concerns about the operation of our governing institutions, the constitution which embraces and empowers them, and the united nation called Canada which he felt to be their proud embodiment. For more than half a century, these were the matters most passionately addressed by Forsey and which attracted, by far, the bulk of his letters. Their number and the interconnected nature of the topics addressed complicates and renders somewhat arbitrary the selection of themes and letters relevant to this section.

Amongst the governing institutions, his comments on the status and functions of the governor general and the Senate have been singled out for special attention. The courts and their role in upholding the rule of law and, since 1982, the interpretation of the Charter of Rights, comprise another grouping.

Constitutional issues and the preservation of a united Canada were, of course, the primary Forsey preserve, the number of relevant letters reaching overwhelming proportions as his battle for Canada heated up in the late 1970s and thereafter. Selection of theme and letter has had to be both arbitrary and subjective, resulting in the assemblage of letters around Forsey's views on Quebec's place in Canada and his last constitutional stand in the battle over the Meech Lake Accord. A fitting closure is provided by his letters which testify to his dedication to a united Dominion, strong and free. For which, in 'True Patriot Love,' he steadfastly stood on guard, 'Keeping the Faith.'

CHAPTER THREE

En Garde! For the English Language

Forsey's way with words was nowhere better displayed than in the corrective letters he addressed to wayward abusers of the English language. Both the perpetrators and the schooling system from which they came received equal doses of his astringent linguistic cleanser. His strictures were laid down with the same vehemence that he used in his letters on the weightiest of constitutional issues. Nor was this just Forsey in his best 'school-marm' guise, for underlying his criticisms was his profound respect for the English language, coupled with his understanding of the power of words to distort as well as to convey meaning. For these reasons, one must grant the sense of serious purpose that often accompanied the more customary 'I gotcha!' motivation. His lifelong mission to ensure that the *facts* were properly disclosed and stated without orotund circumlocution made him a demanding taskmaster. Nevertheless, in these letters we find Forsey's own way with words setting a standard that others found it difficult to emulate – although some dared to try.

The letters which follow are selected from the three dozen or so he addressed to this theme, beginning sporadically in the 1940s but becoming a regular feature during the 1980s. Apart from the more obvious nit-picking letters calling attention to spelling errors, most of the letters focused on the misuse of words. A selected subset in this category included responses to the chosen lexicon of Quebec separatists – such terms as sovereignty association, special status, two nations, and the like, which are included in chapter 9 on Quebec.

One of Forsey's earliest forays as linguistic guardian occurred when, in the 13 September 1949 issue of *Saturday Night* its distinguished editor, B.K. Sandwell, announced a three-month campaign to clarify the uses of 'flout' and 'flaunt,' offering one dollar for examples submitted. Forsey weighed in at the close of the campaign with his own list of literary offences. The sting in the tail of this letter is directed to what Forsey viewed as the anti-labour stand of the magazine.

> I SEE you say you have now said your last word on 'flout' and 'flaunt.' It has been a fine campaign. I venture to suggest that you might now open fire on any one of the following: 'comprise' for 'compose,' 'connive' for 'conspire,' 'substitute' for 'replace,' 'adjust' as an intransitive verb, 'belabor' for 'labor,' 'presently' for 'at present,' 'as much as we detest Mr Blank, we must admit ...' for 'much as we detest Mr Blank ...,' 'different than' for 'different from.'
>
> It mightn't do any harm either to take a shot at ponderous circumlocutions like 'prior to' for 'before,' and 'in the event that' for 'if.' You will perhaps feel particularly eager to deal with the last two when I tell you that they are often used by trade unionists. It's a chance to blame us for the corruption of the English language, as well as for inflation, devaluation, etc., etc.

Not on Forsey's early list was the word 'hopefully,' which he later addressed in a letter to the *Ottawa Journal*, 16 February 1966. This drew a deft response from Professor E.M. Oppenheimer, which is also reproduced below for the light it throws on Forsey's intransigence in the face of the suggestion that perhaps there is room for flexibility and compromise as a language grows. Forsey wrote:

> Do you think you could use your influence to protect the English language against the ravages of the abominable misuse of the word 'hopefully'? A large and increasing number of otherwise literate people, led, or rather misled, by numerous learned men,

> labor under the delusion that 'hopefully' means 'I hope,' or 'we hope.' It does not. It means, 'in a hopeful frame of mind.'
>
> ... Almost certainly, this misuse of 'hopefully' is one of the ghastly literal mistranslations from the German inflicted on us by German-trained American PhD.'s with a shaky acquaintance with English and an apparently ineradicable reluctance to look at a dictionary. If they could be induced to do so, they would find that the German word 'hoffentlich' means 'it is to be hoped,' or 'I hope': the English word 'hopefully' does not appear.
>
> German is a magnificent language. So is English. A pidgin mixture of the two is fit for nothing but to be cast out and trodden under foot of men.

Professor E.M. Oppenheimer countered, 19 February:

> I was more reassured than surprised to find that estimable one-man-academy, Dr Eugene Forsey, standing on guard and not caught napping in the case of 'hopefully.' I share his interest in the modifications of use to which this word is being put, and I agree that there is probably some connection with the German 'hoffentlich.'
>
> But instead of pointing an accusing finger at 'German-trained American PhD.'s' I would suggest that a need for a single adverb to take the place of the phrases 'I hope that' and 'it is to be hoped that' is asserting itself and being filled ...
>
> Of course, such innovations sound faddish and atrocious at first, but I am willing to let the language itself decide, whether it will assimilate or reject a graft of this kind.
>
> As to Dr Forsey's peroration: 'German is a magnificent language. So is English. A pidgin mixture of the two is fit for nothing ...': Exactly 900 years ago, English became the finest pidgin mixture of them all, as witness the writings of G. Chaucer, W. Shakespeare, E. Forsey.'

Professor Oppenheimer's reference to flexibility and the assimilative capacities of the English language had, indeed, been bruited in Sandwell's 'flout' versus 'flaunt' campaign. With the campaign barely started, he found it necessary to produce this disclaimer: 'We have to warn some of our readers that though we are interested in the purity of the English language we have no intention of refraining altogether from the use of colloquialisms in these dignified columns.'

Nearly four decades later, on 26 April 1986, in an exchange on the letters page of the *Globe and Mail* over the use of 'rankle,' Forsey remained his own unbending defender of purity – although in this instance he had to take refuge in his preference for English-English rather than American-English dictionaries: 'Re. Labor Board Rankles Saskatchewan Unionists (April 19): Please tell your headline writer that 'rankle' is an intransitive verb. Something rankles *in* something or *in* somebody.'

On 6 and 7 May, two correspondents took issue, both appealing to the authority of Funk and Wagnall's American-English dictionary that listed 'rankle' as both transitive and intransitive. 'As a transitive verb,' wrote Fraser Simpson, '"rankle" means to "irritate."' He then went on to claim that 'A living language like English has words that change in meaning and use over time. It is unfortunate that this rankles so many.'

Unrepentent, Forsey responded: 'I gather that my comment on "rankle" has stirred up some friends of the American language (letters – May 6 and 7). I still prefer English.'

Forsey seemed prepared, however, to accept a declaration of 'obsolescence' (provided that it came from a proper English source), as when he tackled the misuse of 'fulsome' (*Globe and Mail*, 27 January 1987):

> A linguistic epidemic has struck the House of Commons. It manifests itself in the use of the word 'fulsome' to mean 'full' or 'fuller' or 'fully.' It afflicts all three parties, but the most conspicuous victims are two ministers.
>
> One thanked the Danish Embassy in Tehran for its 'fulsome degree of co-operation.' The other said a colleague had answered a question 'very fulsomely and very forthcomingly.'
>
> Long ago, 'fulsome' did mean 'full' or 'abundant.' But the Oxford English Dictionary says those meanings are now 'obsolete.' For the contemporary meaning, it gives: 'offensive to good

> taste, especially offending from excess or want of measure or from being "overdone." Now chiefly used in reference to gross flattery, over-demonstrative affection, or the like.'
>
> Perhaps the Danish Embassy in Tehran, or the minister whose answer was described as 'fulsome,' will be looking for apologies.

Forsey remained unchallenged, because unchallengeable, in catching out contributors and letter-writers who misplaced words. A typical letter is that of 21 February 1987 to the *Globe*.

> In Edward Babin's interesting and valuable article Time For Canada To End Its Role In Cruise Tests (Feb.9), he says it has been 'stated that Canada has consistently been deleterious in its contributions ... to the common defence of the West.'
>
> My dictionary says 'deleterious' means 'harmful.' This is the first time I have ever heard that anyone, however critical of our defence efforts, policies or contributions, has said they have been harming the common defence of the West, let alone consistently harming.
>
> I should be interested to know who has made this allegation.

On 10 November 1984 Forsey probably took more delight in catching out the distinguished contributors of a collective letter to the *Globe* for their misuse of 'precipitous.' His satisfaction must have been the greater because earlier in the same year (28 April) he had found it necessary, with the use of Fowler's *Modern English Usage*, to lecture both the minister of education and the editorialist for the same offence.

> We all know that, occasionally, 'Homer nods.' But when seven Homers nod in unison, it is an event. In their letter of Oct.11, Louis Applebaum, Pierre Berton, John Hirsch, Ron Ide, Gordon Pinsent, Walter Pitman and Sam Sniderman plead with the Government to consider seriously any question of asking for the resignation or dismissal of Pierre Juneau as head of the CBC 'before taking precipitous action.'
>
> According to the Oxford Dictionary, 'precipitous' means 'of, like a precipice, steep.' It does add: '(rare) – precipitate.'
>
> Rare indeed, and rarer it ought to be.

Nearly the last of Forsey's contributions to the *Globe* (17 August 1990) was reserved for that hardy perennial, the aberrant use of the apostrophe – the more offensive in this case because it had occurred in the course of publishing one of his own previous letters.

> I am beginning to think the English language should get rid of the apostrophe. So few people seem to have any idea of where to use it.
>
> We get 'its' (meaning 'of it') for 'it's' (meaning 'it is'). We get 'citizen's rights' (meaning 'rights of a citizen,' singular) for 'citizens' rights' (meaning the 'rights of citizens,' plural) ... People often seem just to sprinkle apostrophes as if they were shaking them out of a pepper-shaker. The latest example to hit me is in a letter of mine to the *Globe and Mail* (Aug.4) in which I am made to say, 'Ask the Mohawk's at Oka.' This could only mean that there is some particular individual at Oka who enjoys the title, 'the Mohawk,' and that we should ask someone belonging to his or her family ... This is, of course, nonsense. What I wrote was, 'Ask the Mohawks,' the whole lot of them.
>
> Whoever inserted that apostrophe is kin to the student at McGill many years ago who told one of my colleagues that he had no idea at all of punctuation: he just wrote a page and then inserted commas, periods, question marks at random.
>
> This haphazard use of apostrophes is a nuisance. If the schools can't teach people what the apostrophe is, and why it is used, and where, hadn't we better just throw it overboard?

Forsey's battle on behalf of 'this endangered species, the past tense' was also one of his late contributions to this genre of letters. His first corrective piece came on 15 February 1989:

> English and French are the official languages of Canada. 'Fit' as the past tense of 'fit' is neither. Why do reputable, even eminent, journalists persist in using it? Here is one example: Sir John A. Macdonald's National Policy 'fit the times.'
>
> 'Fitted' is the past tense of ' fit,' as 'knitted' is the past tense of 'knit,' and 'flitted' is the past tense of 'flit.'

Are we going to be treated to: 'Year after year, she knit his socks,' or 'The hummingbird flit from flower to flower'? How far will this infection spread? I had an editor at a university press tell me that 'whet' was the past tense of 'whet.'

'This victory,' he wrote, when 'correcting' my English, 'whet the union's appetite.' I dare say he would have written: 'She flirt with her boss,' or 'He rent his house last year.'

To vary Winston Churchill's celebrated phrase: This is bastard English, up with which we should not put.

Forsey's first effusion was greeted by a deft rejoinder from Henry Whitman which accompanied a second letter of 4 March, in which Forsey likened the fate of the past tense to the demise of the passenger pigeon.

Dare I gently needle Eugene Forsey, who throws his pearls while keeping us in stitches? (Tense Situation – Feb.15). Is there a fly in the soothing logic of his erudite ointment?

For if, as Dr Forsey says,
The past of knit is knitted.
Why not then, have in parallel
A past of sit as sitted?
'No! No!' the gentle man declaims,
'The past of sit is sat!'
If that's so sir, may I suggest
The past for knit be gnat.[2]

Forsey shared with other readers the delight in pointing up the sometimes ludicrous quality of bureaucratese, as witness his letter to the *Globe* on 19 November 1982, headed 'Broken English.'

There has recently come to my attention a regulation issued by the Board of Transport Commissioners. It deals with radio communications on the railways.

It specifies that, in such communications, the English number 'three' shall be pronounced 'tree'; 'four' shall be 'fower'; 'five' shall be 'fife'; 'nine' shall be 'niner'; 'thousand' shall be 'tousand'; and the word 'decimal' shall be pronounced 'day-cee-mal.'

It would be interesting to know who decreed this broken English, and why; the more so because there is no indication that the French numbers, in an adjoining column, are to be pronounced in anything but the ordinary French way.

Forsey took even deeper offence to what we might today call inappropriate respect for political correctness when it came to pronouncing or spelling place names in a 'non-English' way. Here is his condemnation of the practice in a letter to the *Globe and Mail* on 8 April 1975.

Norman Webster, in his comments on the René Lévesque–Robert Nixon debate (Dialogue Results in a Draw – April 2) says that Mr Nixon, speaking English, referred to 'the province next door as Quee-beck.'

How did he expect him to refer to it? As Kay-beck? If so, why? When Mr Webster is speaking of the capital of France, in English, does he call it Paree? ...

For an English-speaking Canadian to call Quebec Kay-beck is just affectation ... When we are speaking English, let us stick to the accepted English pronunciation of place names of another language. To do otherwise is as silly as to insist on people's saying spokesperson, for 'spokesman,' or 'personkind' for 'mankind,' or siblinghood' for 'brotherhood.' (What a choice morsel ' the siblinghood of personkind' would be. What a rallying cry for humanitarian causes!)

The accenting of words such as Montreal and Quebec when writing in English drew down equal condemnation. In December 1975 the then editor of *Saturday Night*, Robert Fulford, approved the notion under his Notebook heading, 'The Politics of Style.' Recollecting the affair twenty years later, Fulford admitted that the controversy had started when 'in a fit of pan-Canadianism we decided to use accents on Montreal, Quebec, etc., following the style that the Quebec government of the day followed in its English-language publications.' Fulford's *mea culpa* continues:

> That was a silly idea. But, like most people who get a stupid notion in their head, we stuck to it, becoming more righteous with each passing letter of scorn from our readers. Embarrassment slowly crept up on us. I barely suffered the shame of John Robert Colombo's note about 'Québec City,' admittedly a stunningly wrong-headed usage. Still, we stuck to our guns, such as they were. Then one of our readers decided to appeal to a higher authority. He wrote to Forsey and elicited a letter saying our accent style was a piece of damn foolishness, or some such. Recognizing that our enemies had now acquired superior force, we did the prudent thing and surrendered.[3]

As Fulford admitted, however, the surrender was done silently, 'the way publications always do it,' and Forsey's *coup de grâce* was quietly buried.

CHAPTER FOUR

Moral Arbiter and Civic Censor

Moral Arbiter

It is not surprising to find Forsey, a non-smoker, an early advocate of measures to protect non-smokers from the puffers' pollution of public places. A particular instance which drew Forsey's ire in the *Ottawa Journal* on 30 September 1964 was what he considered to be the excessively permissive approach taken to smokers at the Ottawa Civic Hospital, even though signs pointed out the dangers of smoking where oxygen equipment was in use, and mildly proclaimed that elsewhere in the hospital smoking was 'discouraged.' 'For sheer fatuousness and poltroonery, this could scarcely be surpassed,' Forsey raged. As an erstwhile patient himself, he wrote:

> I recall lying in the corridor of the X-ray division and watching men walking up and down puffing away at pipes and cigarettes like chimneys. When I called a nurse's attention to this breach of what appeared to be an important rule, she replied, 'Oh, that's only the doctors and they know there really isn't any oxygen equipment in use.'
>
> ... If smoking in the Civic Hospital is the danger the hospital authorities say it is, then they should pluck up enough spunk to stop it. If they content themselves with merely twittering at the smoking visitors, they will be derelict in their duties, and deserve to be dismissed, and replaced by people who will behave like

> men, not mice. Surely we do not have to wait till patients die, or till there is a fire and explosion to knock some sense into the heads of the hospital authorities.

Yet another typical contribution to the *Globe and Mail* (6 September 1974) appeared under the heading 'No Smoking.'

> As one of the oppressed minority of non-smokers, I am delighted to find the Canadian National Railways has now, in some of its trains, provided non-smoking sections.
>
> But I wish it would instruct its conductors and trainmen to see that the rules are observed. It is a nuisance to have to ask the staff, explicitly, and sometimes, repeatedly, to request the human chimneys to move to the space reserved for them, so that the rest of us can avoid absorbing the noxious fumes which they emit. All we ask is that these puffing Billies should go to the space reserved for them, and allow us the space reserved for us: surely a modest request. Surely, also, it is not too much to ask the railway staff to enforce the rules the railway has made.

In a nonsense verse, Forsey conducted a debate with himself over the relative offensiveness of 'puffers and pushers.' Although it appears not to have been reproduced as a letter to the press, as a sample of Forsey's whimsical wit at its best, it seemed eminently worthy of inclusion.

> When forth from Ottawa I fare,
> In aeroplanes that cleave the air,
> Whether I travel east or west.
> The rank, I vow, of leading pest
> Goes either to the inveterate smoker
> Or else to the persistent poker.
> The one befouls the atmosphere,
> The other kicks me in the rear.
> One takes the taste from what I eat,
> The other cracks me in the seat.
> Without, how blue and clear the skies!

Within, the smoke gets in my eyes.
Outside, through clouds the aircraft goes,
Inside, the smoke gets up my nose.
While ever smoothly on I float,
Tobacco fumes choke up my throat.
All this I call a major curse;
And yet, perhaps, the other's worse.
The smoker suffocates me, true,
But does not make me black and blue.
The smoker makes me nearly blind,
But does not hit me from behind.
The smoker causes me to frown,
But still allows me to sit down.
The nicotine gets in my hair,
But does not lift me from my chair.
Twixt two such pests the human brain
To hold the scales must strive in vain!
When kicker's feet a trice are calm,
To smoker I award the palm.
And when the smoker lets me breathe,
The kicker gets the laurel wreath.
So both alike I freely curse,
I really can't say *which* is worse
Per se; and yet admit I must
(For I am trying to be just)
The kicker only from the back
His helpless victim can attack;
At but one point this plague is found,
But smokers on all sides abound.
So if I *have* to make a choice
It's number that decide my voice.
In quality, there's naught to choose
In quantity, the kickers lose.
In all but this, they hold their own;
Outnumbered, they must yield the crown.
So there at last you have the answer –
But *will* you *please* not kick my pants, Sir?[1]

As a firm temperance supporter, Forsey censured the National Arts Centre in a letter to the *Globe and Mail* on 16 April 1969:

> I heard, over the air, a few days ago, that the National Arts Centre has applied for 11 liquor licences, and that the Ontario Liquor Control Board had, till that moment, received no objections.
>
> The application, and the lack of objections, alike seem to me shocking. I realize that we live in a society which is more and more alcohol-oriented. But surely, 11 licences for one building, is excessive? Surely the Centre, and the Board, can preserve some sense of proportion?
>
> The welkin rings with expressions of horror by the old at the indulgence of the young in drugs other then alcohol. Eleven licences in one building for the dispensing of this drug is hardly a shining example of moderation, the good sense, the self-discipline, which the young are exhorted to practice.

In similar vein, in the same year (*Globe*, 21 November), Forsey took after 'the older generation.'

> In your report on Organized Heads (Toronto Youths Form Agency to Teach Others about Drugs – Nov. 17), Doug Butler says of young drug users: 'The kids feel parents have their drugs and the kids want their own.'
>
> Margaret Mead, some weeks ago, said much the same.
>
> The moral, for the older generation who deplore youthful indulgence in drugs, seems obvious. Yet many of the older generation seem content to 'compound for drugs they are inclined to, by damning those they have no mind to.' No wonder elderly horror (which I share) fails to impress some of the young.

Ethical concerns always loomed large in Forsey's mind-set; the following four letters reveal Forsey's impatience with practices he felt went beyond proper boundaries.

From the *Globe*, 26 January 1971, 'Essay bank.'

> The Student Liberals' announcement of their essay bank, to facili-

tate organized cheating in the universities, is the most scandalous performance by a supposedly responsible political organization that I can remember.

What are we to expect next from people who are apparently so morally obtuse? A School for Corrupt Practices? Corrupt practices also have 'always existed' and they are one form of that 'direct political involvement' whose 'educative' value John Varley and his friends rate so highly.

To a former policy adviser moving into private consultancy practice, Forsey had this admonition (*Globe*, 14 September 1968), under the heading 'Improper':

I have been waiting and waiting for someone to protest against William Lee's letters to various 'friends,' suggesting that the Prime Minister's office, and the Minister of Transport's office, would be willing to act as a telephone answering service for Mr Lee's new firm until the firm opened its permanent office in Ottawa on (if memory serves) Oct. 1.

Surely this is a most improper proceeding? Mr Lee presumably possesses some local habitation, with or without a telephone, to which anyone wishing to communicate with him might send anything he had to say. But if not, it would at least be more proper for him to avail himself of the services of the Liberal Federation of Canada, which certainly possesses an Ottawa address and telephone number. There are also the General Delivery facilities at the Post Office.

Consultancy fees, at polar opposites, offended Forsey's Gladstonian notions of proper governmental husbandry: 'Liberal Scholarship Plan?' (*Globe*, 25 July 1963) and 'Macdonald's Worth' (*Ottawa Citizen*, 4 March 1983).

I see the Government paid Mr Geoffrey Conway, whom the Finance Minister describes as a 'student,' a living allowance of $1,487.50, and fees of $3,250, for a period of 70 days. (Consultant

> Expenses Defended by Gordon – July 20). This works out to $67.67 per day, or pretty close to $24,700 per year.
>
> Is this the Liberal Scholarship Plan?

> The Citizen of Feb. 23 reports Hon. Donald Macdonald as saying he thinks he is 'worth more' than $800 a day; indeed, as saying, 'I don't think I'm worth more than that – I know I'm worth more than that.'
>
> This is the sort of thing one usually leaves to other people to say about one's value.
>
> But Mr Macdonald evidently takes his cue from Gilbert and Sullivan:
>
> 'For he himself has said it,
> 'And it's greatly to his credit.'
>
> Incidentally, we are told that a large part of the $800 will go to pay the overhead of Mr Macdonald's law firm, McCarthy and McCarthy.
>
> Why?
>
> Mr Macdonald has not been retained by the government of Canada as counsel. He has been appointed a royal commissioner. His work as a royal commissioner has nothing whatever to do with the practise of his profession ...
>
> Appointment as a royal commissioner used to be considered an honor, carrying, accordingly, an honorarium, not a fee for the professional services (let alone the overhead) of any lawyer, physician or dentist so appointed. If this involved some financial sacrifice for the appointee and he felt unable to make the sacrifice, he declined the appointment.
>
> Apparently times have changed, and the public is now charged what the traffic will bear; a notable example of the 'restraint' which all of us, especially the poor, are exhorted to practise.

Forsey's role as moral arbiter often carried him into the arena to protect civil rights and as an advocate of good causes. His position on civil rights is best left to be traced under the theme of 'The Judiciary and Rule of Law,' where his general position on the Charter of Rights is highlighted. Here are reproduced samples of Forsey's advocacy, accompanied by his plea, which must have attracted many supportive endorsements, to reduce junk mail and repetitious appeals. The disastrous flooding of Florence drew a letter of support that Forsey sent broadside to a number of newspapers, that of 11 March 1967 in the *Ottawa Journal* being typical. In a more personal advocacy role, he is found defending osteopaths (*Globe*, 6 August 1982), signing as chairman, Board of Directors, Canadian Osteopathic Aid Society. The third letter, headed 'A Really Good Cause' (*Globe*, 12 December 1983), is one of several where Forsey pleads for more efficiency in the mailings by charitable organizations, one which he also directed to political party fund-raisers ('Making Cents in Cards,' *Globe*, 25 August 1982):

> The recent lecture at the National Gallery has reminded us of the havoc wrought by the November floods on the art treasures of Florence. What has received less publicity is the disaster which the same floods brought to the living inheritors of the Florentine tradition, the artisans and crafts men of Florence whose work is treasured by all who have ever visited the city ...
>
> ... The Florentine Artisan's Fund (FAF) has been set up, under the direct sponsorship of the Mayor of Florence and of various others, including Lady Jackson (Barbara Ward), for the express purpose of helping the artisans of Florence to get started again at their crafts they have practised, father and son, for 700 years.
>
> Contributions should be sent to ...

> I am delighted to see in Zena Cherry's column (July 27) that so many eminent persons have petitioned the Ontario Government to allow osteopathic physicians to practice on the same basis as other physicians, as they already do in every state of the American Union.
>
> For years we of the Canadian Osteopathic Aid Society have been making this request ...
>
> This seems a not unreasonable proposal. It would completely rule out the incompetent and the ill-trained. It would make avail-

able to the public, on a modest scale (for the graduates of osteopathic medical schools are far from numerous), additional medical services of a special kind which many of us find invaluable. These we are now in danger of losing completely because new osteopathic graduates will not come to Ontario, where they are forbidden to use the full range of their knowledge and skills.

I hope the eminent persons will have better luck with their petition than we have had with ours. When we have asked the Government for action, they have replied that it is a matter for the College of Physicians and Surgeons. When we have asked the College of Physicians and Surgeons, they have replied that it a matter for the Government.

Various good causes, in their appeal for funds, tell us we can 'save them a little money' by putting stamps on the envelopes over the 'postage paid' sign.

They could save much more by weeding out the duplicates, from their mailing lists. Very often, I get two appeals from the same organization in a single day's mail (in one case, recently, I got three). They are identical, except for different numbers in one corner. (In fairness, I must admit that one of the two, or three, sometimes manages to misspell my name, or present me with a new Christian name, or new initials. Occasionally they give me a new surname. One envelope was addressed 'Mr. E.A.Fo'; two others were addressed 'Senator & A.' – just the sign for 'and,' no surname, not so much as a number.)

'Senator & A.' really beats even the celebrated 'Five-eighths Smith' of the American Social Security files, or the 'Z. Anybody' who for some years figured in the Ottawa telephone book.

Greg Michalenko (Aug. 18), getting all those PC Canada Fund appeals and the 'lovely embossed card' for his minus contributions, has plainly been a victim of a stuttering (and retarded) computer. As his envelopes arrived, empty, or stuffed with junk mail or, finally, autumn leaves, the computer simply registered each one as a contribution and, when a set number had been reached, spat out the 'Sustaining Member' card.

One wonders how the 'contributions' will be measured: how much junk mail, how many autumn leaves, make a dollar?

The same computer must have been at work issuing all those Toronto-Broadview membership cards. In went the pages of the Metro Toronto Directory, out popped the cards.

If only the Conservative Party could use the same computer in elections, it could announce that its candidates had been elected unanimously. But, of course, the returning officers and the Chief Electoral Officer might register a dissenting opinion.

Forsey's moral sensibilities extended to journalistic ethics as well. A letter addressed to the *Citizen* in 1953 (which seems not to have been published) criticized what he perceived to be the somewhat ghoulish coverage of a mass bereavement. Nearly thirty years later (2 August 1985, 'Revolting Practice') he was castigating the same offence in the *Globe*. However, his most serious response was registered, along with that of numerous other defenders of the good image of the Queen, in the *Journal* (9 October 1968, 'Discourtesy'). A portion of the newspaper's defence, appended in an editor's note, seemed worthy of inclusion, not only for the light it throws on the considerations that enter into the decision to print but also, in light of contemporary press coverage of the royal family, how quaintly decent and old-fashioned were the press attitudes three decades ago.

I protest the printing of pictures of the agonies of the bereaved, such as the one on your front page of July 23, showing a scene at the 'mass burial of the victims in Tesero,' Italy.

Presumably, none of the people concerned will ever see a Toronto paper. But the practice of printing pictures like this is revolting.

– When I read that you were proposing to publish the photographs of the Queen which she had explicitly asked the British press not to publish, I could scarcely believe my eyes. That the paper so long presided over by that great gentleman, Mr P.D.

Ross, should be guilty of so gross a discourtesy to any lady, let alone the Queen, seemed, and still seems, incredible. But, alas! in Friday's edition, the proof was there.

To say that the pictures are 'warm' and 'charming' is nothing to the purpose. The Queen asked that they should not be published, and you published them. I was under the impression that yours was a Conservative newspaper, and that the Conservative party, above all things, was loyal to the Queen. Deliberate, brazen flouting of her express wishes is a strange kind of loyalty. It is not my kind, and I have accordingly cancelled my subscription.

EDITOR'S NOTE: *The sentiments expressed ... are understandable. The conflict between good taste and a newspaper's responsibility in news judgment to mirror the world so that people may see it all is always hard to resolve.*

We do not question the motives or sentiments of our correspondents, nor their loyalty. As to our own loyalty or good taste, the present and previous editors of this newspaper have often had both called into question. It happens to editors.

The Journal *will regret losing any readers, but specially Mr Forsey for we have always welcomed his own trenchant and animated letters of praise, criticism or comment. We hope that on second thought he will remain a reader if only to exercise his own loyalty to Queen and country by writing us to keep us straight ...*

True to his word, over the next three years, the flow of Forsey's letters to the *Journal* dried up, although an article under his byline was published on 13 May 1970 and by January 1972 he had reopened a correspondence that continued unabated until the demise of the *Journal* in 1980.

Civic Censor

The *Ottawa Citizen*, described by one of its former editors as the newspaper Forsey loved to hate, tended to share with the *Journal* his epistolery complaints as a resident of the city.[2] These ranged from a concern for pedestrian safety, unsanitary streets, smoke and noise pollution, to the inroads of developers on the city and environs.

Here, reproduced just as it came from his well-worn typewriter on 27 November 1950, is a typical enraged outcry that appeared in the *Citizen* on 30 November under the heading 'Hunted Pedestrians.'

The Editor,
The Citizen,
Ottawa.

3 Lakeview Terrace,
Ottawa, November 27, 1950.

Sir,

As one of many hunted pedestrians, I should like to know what, if anything, the candidates for municipal office propose to do for our protection. I understand it is illegal to cross the street at traffic light corners except on the green light. But to obey the law is to court death. I have to cross every day at Laurier and O'Connor, and often at Carling and Bronson. Motors to right of me, motors to left of me, motors in front of me, volley and thunder. By the time I have waited for them all to turn, the light has changed to red again. This performance is sometimes repeated until I begin to wonder whether I shall qualify for old age pension before I can get across. I have no doubt other people have the same experience, or worse.

There is one perfectly simple remedy. They use it in Boston. There all vehicular traffic stops on the yellow light, and that light is kept on long enough to allow any reasonably able-bodied pedestrian to cross in safety. If Boston can do it, why not Ottawa?

Pedestrians of Ottawa, unite! Make the civic candidates declare themselves on this question, and make the new Council act to protect us!

Yours truly,

Eugene Forsey.

National Archives of Canada

More restrained was an earlier letter to the *Journal*, offering at some length 'suggestions for improvement of the service,' now 'that the City of Ottawa has taken over the street railway system.'

Another letter to the *Journal*, on 19 August 1961, having to do with stop signs, had a rather broader application, an early revelation of Forsey's lifelong concern to hold his beloved Canada together against the forces of the 'two-nations' sponsors.

> I was delighted to see your editorial, 'Stop-Arretez.' This was the first I had heard of the Ontario Legislature's stupid, narrow-minded, bigoted insistence on English only for such signs.
>
> This is the sort of thing which plays right into the hands of the Quebec separatists and the cranks who say there is no Canadian nation, just a French-Canadian nation and an English-Canadian one. The legislature has made an appalling blunder, and done a grave disservice to national unity. It should take the first opportunity to undo what it has done, and show some sense, not to say some sense of the bi-cultural character of the nation which the Fathers of Confederation thought they were founding 94 years ago.

Rubbish on the streets of Ottawa was greeted with an appeal through the *Citizen* (25 August 1951) to 'people who are otherwise decent and respectable [to] exercise a little self-restraint and consideration for other people in this matter.' His appeal ended with the suggestion 'that the schools could do more than they do to impress on the children that scattering waste paper and other rubbish on the streets is a disgusting and disreputable habit. A good many of the grown ups have never learned this lesson, and are probably past praying for. Can we make a new start with the younger generation?' His appeal seems to have been disregarded, for the *Journal* on 9 June 1952, under the heading 'Porcine Level,' carried this letter from a disgusted Forsey:

> The Driveway is generally considered one of the chief beauties of Ottawa. One might expect Ottawa citizens to have some pride in it, and some desire to keep it as tidy as possible.

> But a lot of them apparently haven't. Last night, on a short walk along the section near Dow's Lake, I found such a litter of rubbish that I went home and got a large waste-basket, and I picked up enough to fill it to the brim.
>
> Some of the rubbish was of a kind that children could have been responsible for ... but a lot of it was cigarette boxes for which, presumably, man (or woman) in all his (or her) glory was responsible.
>
> A self-respecting pig would be ashamed to make such a mess. I wonder if anything can be done to bring the lords of creation up to something like the porcine level?

Offensive billboards were targeted in the *Journal* on 23 February 1957:

> I see Education Week is now once more almost upon us. I should like to suggest to the committee responsible that one useful enterprise they could undertake is to rid us of the sight of that over-stuffed child who leers impudently at us from numerous billboards ordering us to support our community's education 'program.'
>
> The only response that advertisement can evoke in any normally constituted person is a strong desire to put the child through a course of reducing exercises.

Noise pollution received equally short shrift in this letter to the *Journal* on 4 February 1961, headed 'Radio vs. Dogs':

> Hurrah for your editorial on portable radios in OTC buses! Why the Commission allows these infernal squawk-boxes, and at the same time forbids people to take on the buses quiet, peaceable, self-respecting dogs, is beyond me. Up the dogs, down the squawk-boxes, say I!

The public's favourite scapegoat, the postal service, also failed to escape Forsey's satiric attention in a letter headed 'Everything's Relative' (*Globe*, 6 January 1983):

Re Is Mail Service Really Faster? (Dec. 24):

Yes.

On Nov. 25, I received, at my office, a personal letter from the Chief Justice of Canada, posted at the Supreme Court on Nov. 17. It was correctly addressed, postal code and all, and typewritten. The distance is seven blocks.

In 1967, I had a personal letter from the then Minister of Justice, correctly addressed, posted at the West Block of the Parliament Buildings, to my then office in the Ottawa Electric Building. The distance is three blocks. It took nine days.

Seven blocks in eight days is certainly a notable improvement over three blocks in nine days.

There has also been a great improvement over 1977. On Nov. 11 of that year, I sent a letter, correctly addressed, to a well-known private citizen, from the Civic Hospital to his address, 200 Rideau Terrace, Ottawa. He received it on March 26, 1978.

Aesthetic Guardian

Turning from this type of civic censorship, one finds in a category all its own Forsey's vendetta against the Department of Public Works, especially his diatribes against the aesthetic decisions of those responsible for the selection and siting of sculptures in public places. This was a campaign that he conducted not only in the press but also from the floor of the Senate, where he did not hesitate to call into question the credentials of the members of the Art Advisory Committee for the Department of Public Works.

On 5 July 1967 the *Ottawa Journal*, under the heading 'Chuck It?,' carried the first of Forsey's attacks on 'what I suppose is, by courtesy, called the 'sculpture on the Mall, near Elgin Street,' concluding with the advice that 'by any rational standards [it] should grace the city dump.' He renewed his attack in the Senate, his targets in 1973 being 'the monstrosity known as Traffic' opposite the Lord Elgin Hotel (referred to as 'a very large intestine'), a 'performance' in front of the National Defence Building, and 'the thing' outside the Pearson Building described by 'a high personage' as 'Hello, what's this? Something left behind by the builders' labourers?'[3] To his query in the *Citizen* on 8 September 1971, 'Who is responsible for placing in the park opposite the Lord Elgin Hotel that hideous representation of a large intestine?' a reader (K.C. Stein) deigned to enlighten him on 14 September: 'He [Forsey] may be amused to know that it is an artistic representation of the Senate. It goes up and down, around and around, performing no special function at great expense.'

Even when an official response to his inquiry about the membership of the Advisory Committee revealed that it comprised some of the most respected names in the field of art and architecture, Forsey remained unconvinced. Citing the late Healey Willan, Forsey took comfort from Willan's conclusion that 'even the intellegentsia sometimes make asses of themselves.'

When the art critic for the *Globe and Mail* commented adversely on the line of attack spearheaded by Forsey, her column drew the following joint response from Forsey, Ralph Stewart, MP, and Robert Legget, OC, on 5 December 1973:

> 'Kooks' Chorus which drones from Parliament Hill' (Ottawa Showplace for Stunning Art ... Nov. 24) is not an expression that we would have expected to see in the respected pages of the Globe and Mail. It is but one of the insulting remarks that Kay Kritzwiser bestows upon the citizens of Ottawa, its newspapers and, even more unfortunately, upon members of the Senate and the House of Commons in her diatribe about the so-called art that is being placed in and near public buildings in the capital city.
>
> Kay Kritzwiser calls these works stunning. The Oxford Dictionary says stun means to 'knock senseless, overwhelm or temporarily paralyze, or stupefy by shock.' Is it the function of art to knock senseless, to paralyze, to stupefy?
>
> Phrases like soaring rectangles certainly suggest a state of mind bordering on stupefaction.
>
> If, on her visit to Ottawa, this writer had consulted any ordinary citizen she would have found how widespread is the mount-

> ing anger at this profligate waste of public money at the behest of a group of artists, with no public input, let alone any control by elected representatives of the people of Canada. This applies not only to those whose views on art may be conservative but also to the many, such as those who sign this letter, who appreciate true modern art in its rightful place but who have no time for the charlatanry that is now being foisted on us.
>
> In one thing was Kay Kritzwiser correct – there is a sense of fear allied to the city-wide resentment about this waste of public money. But it is not the fear she describes. It is rather the fear that this city's freedom from vandalism may not long continue, so objectionable are some of the items she attempts to defend; fear that this squandering of public money may lead to a reaction against justifiable expenditures from the public purse; fear that, before too long, Ottawa will be a laughing stock instead of a city to admire, as visitors are faced with this utter rubbish and find that as taxpayers they have helped to pay for it.

This letter prompted the eminent Canadian architect, Eric Arthur, to rise to the defence on 11 December 1973, his response couched in terms of his recommendations to the Massey Commission on the Arts which had pleaded for a percentage of the construction cost of new public buildings to be devoted to artistic embellishment. Extolling the results of the 1 per cent contribution for the new legislative buildings in Toronto, Arthur's letter went on to defend developments in Ottawa:

> Since the Government of Canada has accepted contemporary architecture for its public buildings, and one cannot conceive of its doing otherwise, it follows that any embellishment they receive will be done by sculptors and painters whose views on design are compatible with those of the architect with whom they are associated. The association on the Legislative Building in Toronto was admirable ... Equally great and happy in their siting are the works of art in the National Art Centre.
>
> I find the same happy relationship between the External Affairs Building and the sculpture of steel at its base. Your correspon-

> dents write of 'so-called art' in general in the capital, but I assume I am not far off in referring to that building and its sculpture which I have seen. What surprises me is that your three traditionalists have no criticism of the building itself, which gives one ground for hope that their cultural development is approaching a point where modern sculpture will be equally acceptable to them. It is clear that, like many hundreds of their fellow citizens, they have become accustomed to modern architecture in steel and concrete, the materials of our time in the Western world. They may even enjoy it. In doing so, they would not be blind to the architectural qualities of the buildings on Parliament Hill or the spectacular interior of the old library.
>
> It may interest them to know that the most enthusiastic visitor that I have ever shown the buildings was Alfred Barr, the director of the Museum of Modern Art, in New York. I wonder whether the contents of that museum are known to your correspondents who claim to 'appreciate true modern art in its rightful place.' Perhaps on another occasion they will tell us what is 'true' and where is the 'rightful place.' I am unable to anticipate the former, but, regretfully, would hazard a guess at the latter.[4]

Forsey's response to Arthur never reached the printed page but is revealing of the private correspondence which so often accompanied his published letters and also revealing of his literary style and the range of his well-stocked mind that it is worth reproducing. To Professor Arthur, from the Senate on 5 January 1974, Forsey wrote:

> I hoped to send the *Globe and Mail* a letter in reply to yours in its issue of December 11. But pressure of work prevented (you will say, perhaps, that Providence had a hand!)
>
> None the less, I feel I must offer you my comments on what you wrote, even though they may be less than congruent with the respect I owe you, and feel for you.
>
> First, I appreciate the courtesy with which you wrote. A good many of the those who disagree with the view Dr Legget, Mr Stewart and I expressed, become very abusive.

Second, I wonder whether you would be as pleased with the fibre-glass affair opposite the Lord Elgin Hotel as you are with the steel production outside the External Affairs building ...

Third, you are 'surprised' that we had no criticism of the External Affairs building itself. Well, why should we [be] expected to? A distressing assumption, which you appear to share, often appears in the replies to, or attacks on, us: namely, that we object to anything new in art. This is not our point at all; certainly not mine. I think the External Affairs building is both handsome and interesting. Like the buildings at Simon Fraser University, it seems to me to have echoes of the Mayans (I suppose that shows I am a worse-than-hopeless 'traditionalist,' longing for the prehistoric!). I find it also a relief, an agreeable contrast, to the many modern buildings which belong either to the packing-box or the penitentiary school of architecture.

Why should anyone be expected to admire, or condemn, everything that's new? Why should we not use our critical judgement ...? Surely any reasonable person does this with ideas; why not with works of (real or claimed) art?

We are often reminded that various new developments in art in the past, now acclaimed universally as superb, were, in the beginning, denounced or condemned. True. But some new developments in art, acclaimed at the beginning as superb, are now universally denounced, condemned or merely laughed at. There was a time when the Albert memorial was considered a masterpiece; also, I think, Keble College chapel, and the horror with which Butterfield replaced our fifteenth century chapel at Balliol. You will recall Lytton Strachey's account of how that traditionalist, Lord Palmerston, prevented Sir Gilbert Scott from doing Whitehall in Victorian Gothic.

'De gustibus non est disputandum,' I know. But surely there is nothing reprehensible in refusing to abdicate our faculty of judgment and declining to prostrate ourselves before *any*thing (or everything) new (even if it is warranted a work of genius by the aesthetic Establishment)? ...

You hope the new National Gallery will be 'provocative'? Why? *I* hope it will be beautiful, and suited to its purpose.

> Whether or not it is 'provocative' seems to me to be beside the point; unless, of course, the purpose of art is to make people angry as well as to 'stun' them ... But is either of those its *purpose*? Surely anger or bewilderment are by-products, or *may be* by-products, of good art ...
>
> I find the whole cult of the new equals the good, or the odd equals the good, or the provocative equals the good, very depressing. It seems to me part of the 'flight from reason' which Dorothy Sayers deplored; and I do not subscribe to the notion that reason and emotion are antithetical terms (see John MacMurray's 'Reason and Emotion'). Of course these simple equations make it easy for any jackass, any humbug, with enough gall and enough contempt for his fellow-citizens, to set up as a critic, and in the paradise of humbugs which is Canada, to get himself accepted as a sort of aesthetic Pope; especially if he lards his dicta with phrases like 'soaring rectangles.' But I cannot imagine for a moment that you would subscribe to any of these equations.
>
> Finally, one thing that some of us object to is the virtual monopoly of the decoration of our public buildings and our parks by one particular school of aesthetic thought. Even if all these things are the imperishable masterpieces you and your colleagues think them, surely they are not the *only* aesthetically respectworthy kind of art? ...
>
> There is, of course, no need to answer this letter. But I do hope you have managed to read to the end, and may find in it something that deserves a moment's reflection. It seems to me it would be a pity if you seemed to be giving your distinguished imprimatur to any kind of 'provocative' extravaganza, sight unseen, which the Public Works Department's mandarins of art may see fit to impose upon us. [A hand-written postscript to this long letter reads, 'I enclose some quotations from Jung which may be in point.'][5]

Forsey himself proved that he was not immune to the charge he levelled in his letter to Eric Arthur, namely, criticizing a work of art sight unseen. In a letter to the *Globe*, on 24 July 1975, he mounted a campaign against a sculpture called *Love*, destined to grace a federal government building in Hull.

> I have been contemplating the picture, in your issue of July 11, of one of the three parts of the 'sculpture' called Love, to be erected outside a federal Government building in Hull. This steel and plastic concoction, you say, will cost $88, 000.
>
> It gives every sign of being another of the practical jokes at the taxpayers' expense which are becoming so notable a feature of the landscape in the National Capital area.
>
> I can already surmise the reaction to what I have just written, from what Dr Healey Willan used to call 'the intellegentsia – though God knows why they're called so.' It disturbs me not at all. Precisely the same would probably have been evoked from their predecessors by any criticism of the monuments of Victorian 'art' at which today we gaze with incredulity and horror.
>
> I wonder what our descendants will say of us when they look at the current 'masterpieces,' and are told we paid for them the astronomical sums we did.

This outburst was greeted on 30 July with a gentle reproof from John Meisel, who chided Forsey for judging the sculpture on the basis of a studio photograph, thereby directing to Forsey the same criticism the latter had levelled at Arthur for seeming to give his 'imprimatur ... sight unseen.'

> I am one of the many Canadians who greatly admire and respect Eugene Forsey for his qualities as a fine, fair-minded person and for his outstanding intellect. Until I read his letter to you printed on July 24 (Senator Sees Sculpture as a Joke at Taxpayers' Expense). I would in fact have called him an ornament of Canada's intellegentsia. While I do not always agree with him on all issues, I delight in his irrepressible sorties into public controversies and in the zestful presentation of his views.
>
> His justifiably high reputation rests on a prodigious knowledge of the constitution and of historical precedent, and on his habit of smiting all opponents with precise facts and hard-to-refute evidence.
>
> I was therefore startled to see him leap into print, averring that a new piece of sculpture he has not even seen 'gives every sign of

> being another practical joke at the taxpayers' expense ...' To judge a three-dimensional work of art from a photograph is hazardous and, to my mind, unfair. To do so on the basis of only part of a sculpture, photographed in a studio rather than at its proper site, is worse.
>
> As for the cost, surely those who produce sculptures are as entitled to remuneration as are senators.[6]

Inevitably, Forsey had the final word in the *Globe* on 15 August. Indeed, the difficulties of putting the sculpture in place gave Forsey an additional opportunity, in a letter to the *Ottawa Journal* the previous day, to deliver his curtain-ringing blow:

> No doubt I should be much chastened by John Meisel's reproaches (Eugene Forsey and Sculpture – July 30). But an item in the *Ottawa Journal* of Aug. 8 only confirms me in my opinion of the 'sculpture,' Love, which is to be erected outside the Place du Portage in Hull.
>
> The item quotes Henry Wanton Jones, who 'designed the sculpture,' as saying: 'The bottom section is shaped in the form of an inverted knee; the centre section in the form of a woman's breast or a human posterior depending on how you look at it, and the top section is in the form of a three-dimensional heart.'
>
> If this is Mr Meisel's, or the Government's, idea of either art or love, they are easily pleased. They, and Mr Jones, might do better to cultivate 'an attachment a la Plato for a bashful young potato, or a not too French bean!'

As Forsey typed this letter he must have been taking extra pleasure in the report in the *Citizen* of 12 August revealing that the mammoth mid-section of the sculpture still had not been able to be budged from Renfrew and united with the upper and lower parts that had been successfully transported to Hull. Even deploying a heavy-duty helicopter failed to do the trick, an apparent confirmation on high of the correctness of Forsey's judgment which he underlined in his letter to the *Journal*:

> So Henry Walton Jones' $88, 000 practical joke at the taxpayers' expense proved not so practical after all. The helicopter gagged and the citizens of Hull have at least a respite.
>
> But the admirers of modern 'sculpture' need not despair. Two superb examples are already on display outside the National Gallery ... They bear the inscription 'Anthes' and resemble elongated stove pipes.
>
> They are, at the moment, being used to convey rubble from the roof of the Gallery to the ground. But once the renovations to the building are finished, they could easily be transported to Hull for the Place du Portage. In time, they would no doubt rust and come to resemble, but surpass, the rusty stove pipe masterpieces at Carleton University.
>
> The director of the National Gallery would perhaps be reluctant to part with them but she could surely be persuaded that Hull's need was greater than the Gallery's.

A final testimonial to the tenacity of Forsey's one-man campaign as aesthetic censor is provided in this outraged letter to the *Citizen* on 29 April 1982:

> Now that the tulips are about to bloom along the Driveway by Dow's Lake, can anything be done about the hideous fake 'sculpture' with which the National Capital Commission has defaced what used to be one of the loveliest park areas in the city?
>
> Why the thing is allowed to masquerade as 'sculpture' passes the wit of any normal person to conceive ...
>
> The National Capital Commission should be bombarded with letters demanding that this eyesore be taken away to the garbage dump where it belongs, or returned to the perpetrator for his own back yard.
>
> What would the authorities do if private citizens ransacked their cellars, their garages and their attics for all the old cast-off wood and scrap iron they could find and dumped the results ... at selected spots along the Parkways or in front of public buildings? Would they be suffered to remain? Hardly. Yet 'artistic' practical

jokers are not only permitted but paid to plant their hoaxes on us at our expense.

... These things are an intolerable outrage, and the public should howl against them till they are got rid of. The howls should be directed not only to the commission but to the mayor and aldermen, and the local MPs who ought to be protecting us against such bureaucratic impositions and fleecings.

A Missed Opportunity: Metric Conversion

Given Forsey's devotion to all things British, it was to be expected that he would attack the program of metric conversion. In fact, the program was well into its final phase of adoption when Forsey, on 6 December 1978, became the sole contributor to a debate in the Senate on the Statute Law (Metric Conversion) Amendment Bill.

I rise to sing a threnody on a dirge for the passing of the system of weights and measures to which we have become accustomed for most of our lives. It is a matter of lasting grief to me that when this thing was first brought up it slipped past me unnoticed. The result of its passing, regardless of whether I noticed it or not, is that my declining years are being embittered by a constant series of exercises in mental arithmetic. I realize that I am speaking against progress ... but I do want to register my expiring wail on this subject. I am going to read into the record of the Senate some verses which I wrote on this subject.[7]

These verses, under the title 'Lament for the Old Weights and Measures,' had actually appeared two years earlier (31 January 1976) in the form of a letter to the Ottawa *Journal*:

The foreigners have taken over!
They've leapt across the Straits of Dover
And robbed us of our simple pleasures,
Our good old English weights and measures.

Henceforth, alas! to us it's barred
To buy or sell goods 'by the yard.'
No, no! It must be 'by the metre,'
And drinks are poured out by the litre.
An icy stare the chappie courts
Who asks for his in pints and quarts.
Butter in kilos now we're bound
To purchase; no more by the pound.
The wheat that's needed by our bakers
No longer comes from good broad acres.
In centigrade degrees we're told
Whether it's hot, or mild or cold;
And snow no longer falls in inches:
A thought at which the skier flinches.
No flight of miles our drivers heed:
The kilometer limits speed.
The only counting left that's ours
Is years and months, weeks, days and hours.
As in old times, these still are reckoned
By minute, and un-metric second.
For this small mercy let's be thankful,
As all else daily gets more crankful.

CHAPTER FIVE

'You've Got Me Wrong!'

Many of Forsey's letters were directed to correcting errors of fact in such a decisive manner as to charm every reader not implicated in his strictures. In addition to asserting 'You've got it wrong!,' Forsey was often obliged to insist that 'You've got *me* wrong!' Letters of this sort were directed to complaints against journalistic errors in reporting his views wherever expressed or, much more serious, countering letters or reports that impugned his motives and affronted him personally.

'I've Been Misquoted'

Letters in the first category were triggered by Forsey's high visibility in the numerous forums to which he had access and where he seldom failed to provide quotable copy. His racy way with words and rapid-fire delivery often necessitated damage control and led to what has been previously noted as the multiplier effect on Forsey's public utterances. Here are included a small representative sample of the many letters in this first category.

From the *Globe and Mail*, 10 June 1972:

> I see Mr Michael Valpy accuses me of having, at the Heritage Ontario Conference, 'talked about Canada's two founding peoples immediately after Walter Currie had said the phrase 'was a particular irritant to the red man.'

> I have no recollection of having used the phrase at all. The tape recording (which I understand was taken) will show whether I did or did not. I can see no reason why I should have used it, as I was talking exclusively about the British, and more particularly the English, contribution to Ontario's heritage.
>
> In any event, if I did use the phrase, it was solely in the context of the law and the constitution, where, like it or not, the French and the British most emphatically were the two founding peoples.
>
> I am sorry if I offended Mr Currie, or any Indian or Eskimo, or any of their sympathizers (of whom I thought I was one), or anybody else. But I hope they will all, if they remember what I said, try to remember the context, and acquit me of any intention of hurting anyone's feelings.
>
> This is the kind of thing that scares people into writing out a text and reading it, which is a bore for all concerned.

Reporting on the emergency debate in the House of Commons on the collapse of the oil sands and northern pipeline projects and the efforts of the opposition to dislodge Marc Lalonde, the minister of energy, Michael Valpy concluded: 'The British, who gave Parliament to the world, are sensitive about these matters. Their ministers resign at no more than the whiff of maladministration ... Canada's parliamentary expert, Eugene Forsey, yesterday contrasted British sensitivity to the Canadian practice: "Here," he said, "you need a crowbar to get them out"' (*Globe*, 6 May 1982).

Forsey's response, in full, came on 12 May:

> Michael Valpy's You Need a Crowbar (May 6) quotes me correctly. But I should like to make it clear that I was commenting on general practice in Britain and Canada, not on the question of whether Energy Minister Marc Lalonde should or should not resign. That question I explicitly refused to discuss.

On 11 August 1975, the *Globe and Mail* provided a typical heading to spotlight a lengthy correction: 'Forsey Was Concerned about Expectations of Centralizing Judgments.'

> John Beaufoy (Supreme Court's Calls Unpredictable – Aug. 6) attributes to me the opinion 'that the court will, if pressed, decide more cases for federal Government in the future'.
>
> The only time I can recall discussing this matter with any journalist, the conversation took place in French, and my inadequate French may have led to a misapprehension. What I tried to say was that the court, for reasons that Mr Beaufoy quotes correctly, might decide more cases in favor of the Dominion in the future. As for the 'if pressed,' I am at a loss to understand how, even in my imperfect French, I could have left any such impression. The suggestion that the court is open to pressure of any kind, except the pressure of facts and argument, would be wholly unwarranted and grossly improper; and no such idea ever entered my head.
>
> In the conversation which took place, I was concerned to rebut the notion that the appointment of the present Chief Justice [Mr Bora Laskin] would lead to a series of revolutionary, centralizing judgments. I pointed out that he was only one of nine judges; that sudden reversals are not part of our judicial tradition, that people sometimes change their minds, and that a judge, faced with new evidence and argument, may well decide that an opinion he expressed in a previous academic incarnation, was inadequate or mistaken.

Wherever Forsey spoke, he kept a weather eye peeled on any subsequent newspaper account of the event, hastening to correct even the slightest misrepresentation of his views lest he be accused of the same sins of factual error for which he chastened lesser mortals. Because his forays out of Ottawa were frequent and geographically extensive, his corrective letters were widely distributed. The *Vancouver Sun* on 12 July 1973 was obliged to publish a corrective blast because it had misreported a Forsey speech in the Senate. The *Charlottetown Guardian* on 15 October 1976 carried Forsey's letter correcting errors in the reports on a speech he had delivered in that city on 4 October. To the *Kingston Whig Standard* on 4 December 1985 he wrote to straighten out the reporter's coverage of his speech to the local Canadian Club in which he was alleged to have said: 'the Senate is riddled with dead-heads, duds, spavined horses, and hatchet men. Forsey said that part of the problem is antiquated and ridiculous Senate rules. For instance, the former senator said, he has seen other senators literally "wheeled into the chambers in wheelchairs and stretchers, and then wheeled right out again" to meet attendance requirements – and thus collect their generous salaries.' After quoting this portion of the report Forsey continued:

> My unfortunate habit of speaking too fast must have misled Mr McKay [the reporter].
>
> I did not say the Senate was 'riddled with dead-heads' and the rest of it. I said that if provincial governments made the appointments, that is what we'd probably get.
>
> I said nothing about 'Senate rules.' What I said was that the Constitution Act, 1867, stipulates that if a senator does not turn up at least once in two consecutive sessions, he loses his seat; and that this was not good enough, especially as a single session may now last for three years.
>
> I did not say I had seen a senator wheeled in on a stretcher.
>
> I said I had heard of it. It was long before my time, back in my boyhood.
>
> I did not mention salaries.
>
> And I did not say 'no room for change,' as the line under my photograph suggests.
>
> I am sorry to take up your space with this. But if I leave that statement about 'dead-heads' uncorrected I shall lose about half my friends.

Forsey's frequent comments on the Senate seemed particularly prone to journalistic misrepresentation. In 1980, after his departure from the Senate, a *Globe and Mail* editorial referring to his testimony before a committee of the Ontario legislature, drew this letter from Forsey under the heading 'No Suggestion of "Senility" in Senate' (23 August 1980).

> Your editorial Forsey Confidential (Aug. 16) says I told the

Ontario Legislature's committee on constitutional reform that 'a few members' of the Senate 'were growing quite senile.'

This is incorrect. I did not use the word 'senile' about anyone, in the Senate or out of it. Nor did I even suggest that Senators were getting that way, or even hint at such a thing. Nor did I say that 'retirement' of Senators 'at 75 has the virtue of forcing incompetent ones to leave.'

I was asked, in reference to Senator Croll's committee on retirement age policies. whether I favored a compulsory retirement age in general. I said yes ...

I also specifically said that the 75-year age limit had cost the Senate ... excellent members ... Discussing the advantages of having the national Government appoint Senators from lists submitted by provincial Governments, instead of direct provincial appointments, I said that the Prime Minister, looking at such a list, might say of the first name on it, 'Oh! No, no! He's past due. He'd be worse than poor old Forsey.'

So the only person I even hinted might be senile was myself; and, for the moment at least, I can bear the 'soft impeachment.'

Even before his retirement from the Senate, Forsey had been obliged to correct the *London Free Press* report of one of his speeches dealing with current proposals for reforming the Senate, in order to remove any suggestion that his opposition was tainted by self-interest. ('Senator Protests Report of Speech Gives Wrong Impression of His Position,' 21 November 1978.)

The report of my speech to the University of Western Ontario law students, in the Nov. 1 Free Press, is seriously misleading.

First, the headline 'Forsey wants a "hands off" policy on Senate by Trudeau,' is wholly false. I never said anything remotely resembling this. On the contrary, I said no senators, or almost none, would take such a position.

Second, I did not say: 'Leave the Senate alone or the body will be nothing but a "nuisance".' I said the proposed new House of the Federation would have only the power to make a nuisance of itself.

> Third, it is false to say that I 'admitted to being outspoken on the constitution mainly because I retire from the Senate in May.' What I said was that no one could accuse me of self-interest in my criticisms of the constitutional amendment bill, for the simple reason that in May I would be out of the Senate and it would make no earthly difference to me personally whether it had been abolished and replaced or not ...
>
> Fourth, I did not suggest that the government should 'change the constitution ... to "get rid of dead wood".' I said many senators thought it would be desirable to get rid of dead wood. Whether this would require a change in the constitution is questionable.

In the same year, the *London Free Press* was obliged to publish another Forsey correction. The following excerpts demonstrate Forsey's technique of point-by-point refutation and, indirectly, reveal how his propensity to use colourful language in his speeches can so capture the hearer's attention that the true meaning and intent of his discourse is overlooked or simply misunderstood.

> The Free Press of May 8, purporting to report my speech to the United Empire Loyalists, May 6, describes me as saying that 'Quebec Premier René Lévesque is one of many "odd characters" in Canadian history who have tried to destroy a responsible cabinet system of government and replace it with "a series of road blocks".'
>
> I mentioned Lévesque and W.A.C. Bennett, William Aberhart, Mitchell Hepburn, Ross Thatcher, Joey Smallwood, and Maurice Duplessis as 'odd characters.' The rest of what your reporter attributes to me is the worst piece of garbling I have ever seen ...
>
> I never said one word about any of these people having 'tried to destroy a responsible cabinet system of government and replace it with' anything whatever. Such a statement would have been nonsense ...
>
> Your reporter also says I said that 'Quebec radicals use "dreadful fairy tales" about the intentions of English-speaking Canadi-

ans to "inflame delicate national issues".' He adds that Forsey said: 'It's more subversive than anything the Communists can say, but it's inviting the Communists to come along and pick up the pieces.'

This is the worst jumble of all. I did mention constitutiomal fairy tales, and I did say they inflamed discussion of delicate issues. I did not attribute them particularly to Quebecers, let alone 'Quebec radicals.'

'You've Done Me Wrong'

While Forsey was quick to use letters to correct misrepresentation of views he expressed in lectures and speeches (including speeches in the Senate) he was even more concerned to correct references in the press which he deemed to be inaccurate portrayals of his own person. In the main, such corrective letters concerned his political party preferences which, in view of his principled independent stance leading to dramatic shifts in his party allegiances, did require clarifying reminders. In the extreme case of the accusation that he was a communist, the correspondence was especially intense.

Before presenting samples from the political arena, we may start with a lighter-hearted correction to the *Ottawa Citizen* on 31 January 1979, titled 'Not a Director.'

> Recently you carried a report which described me as 'a member of the Board of Directors' of the Royal Bank of Canada.
>
> I have never been even qualified to be a director of any bank. I have never had enough shares, and I am now also much too old. I am a very, very small shareholder of four companies, including two banks. I have never been a director of any company whatsoever – and the mere suggestion of such a thing would freeze the marrow of every shareholder qualified to be a director.

The vigour with which the following denial of personal association is expressed is difficult to explain, unless we presume

Forsey possessed some gift of prevision that enabled him to foresee the approval of anti-union legislation by the Smallwood government some eight years later, in 1959. As can be seen, Forsey sought wide distribution of his rebuttal; the original copy, dated 29 May 1951, was written on the letterhead of the Canadian Congress of Labour; the following published version comes from the *St John's Evening Telegram*, 5 June 1951.

Would you kindly publish the following which is self explanatory.

EUGENE FORSEY

The Editor,
The Western Star,
Corner Brook,
Newfoundland.

Sir, – I have just received a clipping, apparently from one of the St John's papers, reproducing what purports to be an article from your paper early this month. One paragraph of this article reads:

'And what of Mr Smallwood's reported friendship with Eugene Forsey, the Ottawa socialist? The Press Gallery of the House of Commons has long buzzed with rumors that the Newfoundland premier and Mr Forsey are the closest of friends, and that Mr Smallwood frequently called on his socialist friend during his visits to Ottawa. This rumor is so widespread that it must have reached Mr Smallwood; yet we have heard no details.'

Well, you hear one now, and if I had got wind of this rubbish sooner, you would have heard one long ago. The whole story is false, from beginning to end. I have never met Mr Smallwood. I have never seen him in person, in the movies, or on television. I have never heard him speak, in person, in the movies, on the radio, or on the telephone. He has never communicated with me, directly or indirectly, nor I with him, by word of mouth, by letter, post card, telegram, telephone or wireless. I hope this denial is complete. If you can think of any way to make it more complete let me know, and I shall immediately plug any loopholes you may think you have found.

I am sending a copy of this letter to each of the St John's papers and to the President of the Parliamentary Press Gallery.

The contingent nature of Forsey's loyalty to a political party of any stripe brought about by his stubborn but principled independence created difficulties for the press in keeping abreast of the changes in his formal adherence to a party. Such letters as Forsey felt obliged to address to correcting misrepresentation of his party connections were surprisingly few and normally occurred sometime after the event. In fact, there appear to be no letters bearing on his earliest years when his personal loyalty to Arthur Meighen, the Conservative leader, seemed to conflict with the socialist leanings that made him a founder of the CCF. Perhaps Forsey's description of himself as a 'Sir John A. Macdonald Conservative' helps to account for his ambivalence towards organized political parties. This caused him to resign from the CCF when it changed its name to the New Democratic Party, and his subsequent joining and then resigning from the Liberal party. But, as Forsey noted in his memoirs, when describing his departure from the NDP, 'My resignation produced a small item in the newspapers, in which David Lewis "regretted" my decision.'

Forsey's subsequent changes of political adherence are recorded in the following two entries, from the *Globe*, 16 August 1978, and the *Toronto Star*, 15 May 1982.

> The much too kind Canadian Press story on me (Senators to Begin a Study of Trudeau's 'Infernal Bill' – Aug. 8) has one small error of fact.
>
> I did not 'join the Liberals after quitting the New Democratic party in 1968.' I left the NDP in 1961, a few weeks after its formation, because I could not swallow the 'two nations.' I did not become a member of the Liberal Party till after I was appointed to the Senate, [in 1970] and I may add that the Prime Minister, inviting me to accept the appointment, told me explicitly that he did not care where I sat.

> You say (May 1) that I resigned from the Liberal party in a 'huff.'
>
> This is nonsense. What on earth had I to be huffy about? Throughout my time in the Senate, and since, despite my frequent obstreperousness, I have received nothing but kindness and

consideration from the Liberal party. I joined the party in 1970 for reasons of principle. I have resigned from it for reasons of principle. Is that incomprehensible?

Incidentally, your report is askew on two other points.

First, I did not leave the NDP 'shortly after its formation to join the Liberals.' I left the NDP in 1961. I joined the Liberals in 1970. I never even voted Liberal in my life until 1968. I voted Conservative in 1962, 1963 and 1965. I had left the NDP because it had embraced the 'two nations' policy. When the Conservatives appeared to be following suit, and the Prime Minister [Mr Trudeau] made his first big speech on national unity, I had no choice but to support him.

Second, one of my two reasons for leaving the Liberal party, some months ago, was what seemed to me the government's incomprehension of 'the rule of law.' Some reporters' ears are evidently even worse than mine.

Two other readers commented on the same report of Forsey's resignation from the party. Mr Stan Obodiac, noting that one of the reasons given was that Forsey had claimed there was 'too much power and authority in the Prime Minister's job,' wondered whether Forsey minded 'the power and authority in Trudeau's job which gave him his senatorship.' More supportively, Mr Perrin Beatty, then a Conservative MP, wrote: 'As the article itself makes clear, Dr Forsey left the Liberal party over two questions of principle: The government's undemocratic cancellation of 20 per cent of VIA Rail's services and the Liberals' handling of the report of the McDonald Commission [on the activities of the RCMP].'

No doubt the most serious charge that Forsey had to counter was that, if not a member of the Communist Party, he was at least close to being a fellow traveller. The charge was first levelled in the heat of Forsey's three eventful but unsuccessful ventures into electoral politics as a CCF candidate. On the first occasion, running in the Ontario election of 1945, he was defeated by a Progressive Conservative cabinet minister, George H. Dunbar. The following letter to the *Toronto Star*, 28 May 1945, written as spokesman for the Canadian Labour Congress, carries on the story.

> Since you were kind enough to take up the cudgels on my behalf against Hon. George Dunbar, when he accused me of being a confessed former Communist, perhaps you and your readers would be interested in hearing what has happened since. Mr Dunbar, you will recall, told the legislature on March 25 (p.1555 of the provincial Hansard) that 'Dr Eugene Forsey admitted, said in Carleton county, at Richmond, that he had been a Communist but he had changed. He never to this day set up any change.' I immediately said that Mr Dunbar was a liar, and that if he would repeat his charge outside the house I would sue him.
>
> On March 26, asked in the legislature either to retract or to repeat his charge outside, he firmly refused to do either. On the contrary, he cited Mr Grattan O'Leary as having said at the time: 'He says he was a Communist once, let him tell us was it two years ago, was it one year ago, or did he change his mind right on the platform?' 'Why,' added Mr Dunbar, 'did he not take action against Grattan O'Leary?' (p.1578)
>
> There was, of course, a very simple answer to that. I had never heard of any such statement by Mr O'Leary. Neither had Mr O'Leary. The moment I got the Hansard, April 8, I telephoned and wrote him, and he indignantly denied anything of the sort. He also wrote Mr Dunbar, April 25, informing him, among other things, that the statement in Hansard was 'untrue.' He added: 'I have never said nor thought that he (Forsey) was a Communist, and from what I know of him, do not think he could ever be a Communist.'
>
> On April 8, I also wrote Mr Frost [the premier], setting forth the facts ...
>
> I have now a reply from Mr Frost. It is not marked 'personal' or 'confidential.' It contains this paragraph: 'May I say that I am quite prepared to accept your statement that you are not now, nor have you ever been, a Communist.'
>
> I think Mr O'Leary's and the premier's letters speak for themselves.

Obviously, the Canadian Labour Congress was as intent on distancing itself from accusations of communist infiltration as was Forsey in clearing himself of these charges. Even so, the issue was revisited in 1949 by J.O. Wyse, a regular letter contributer to the *Montreal Gazette* who had previously sparred with Forsey on labour issues.[1] The exchange began with a Forsey letter on Quebec's Padlock Law, a measure passed by the Duplessis government ostensibly to curb the publication of communist literature. Forsey, along with Frank Scott, his scholarly colleague at McGill, had been inveighing against this repressive legislation, especially in the pages of the *Canadian Forum*, ever since its passage in 1937. Hence the moralizing tone of this first letter, of 24 August 1949.

> A dispatch in your issue of Saturday quotes Mr Duplessis as saying that his padlock law 'though beneficent and salutary' had been 'hotly criticized by the Liberal party at the time of its passage.'
>
> This will certainly be news to those who really did fight the padlock law at the time of its passage. I was one of them, and I recall the whole business very clearly. Not one member of the Liberal party in either House of the legislature voted against the bill; and I cannot call to mind the name of a single Liberal of any importance outside the legislature who so much as let out a squeak on the subject.
>
> The padlock law is, was, and always will be, an infamous piece of legislation, not because it attacks Communism but because it does so by the methods of the police state. As the Canadian Bar Association committee commented at the time: 'The Act gives the Attorney-General powers which he can exercise in the first instance without the slightest judicial restraint, and takes away all the safeguards which even an ordinary criminal enjoys before conviction ... It might be as well to observe that possibly it is under laws such as this that in other lands the homes of respectable and law-abiding citizens are ransacked simply because their owners do not wear a brown or a black shirt.'

This letter triggered the response of J.O. Wyse, on 1 September

1949, relying on exchanges that had occurred in connection with Forsey's electoral battle against George Drew for a federal seat. Wyse began by asserting that he himself did not like the padlock law; nevertheless, he could see why Mr Duplessis thought it a good one and why the Liberals had made no objection to it. Having thus isolated Forsey as odd man out, Wyse went on to suggest that this seemed to place Forsey among those whose opposition to the law was suspect, concluding that:

> Eugene Forsey may not be a Communist now. He knows about that. Certainly, at the time when, as he asserts, he was one of a small band of opponents to the Padlock law, he was issuing statements that the Christian religion was not enough to win salvation, and that people could only go to heaven if they accepted the gospel according to Karl Marx. It is easily understood why Mr Duplessis might not pay much attention to that sort of opposition.

Forsey's immediate reply was published on 3 September 1949.

> Mr Wyse says I 'may not be a Communist now.' If it will ease his mind, I can assure him I never was a Communist. His garbled quotation from something I wrote (not 'statements I issued') a dozen years ago is just a rehash of some election propaganda of last December with which I dealt at the time. [A reference to his campaign in the federal election against George Drew.]
>
> Mr Wyse does not need to take my word for it that I am not a Communist. He can look up the Communists' propaganda organs. He will find that I have been the recipient of some very choice abuse, nicely seasoned with mendacity, from these gentry.
>
> I observe that, with prudence which I cannot too highly commend, Mr Wyse refrains from comment on what the Canadian Bar Association's committee said about the Padlock Act in 1937. Doubtless for him, it is 'easily understood why Mr Duplessis might not pay much attention to that sort of opposition.'

Mr Wyse returned to the attack on 23 September, this time triumphantly quoting from Forsey's contribution to a book,

Towards the Christian Revolution, in which he had written: 'This generation seeketh after a sign, and there shall be no sign given but the sign of the prophet Marx. Until Christians learn to understand and apply the lessons of Marxism they cannot enter the Kingdom of Heaven – nor probably, can anyone else.'

Wyse continued to rub it in: 'Dr Forsey says that he disposed of this question during a recent election. When Mr Drew and the *Ottawa Journal* used the quotation, Dr Forsey wrote to the *Ottawa Journal* to say that this statement was made twelve years ago, and that he had changed his mind. That disposes of Dr Forsey, but has he done anything to undo the damage which this and other teachings did to young men and women at McGill at that time?'

Forsey's rejoinder came on 27 September:

> The best reply to Mr Wyse's latest letter is, 'Oh! rats!'
>
> However, perhaps you will permit me to add: (1) There is a difference between understanding and applying the lessons of something and swallowing it whole. (2) The 'damage' I did at McGill is perhaps best illustrated by the fact that ex-students of mine were candidates for four different parties (Liberal, Progressive Conservative, CCF and LPP) at the recent election. (3) I can produce documentary evidence, plenty of it, that I have been fighting Communists for years. (4) I am not responsible for silly notions gullible people may have formed about my political opinions. In 1943, the Winnipeg Free Press accused me of a Tory conspiracy to bring Mr Meighen back into public life. (5) I never claimed that I and the people associated with me were 'the only opponents of the Padlock Law.' All I claimed was that the Liberal party did not oppose it. That is not quite the same thing.
>
> Your readers can hardly be more interested in a prolonged discussion of my opinions, real or alleged. I venture to suggest that Mr Wyse would contribute more ... if he could be persuaded to return to the original subject of discussion: the Padlock Law and its merits and demerits, and the attitude of the Liberal party thereto.
>
> I am perfectly ready to engage in any such discussion; but I do

> not propose to waste my time or your space in further pursuit of any rabbits Mr Wyse produces out of his hat.

For once, Forsey did not have the last word: on 6 October J.O. Wyse responded in a letter that began: 'Dr Eugene Forsey must forgive me for saying that an attempt to close an argument by saying "Oh! rats" is less becoming to one who is now a sort of elder statesman than it would have been to a rather exhibitionist young instructor trying to impress his more gullible students.' Then, following a somewhat heavy-handed rebuttal, Wyse also concluded that 'I am quite willing, as Dr Forsey suggests, to let the discussion drop.' And, indeed, that particular charge never surfaced again, although, as previous letters show, Forsey's fierce independence obliged him to explain, first his departure from a party he had helped found and then his apostasy from a party that he joined because of the strong centralist stand of its leader, Mr Trudeau, and departed because of what he deemed to be its disloyalty to true liberal concerns for the supremacy of Parliament and to the rule of law. As other letters will reveal, Forsey remained unshakeably dedicated to these two pillars of the constitution.

CHAPTER SIX

The Governor General and the Reserve Power

Loyal monarchist that he was, Forsey was an ardent defender of the office of governor general, the embodiment in Canada of the monarchical inheritance from Britain. He was in agreement with Walter Bagehot's classic formulation of the role of the monarch, as applied to the governor general: that is, the right to be consulted, to encourage, and to warn. The performance of these functions demanded complete neutrality amid the partisan passions of political parties, vying for command of the levers of government.

The surrogate in Canada for the neutrality of the British monarch was originally presumed to lie in the appointment of a scion of the British aristocracy – an outsider – to the office. Gradual modifications in the mode of selection which placed the right of nomination (if not of formal appointment) in the hands of the Canadian prime minister, contributed to the nationalistic demand for the appointment of a 'home-grown' governor general.

Forsey fought (unsuccessfully as it turned out) against taking this step, as this letter to *Saturday Night* of 1 December 1951 makes clear:

> Frank Flaherty (in the Nov. 17 issue) says the Governor-General's 'acts of state are nearly all on the advice of his ministers which he may not reject' ...
>
> This is just Liberal party folk-lore. Curiously enough, it has not

even the authority of the late Mr King, who, in 1926, three times explicitly admitted that there were circumstances in which the Governor-General would be justified in refusing dissolution ...

It is precisely because the Governor-General has certain reserve powers, because he can, in very special circumstances, refuse the advice of his ministers, that it is desirable to have a Governor-General with no past connection with any Canadian political party. He need not be an Englishman, a Scotsman, an Irishman or a Welshman; he could equally well be an Australian, a New Zealander, a South African, or a citizen of any other Dominion, and a Canadian might well be a perfectly satisfactory Governor-General of one of the other Dominions. But a Canadian will not be a satisfactory Governor-General of Canada.

The appointment of a Canadian will throw the office into the whirlpool of national politics and sectional, racial and sectarian feeling. The French-Canadians will insist, most reasonably, that every second, or at the very least, every third, Governor shall be French-Canadian. The Irish Roman Catholics will insist on one of their number every once in so many times. The various Protestant denominations will want their turn. The Maritimes will jib at a succession of 'Upper Canadian' Governors. ... Indeed, it may well prove that each province will press its own particular claim. One would think we already had enough of this kind of trouble without deliberately inviting more.

No, the appointment of a Canadian Governor-General of Canada still remains what Laurier called it: 'a laudable but misguided expression of national pride.' Let's stick to something that works.

Vincent Massey's appointment in 1952 as the first home-grown governor general seemed to put paid to Forsey's concerns. That he continued to harbour them is revealed when, thirty years later, he admonished the then governor general, Edward Schreyer, for publicly speculating on a return to a political career after his term of office had expired (*Globe and Mail*, 30 April 1984):

Thomas Walkom has already reported fully and accurately ... my opinion of certain statements in the Governor-General's recent interviews (Forsey Outraged at Schreyer's Career Musings – April 20).

There is, however, one relevant point I failed to make, and one comment on Prof. Edward McWhinney's observations that I want to make.

Governor-General Edward Schreyer says 'there is nothing written ... about the constitutional propriety or inadvisability of a former Governor-General entering or re-entering politics.'

Of course there isn't. There is also nothing written about the propriety of a Governor-General opening Parliament in his nightshirt.

He adds that 'there is nothing even understood' about the constitutional propriety or inadvisability of a former Governor-General's entering or re-entering politics.

This betrays a fundamental failure to understand the limitations of the vice-regal office, imposed by the fact that its occupant must be absolutely free of even the slightest suspicion of partisanship. This he (or she) cannot be if Rideau Hall is to be accepted as a stopping-place on the road to 24 Sussex Drive.

Prof. McWhinney, endorsing Mr Schreyer's proposition, asks plaintively, 'What do you do with a 48-year old? ... What is a 48- or 50-year old to do? Become president of a university? Write his memoirs?'

This gets the whole thing wrong way 'round. It is not Mr Schreyer's or anyone else's private welfare which is at issue. It is the office of Governor-General and the responsibilities and limitations it carries with it. A former Governor-General is not left destitute. He (or she) has a respectable pension. There are any number of careers he (or she) can take up with perfect propriety. He (or she) can enter the diplomatic service (as Mr Schreyer is doing) ...

But when a person accepts the office of Governor-General, he (or she) forfeits his (or her) right to go into politics, on retirement or at any later date. Anyone who is not prepared to accept that limitation should not accept the office. To vary Harry Truman's words 'If you can't stand the cold, stay out of the refrigerator.'

21 April 1984. Reprinted with permission from the *Globe and Mail*

Apparently, Forsey's admonitions fell on deaf ears, for he felt obliged to recycle his letter, somewhat more fully expressed, in *Saturday Night* in January 1988, when Mr Schreyer reverted to his musings about a political career as his diplomatic posting was coming to an end. That Forsey's objections were not driven by any personal animosity but directed to preserving the status of the office of governor general is confirmed by this 23 February 1982 letter to the *Globe*:

> Your issue of Feb. 17 says that 'an External Affairs Department official' has 'said that it is expected that,' during his official visit to Romania, the Governor-General 'will discuss the sale of Candu nuclear reactors and maintenance contracts for them with officials' of the Romanian Government ...
>
> Who is responsible for this attempt to turn the Governor-General into a commercial traveller?
>
> The sale of Candu reactors to a Communist state is highly dubious and controversial, to say the least. But even if it were cottage

cheese and its refrigeration the Government was asking him to peddle, the assignment would be an insult to His Excellency and a perversion of his office.

Forsey's insistence on the office of governor general standing aloof from partisan politics – even more necessary once the decision was taken to appoint a home-grown candidate – was based on his doctoral dissertation, published in 1943 as *The Royal Power of Dissolution in the Commonwealth*. One could say that Forsey's growing recognition as *the* constitutional expert was built on this treatise and the fanfare it aroused through the violent dispute with Dafoe and the attendant echoes that reverberated from that controversy.[1]

The centrepiece of this study was the King–Byng affair in which the reserve power of Governor General Byng had been deployed in such a fashion as to suggest that Byng had compromised the neutrality of the office by rejecting Mackenzie King's advice but subsequently having to accept Meighan's advice to dissolve Parliament. Forsey had occasion to return again and again to defend his account of this exercise of the reserve power, both in his lectures and in his letters to the press. As one of his former students at McGill University recalled: 'We had Meighen for breakfast, Byng for lunch, and King for dinner.'[2] Nonetheless, references to the King–Byng affair kept cropping up over the years, each time necessitating long, heated letters of correction from Forsey. Academics and journalists alike were pilloried for inaccurate portrayal of the events surrounding the affair, sometimes to vindicate the role of his hero, Arthur Meighen, and always to reaffirm his own conclusions which assumed the status of the Authorized Version.

Arcane as some of these debates may now appear, there was a reason why Forsey's original exhaustive analysis of the reserve powers of the governor general had continuing relevance and why his fixation on getting the historical precedents correctly cited was so constantly brought in play. The reason is to be found in the peculiar nature of the Canadian constitution. It is in part a formal document and in part an inheritance of British institutions that operate according to unwritten rules. This leaves room for interpretation of the precedents that accrue over time as working conventions of the constitution. Thus, the operation of a system of representative parliamentary institutions in combination with the Crown prerogative, here defined as the reserve power, at times could call upon the expert on precedents to guide politicians on what appropriate procedure should be applied to particular circumstances. The emergence of a multiparty system rather than a two-party system, both in national political life and within most of the provinces, meant that questions about the reserve powers of the Crown (whether governor general or lieutenant-governor), have been frequently tested in Canada. Australia, too, has had its share of such crises. For such occasions, Forsey was always at hand, contributing not only his letters but lengthy and learned treatises, often reproduced as a series of articles. The extracts reproduced here are from letters that sought to illuminate a particular aspect of the involvement (or not) of the Crown's reserve power.

Can a Prime Minister Be Dismissed? (*Toronto Star,* 4 February 1982).

> Your article (Jan. 22) on the Governor-General's recent pronouncements reports me as saying that the Crown has the right to advise, encourage and warn. So far, so good. But the article further quotes me as saying that any stronger interpretations of the Crown's authority are 'obsolete.'
>
> That statement is not true, and I did not make it. I have spent a good many years insisting that in fact there are circumstances in which the Crown can, and should, refuse to act on the advice of the government in office, provided it can find an alternative government to take the responsibility for such action.
>
> Beyond question, the Crown (which, of course, means in Canada, also the governor-general and the lieutenant-governors) can dismiss a government. But it would have to find an alternative government to take responsibility for the dismissal.

It is, I think, common ground among constitutional authorities that if a prime minister were faced with serious charges of bribery and corruption and refused to advise the summoning of Parliament to deal with the charges, the Crown could dismiss him and appoint a new prime minister who would tender the necessary advice.

Who Prolongs the Life of Parliament? (*Globe and Mail*, 19 March 1979).

There is a yarn going the rounds that the Prime Minister might go to the Governor-General, tell him there is an emergency, and advise him to prolong the life of Parliament beyond July 31, when it will have reached its normal life of five years.

This is unadulterated nonsense.

Only Parliament (the two houses) can prolong the life of Parliament beyond five years, and only 'in time of real or apprehended war, invasion or insurrection,' and even then only if two-thirds of the House of Commons votes for its prolongation. That is laid down plainly in section 91, head 1, of the British North America Act. The Governor-General can no more prolong the life of Parliament than I can.

What about the Reverse Situation, the Power to Dissolve Parliament? Here, Forsey always opted for the application of 'common sense' interpretations, with the object of avoiding unnecessary elections whenever possible. In a letter to the *Toronto Star* on 21 September 1962, he even takes on his old colleague and expert in parliamentary procedure, Stanley Knowles:

Stanley Knowles of the New Democratic Party is reported (Sept. 17) as saying that Mr Diefenbaker may call an election the day Parliament opens.

I find it difficult to believe that any responsible person can be contemplating so blazing and scandalous a violation of the constitution.

If parliament has any rights at all, it must have the right at least to meet and attempt to transact public business. Only if it proves unable to do so would it be proper to have recourse to an immediate second election ...

If our new House of Commons proves unable to elect a Speaker, Mr Diefenbaker would have no choice but to ask for an immediate second dissolution, and the Governor-General would have no choice but to grant it.

But a request for dissolution before a Speaker could be elected, or after he was elected but before the House could do any business, would be subversive of the most basic rights of Parliament. It would therefore be the Governor-General's constitutional duty to refuse. If the government declined to accept the refusal, it would be the Governor-General's constitutional duty to send for Mr Pearson and Mr Pearson's constitutional duty to accept office, so that Parliament could at least try to transact the public business it was elected to transact.

Elections are not held for fun. Nor are they held to give any leader a majority ... The country ought not to be put to the tumult and turmoil – and huge expense – of electing a fresh Parliament until the Parliament it has just elected has had a chance to function.

Mr Knowles is also reported to have said that if Mr Diefenbaker asked for dissolution the day Parliament opened he would be 'emulating' Mr King's action in 1940, when that personage met Parliament on the afternoon and dissolved at supper time.

This is not fair to Mr King. His action was an outrage, true. But the Parliament dissolved on January 25, 1940 had held four full sessions and a special session. It would have reached the end of its maximum term in November, 1940.

There is all the difference in the world between dissolving such a parliament which has met five times and sat for 532 days and dissolving a Parliament which has barely met at all and sat for less than one day.

Probably the most contentious issue involving the dissolution of Parliament arises when a government receives an adverse vote in the House of Commons. A notorious case occurred in

1968 when the Pearson government was defeated by being ambushed by the opposition on a vote on a tax measure. In defending the decision not to accept the vote as a vote of non-confidence, requiring the resignation of his government, the prime minister cited Forsey in his defence. At the same time Dalton Camp, in an address to the annual meeting of the Progressive Conservative Student Federation in which he denounced the government for its refusal to resign, also leaned on Forsey in support of his position. On 24 February 1968 the *Ottawa Journal* sought Forsey's aid to resolve the conflict:

> 'Mr Pearson was quoting me in context,' he said. 'Mr Camp missed the operative word.'
>
> Here is the quote Mr Camp used ... 'This (meaning the arguments advanced earlier) could force a minority government to hark back to Macdonald's commonsense position of simply accepting defeats on any question except censure or want of confidence on some measure which he considered vital to his policy.'
>
> In this article, Dr Forsey said he was discussing the position of the government of Sir John A. Macdonald between 1867 and 1872.
>
> And the operative word, declared Dr Forsey is 'considered.'
>
> 'The point is,' said Dr Forsey, 'the government should decide whether it considers a matter on which it was defeated in the House vital to its policy.'
>
> If the government doesn't declare the legislation a matter of confidence, he said, then there is no question that the government can stay in office – at least until it formally declares a motion a matter of confidence and loses or the opposition moves a motion of censure or want of confidence and wins.
>
> Dr Forsey described how the Macdonald government was defeated a number of times between 1867 and 1872 but did not resign because it would not consider any of the matters on which it lost vital to government policy.
>
> He said there were many other precedents in Canada and Great Britain for this type of government decision.
>
> In the past, he explained, these decisions were justified by the

number of independents or 'loose fish,' as they were called. These meant that governments were often easily defeated.

In modern times, he said, these precedents are valid because the splinter parties make it just as likely there will be minority governments which can be defeated with ease.

About the Liberal government's decision to stay in office after their Monday vote and place a motion of confidence before the House, he had this to say: 'It is a perfectly proper and common-sense way to meet the problem.'

In the *Ottawa Citizen* on 23 February 1968 Forsey corrected other erroneous constitutional interpretations:

> Greg Connolley says that after the defeat of the government on Monday, it was open to Mr Pearson to 'resign and ask a cabinet colleague to take over the government.' You yourself say that it was open to Mr Pearson to 'resign and ask the Governor-General to send for Mr Stanfield.'
>
> Neither statement has any warrant in constitutional practice. A prime minister who resigns, even because of ill-health, let alone defeat, has no right whatever to tender any advice as to his successor. Only if the Governor-General asks for his opinion has he any right to open his mouth on the subject; and even then the Governor-General is perfectly free to disregard the opinion ...
>
> The correct constitutional doctrine is set forth fully in Sir Robert Borden's official statement of July, 1920 ...
>
> In the case of a defeated prime minister, there is also the small matter of common sense. If he decides to resign, it is clearly outrageous that he should have the right to designate his successor, whether from his own party or from among his opponents.
>
> If a defeated prime minister resigns, the Governor-General must send for the leader of the opposition. This is the established rule, firmly grounded on the triple foundation of precedent, authority and common sense.

Journalists were not alone in being targets for Forsey's corrections, for in a letter to the *Globe* on 11 March 1968 dealing with the same crisis and expanding on the points made in his earlier letters, the constitutional expertise of Professor Edward McWhinney was exposed to a chapter and verse rebuttal, with side-bars directed to the *Globe*'s reporter, Anthony Westell.

What Happens after an Indecisive Election Result? Among the many letters Forsey felt obliged to write in order to correct misrepresentations of the proper constitutional practice was one to the *Ottawa Journal* on 30 December 1978:

> The true constitutional position can be stated very simply. It is not the business of the Governor-General, even on the basis of assurances (very possibly ill-founded) of any party leader, to decide who should form the government. That is the business of the people's representatives in the House of Commons.
>
> It follows that if no party gets a clear majority in a general election, the government in office has the right, if it chooses, to stay in office and meet the new Parliament, though it must summon Parliament as promptly as possible. The new House of Commons will then decide whether to keep it in or throw it out.
>
> If the House votes want of confidence, the government resigns, and the Governor-General calls on the opposition to form a new goverment.
>
> If the government fails to summon the new Parliament within a reasonable time, the Governor-General can, and should, insist that the delay must end; and if the government still procrastinates, he can, and should, dismiss it and call on the leader of the opposition to form a government which will summon Parliament forthwith.
>
> Similarly, if the government which has come out of the election without a clear majority, and meets the new House promptly, and is promptly defeated, asks for a fresh dissolution, the Governor-General can, and should, refuse, and call on the leader of the opposition to form a government (unless, of course, there is clearly no possibility of an alternative government in the existing House of Commons).
>
> Apart from these circumstances, the role of the Governor-

> General is purely passive. He can, and should, intervene in the process only to stop any attempt by a cabinet to prevent the people's representatives from deciding who should form the government ...
>
> I may add that if a general election gives no party a clear majority, and the government party is not even the largest party, the government is still constitutionally entitled to meet the new House of Commons (though, again, it must do so reasonably promptly). The Governor-General would not be entitled to dismiss it and call on the leader of the largest party. It would be for the House of Commons to decide whether the existing government should remain in office, or whether it should give place to a new one headed by the leader of the largest party.

The Office of Lieutenant-Governor. What Forsey had to say about the role of the governor general also applied at the provincial level to the office of lieutenant-governor. In a letter to the *Globe* on 26 February 1969, he had these clarifications of the special functions of the office:

> Donald Newman ('Primacy' for Ottawa – Feb. 6) has got three distinct things mixed up.
>
> A Lieutenant-Governor, presented with a bill, may (1) assent to it, (2) withhold assent, (3) reserve it for the signification of the Governor-General's pleasure.
>
> If he assents, the bill becomes law, but this bill may be disallowed (wiped off the statute book) by the Dominion Government at any time within one year of receipt of the Act at Ottawa. One hundred and twelve Acts have been so disallowed, the last in 1943.
>
> If the Lieutenant-Governor withholds his assent, the bill is dead. It does not go to Ottawa or anywhere else, for action to anyone. To the best of my recollection, 20-odd provincial bills have suffered this fate, the last, in Prince Edward Island, in 1945.
>
> If the Lieutenant-Governor reserves a bill, it goes to Ottawa in a state of suspended animation; and, unless the Governor-General (on the advice of the Dominion Cabinet) assents to it, within one year after its receipt at Ottawa, it does not become law. My recol-

lection is that some 70 bills have been so reserved, the last in 1961, and that only 14 ever received the Governor-General's assent.

Forsey found he had to deal at the provincial level with the same misrepresentation of the working practices of the constitution that he had repeatedly addressed at the national level. The events surrounding the end of the four-decade rule of the Progressive Conservative party in Ontario provided Forsey with a glorious opportunity to instruct the journalists one final time in 1985.

On 11 May 1985 he took on the *Globe and Mail*:

> The Globe and Mail informs us that Ontario NDP Leader Bob Rae's 'statement' about what he will do when the legislature meets 'means that Frank Miller will at least have a chance to form a government' (Ontario NDP Invites Bids for Support – May 7). Premier Miller formed a government weeks ago, when he was elected party leader. It is still there. It will remain there until it resigns.
>
> The previous day had offered an even worse howler: 'Under provincial, and federal precedent, when a government is defeated on an issue of significance, such as a Throne Speech or budget, the lieutenant-governor can order a new election or ask the next largest party (in this case the Liberals) to attempt to form a government' (Liberals Ready to Govern If PC Minority Defeated).
>
> If Mr Miller is defeated on the address in reply from the Speech from the Throne, he can advise the lieutenant-governor to dissolve the newly elected legislature. But the lieutenant-governor could not, in conscience, accept such advice. Mr Miller would have no right whatever to drag us through the polling booths by the scruff of the neck when there is, plainly, the possibility that Liberal leader David Peterson could form a government and carry on the public business with the support of the NDP. Of course, if the NDP refused to support either Mr Miller or Mr Peterson, then a fresh election is the only way out ...
>
> All this talk of a fresh election in a matter of months is nonsense, and an insult to the people of the province.

As the Miller government's political foothold became more tenuous, Forsey was obliged to instruct both the *Globe* and the *Ottawa Citizen* on proper procedure. To the *Citizen*'s reporter, on 10 June, Forsey gave his usual lecture on unnecessary elections, opening and closing his letter as follows:

> Susan Hanna ... says the Lieutenant-Governor 'is now searching his soul and consulting legal and constitutional precedents in anticipation of the historic decision he will be asked to make.'
>
> Decision as to what? Whether, when Mr Miller is defeated in the legislature, to grant him a fresh election, or to call upon Mr Peterson to form a government.
>
> He need not search long.
>
> Only once in the whole history of the Commonwealth, has a prime minister defeated on a vote of want of confidence in a newly elected Legislature or Parliament, at the very outset of its first session, even asked for a fresh election. That was in New Brunswick in 1883. The request was refused.
>
> It had to be. To have granted it would have been contempt of Parliament. If parliamentary government means anything, it must mean that at least a newly elected Legislature is given a chance to transact public business. If it is not given that chance, then we might as well not bother to have legislatures at all, but just govern by plebescite ...
>
> Ms Hanna cites the case of 1977, when a Conservative minority government asked for and got a fresh election. Yes, but after two years, not six or eight weeks. If Mr Miller were able to keep a majority in the House for two years, of course he could get a fresh election. But, though the fact seems to have escaped him, and the journalists who have been purveying all this solemn nonsense about 'decisions,' and 'alternatives,' this is 1985, not 1987.

The *Globe's* reporter fared no better, as Forsey's parting shot came on 4 June:

> John Cruickshank says the Liberals and NDP believe their alliance means [Lieutenant-Governor John Black] Aird will decide to

> offer the Liberals a chance to govern instead of calling an election (PC's 42-year Rule to End As NDP Chooses Liberals – May 25).
>
> Mr Aird will not have to 'decide' anything. If the newly elected House defeats Premier Frank Miller, the constitutional duty of the Lieutenant-Governor is to call on the leader of the Opposition.
>
> The Lieutenant-Governor does not 'decide' to call an election. He dissolves the Legislature only on the advice of the Premier ...
>
> Where on earth do reporters get these quaint, antediluvian notions of the power of the Crown and its representatives?

Last Thoughts on the Reserve Power. Forsey spent much intellectual energy over the course of his life in establishing the true parameters of the discretionary power of the crown's representative in Canada. His views were initially contested but ultimately became the 'official' version, as his reputation as a constitutional authority gained credence. It was, therefore, ironic that, in one of his unpublished think pieces on the monarchy, written in the 1980s, he expressed serious reservations about what he thought to be ill-conceived proposals for expanding the reserve power of the governor general.[3] He observed that the electoral system was forcing major parties to confront 'serious feelings of alienation in one or other region' (a result of their inability to capture seats in all parts of the country). 'But that giving the Governor General a massive increase in personal, discretionary power would provide a remedy is, to say the least, far from clear, and the remedy might well prove worse than the disease. The proper remedy for defects in the electoral system is change in the electoral system. If plumbing does not work properly, we do not tear off the roof.'

CHAPTER SEVEN

The Senate

The attention our founding fathers gave to the composition and functions of the Canadian Senate testifies to the key role they expected it to play in the new federation. The Senate was the crucial compromise, offsetting the dominance of the most populous provinces in the elective House of Commons by an appointed Senate that represented the provinces, without regard to their population. The passing years have witnessed no relaxation of the attention devoted to the Senate, with proposals to reform or abolish it always claiming the limelight over any reform of the House of Commons. Forsey's letters reflect the same obsession. They also reveal one of the few topics on which he openly acknowledged a change of mind. As a thrice unsuccessful CCF candidate, in the 1940s he wholeheartedly endorsed that party's formal policy of abolition. However, even before his appointment to the Senate, he had changed his mind about abolition and, during his decade of service in the Senate and thereafter, was even sceptical of the many proposals for reform, particularly those that would have created a new institution embodying more fully the interests of the provinces. Forsey's stand-pat position was reinforced by successive alterations in the constitutional amending processes that made such serious changes to the Senate as those envisaged in a House of Provinces or a 'Triple E Senate,' increasingly problematic.

The letter to the *Globe and Mail* on 7 September 1977 contains

Forsey's response to the accusation of apostasy and his extended apologia defending his change of mind.

> G.W. McCullough (Senate – Aug. 16) quotes me as saying, in 1945, that the 'first act of a minority CCF government' would be to 'bring in a bill to abolish the Senate, go to the country, and win, hands down.'
>
> The quotation is no doubt correct. But several years before I was summoned to the Senate I had reached the conclusion that very few people had the faintest interest in abolishing the Senate, and very few ever would have unless the Senate did something plumb crazy. Most people are far too concerned with practical problems like unemployment and inflation. If the House of Commons produced solutions for these, or if it passed some great measure of social justice or economic reform and the Senate threw the bills out, then a party that proposed abolition of the Senate might well 'win, hands down.' But can anyone in his right mind see the Senate doing anything of the sort? It hasn't enough political base, or clout ... And if we did abolish the Senate we should have to create a new one. Every federation in the Western world has an Upper House, for the simple reason that every federation must have a House which represents the constituent communities (states or provinces) as such. It took me a disgracefully long time to realize this; but, by the time the Government published its (very foolish) proposals for Senate reform in the February, 1969, White Paper, The Constitution and the People of Canada, this plain fact had at last penetrated my skull, and that is on the record, in print.
>
> The Senate is not going to be abolished unless it does something simply lunatic. It may, some day, be reformed (though talk of such reform always recalls to my mind Arthur Meighen's scornful comment on Mackenzie King's 1925 announcement of his intention to undertake an unspecified reform: 'So that old bird is to be provided with wooden wings and told to fly again!'). The trouble is that they would have given the Senate more real power than it has now (it has not thrown out a bill in the last 40 years), which would mean giving it more power to make a nuisance of itself (or worse); which ought not to be its function.

> The probability is that, with all its faults, the present Senate is a good deal better than anything the 'reformers' might put in its place. Most of its faults could be cured by the modest proposals of the Joint Parliamentary Committee on the Constitution (1972) and by such other, easy and relatively minor changes as I ventured to suggest in your columns last month. It will be hard enough to get the public interested even in these, let alone grandiose schemes of fundamental 'reform' or apocalyptic visions of abolition.

The letter containing the modest reform proposals referred to (19 August 1977), and headed 'Forsey Suggests Four Ways Senate Could Be Helped to Get through Load,' also provides such a concise description of the working practices of the Senate that it is worth reproducing as a textbook entry.

> Your editorial, The Senate at its Leisure (Aug. 3), was printed on the very day when the Senate wound up a week of incessant work, on a variety of large, complex, important, and often highly dubious bills, dumped on us at the tailend of a session. Most of the careful consideration the Senate is supposed to give to such bills – and would undoubtedly have given had they reached us at the proper time, is of course given in committee. When four or five complex bills are before different committees at the same time, it is often impossible for their critics to do their job, for the simple reason that no one can be in two or more places at once. This was certainly my situation. It was also, very markedly, the situation of Opposition senators. There are only 15 of them, and during that week a number of those 15 were ill.
>
> The Opposition, with some help from the Liberals (I sided with the Opposition in, I think, every case), put up a stiff fight on two of the bills ... By the time we got to the gun-control and wire-tapping bill, those of us who were critical were pretty thoroughly discouraged ... On this bill, the situation was further complicated by the fact that it was an omnibus bill, dealing with several totally different matters. Senators who favored the gun-control provisions might be opposed to the wiretapping provisions and vice versa.

There is a limit to the number of times most people are prepared to fight in the face of certain defeat.

You may perhaps say that the Senate could have done with other bills what it has done with the Maritime Code bill, which is still before the Transportation and Communications Committee, which will meet again during the recess to consider some 130 proposed amendments. But in this case, the bill was ... so appallingly drafted that no one was prepared to let it go through without a thorough overhauling.

The remedies for this situation are four: (1) the appointment of more Opposition senators; (2) the introduction of more of these complex, non-money bills in the Senate; (3) prompter disposition of the bills in the House of Commons, so that they come to the Senate well before the end of the session; (4) more use of the Hayden formula.

This last is the procedure which Senator Hayden initiated for complex bills coming before the Banking, Trade and Commerce Committee. The moment such a bill is introduced in the House of Commons, Senator Hayden moves to have 'the subject matter' (that is, in reality, the bill itself) referred to his committee ... In the case of the tax reform legislation, both the White Paper and the bill were referred, and the Senate committee put in six months solid work on the subject before the bill passed by the House of Commons ever reached us. Consequently, by the time it did reach us. the committee had heard over 100 witnesses and examined well over 200 briefs, and had suggested 53 changes in the original plan, all of which had been accepted by the House of Commons. So when the bill finally got to us nearly all the work on it had been thoroughly done; and the very few further amendments ... it got ... within the next two years.

Despite Forsey's praise for the value of the Hayden formula for improving the effectiveness of the Senate, in 1984, without any formal constitutional change and without fanfare, the Senate on its own motion dropped the procedure. Clearly, it is within the Senate's own power to effect important procedural changes. However, basic changes up to and including abolition of the Senate require more fundamental interventions.[1]

During his early abolitionist phase, Forsey launched a long attack on a *Free Press* editorial which defended the Senate and pointed up the difficulty of abolition (24 December 1943). In the course of a long and richly ornamented rebuttal of 'the utterances of a lay pope,' Forsey made the point that the constitution (the BNA Act) permitted Canada's Parliament to pass legislation that would abolish the Senate, a point which he was to reiterate until the constitution was patriated in 1982 with much more rigorous amending procedures applicable to Senate reform or abolition. Ironically, Dafoe's appended 'Ed. Note' forecast Forsey's own change of heart:

> The circumstances which make it quite impossible for Mr Forsey and others of his like to 'scrap the constitution' with the celerity he prophesies are not affected in the least by his oracular deliverances. While the Canadian federation endures, there must be a second chamber – as he would know if he were familiar with the basic facts of our Confederation. The present senate may be changed into a more effective second chamber, but when this is desired by them it will be attended to by the Canadian people themselves by orderly means.

Forsey, as we have seen, did embrace Dafoe's position and then directed his letters to the flood of reform proposals that arose in the 1970s and 1980s and continue, seemingly as regular as the ocean tides – but now beyond the reach of Forsey's admonitory voice.

On a 'back-door' proposal for senate reform in a *Globe* editorial on 27 April 1976, he had this rejoinder (30 April):

> Your editorial ... suggests that 'The Prime Minister might be forgiven' for not filling Senate vacancies 'if he were undertaking to abolish the Senate by attrition.'
>
> If you are under the impression that the Senate could be abolished simply by not appointing new senators, and waiting till all

the present ones died, or resigned, or vacated their seats automatically on reaching the age of 75, you are under a misapprehension.

If all the present senators died, resigned, or vacated their seats because of age, the result would simply be that no legislation could be passed at all. No bill can become an act without the consent of the Senate. If all the senators had disappeared, then there would be none left to pass a single proposal into law. The House of Commons would be powerless.

[Forsey then re-stated the procedure applicable until 1982.] The only way to abolish the Senate is by an act of Parliament, passed by the House of Commons and the Senate and assented to by the Crown. Incidentally, this can be done, under our present Constitution, by a simple, ordinary act, in exactly the same way that we amend the Criminal Code, the Food and Drugs Act or any other law.

The passage of the Constitution Act, 1982 not only altered the procedures required for abolishing the Senate but also those involved for reforming the Senate. Since such proposals proliferated in the 1980s, Forsey's special aptitude for keeping the record clear was often put in play, as in the following correction of the *Globe* columnist, Jeffrey Simpson, on 24 September 1987.

Jeffrey Simpson (A Comic Opera – Aug. 26) says, correctly, that neither a simple resolution of the House of Commons nor an Act of Parliament of Canada could abolish the Senate. For one thing, 'the Senate would have a say in its own demise.' (It would, but it could hold up a constitutional amendment only for 180 days.) 'More important, so would the provinces since the Supreme Court ruled unanimously a few years back that Ottawa alone could not change the Senate.'

This is a little out of date. The Supreme Court was ruling on then head 1 of section 91 of the Constitution Act, 1867. That provision of the Constitution disappeared in 1982. The situation now is that, under section 41 (e) of the Constitution Act, 1982, the Senate could be abolished only with the unanimous consent of the provinces. This is because the Senate is a part of all the amending

> formulas, and section 41 (e) says the amending formulas can be changed only by unanimous consent. Any one province could now veto abolition of the Senate.
>
> Further, any change in the powers of the Senate, the number of senators from any province, and the method of selecting senators, must, under section 42 (1) (b) and (c) have the consent of at least seven provinces with at least half the population of the 10. The Meech Lake accord would change this to unanimous consent; so that, under the Meech Lake accord, any one province could veto any change to an elected Senate, or any change in the Senate's powers, or any change in the number of senators from any province.
>
> In exchange, the Meech Lake accord gives the provincial premiers, and the Prime Minister of Canada, a guaranteed right to propose, once a year, changes in the Senate, or abolition. One hopes the Senate reformers will be suitably grateful for this ineffable privilege.

In the late 1970s and throughout the 1980s, proposals to make the Senate both more powerful and more representative of provincial interests increased, particularly from the alienated Western provinces, one of whose spokesmen, Joe Clark, began to speak of the Canadian federation as a community of communities. From his seat in the Senate and even more vigorously after retirement, Forsey challenged the proposals of the 'provincial warlords,' viewing them as undermining the very edifice of a strong Canadian government. To one of these proponents, Forsey addressed this letter in the *Globe* on 14 January 1978:

> Flora MacDonald, MP (A Vision of a Revitalized Canada – Jan. 9), suggests that the Senate 'could be changed to become a veritable House of Provinces.'
>
> How? By giving provincial governments the power of appointment? A first class way of giving them power to paralyze the operations of the national Government and Parliament. The existing Senate has not thrown out a bill for over 40 years ... It has refrained from using its power of veto because it has little political

clout. [From the mid-eighties on, the Senate was to assert its veto and suspensive powers in unprecedented fashion, with consequences noted below.] But a Senate appointed by provincial governments would have plenty of clout. Can anyone be innocent enough to suppose it would not use it, especially if it had been given, as Miss MacDonald also suggests, 'more power'?

And what extra powers would she give it? It already has an absolute veto over all legislation: it can throw out any bill as often as it likes. [This was true until 1982, as Forsey shows in next letter.] It has, in the past, thrown out a particular bill as often as four times. The only additional power it could be given would be power to initiate money bills. The House Commons is not likely to consent to that.

Would Miss MacDonald give our Senate executive powers also, like the American Senate? Power to veto the appointment of judges, ambassadors, heads of regulatory agencies? Power to veto treaties? The present Government proposed this sort of thing some years ago, but dropped it. Is Miss MacDonald proposing to borrow old clothes from a Liberal rag-bag?

She thinks her 'House of Provinces' could 'become a forum for constant federal-provincial negotiation.' The provincial Premiers would, of course, willingly stand aside. ...

Forsey greeted the reformers' choice of the 1980s, a Triple E Senate, with the same dismissive letters, that to the *Globe* on 25 April 1987 being typical:

The proposal for a 'triple E' Senate (equal, elected, effective) includes provision for six senators from every province. That alone is enough to prove that it is just flailing the air, whistling in the wind, blowing soap bubbles.

Nova Scotia and New Brunswick would drop from 10 seats to six. Quebec and Ontario would drop from 24 seats to six.

Anyone who believes that ... is capable of believing that the moon is made of molasses.

But, under the Constitution Act, 1982, any change in the number of senators from any province must have the consent of the

11 March 1985. Reprinted with permission from the *Globe and Mail*

legislatures of at least seven provinces with at least half the population of the 10.

If four provinces balk, the proposal is dead.

Before 1982, it was possible to argue about how many provinces had to consent, or which ones. All? A majority? A 'substantial number' or 'substantial majority'? Quebec? But now it is all set down in black and white in the supreme law of the land. For some amendments (for example, abolishing the Senate), you must have the consent of all 10 provinces; for most of the other amendments, the consent of seven, representing half the total population of the 10 ...

And if you can't get the consent of the 10, or the seven, within three years, your proposed amendment is dead. One province (for some amendments), four provinces (for most of the others), just dragging their feet, is enough to kill it.

> It is astonishing how many people simply cannot get it into their heads that we now have a very rigid Constitution. It is going to be the devil of a job to get anything new of importance into it, or anything old of any importance out of it.

Forsey probably took comfort from the closing lines of the foregoing letter, for he repeatedly returned to the theme that we now had one of the most rigid constitutions in the world. Such rigidity made academic the ambitions of abolitionists and root-and-branch reformers of the Senate. But, as his letters revealed, he favoured only modest procedural reforms that could be accomplished without invoking formal amendment procedures – and, even here, remained a staunch defender of one of the historic functions of the Senate as a so-called court of sober second thought. It was the appointive nature of the Senate (until 1965, for life), making it a legislative body without a constituency, together with its original endowment of absolute veto powers over the House of Commons, that attracted Forsey's denunciations during his CCF days. Later, Forsey became a strong defender of the Senate's role as a check on the popularly elected lower house.

Among the most misunderstood checking powers of the Senate was that exercised with respect to so-called money bills – measures for the expenditure of public funds which can only be initiated by ministers of the Crown. A crisp letter to the *Ottawa Citizen* on 5 December 1987 clarified the Senate's role:

> Don McGillivray (Nov. 24) quotes Mr Blenkarn, MP, as saying that the Senate 'can neither amend nor veto' a money bill; and that 'they can only delay it for a maximum of six months. Then it automatically becomes law.'
>
> Someone has been leading Mr Blenkarn up the garden path.
>
> A very brief inspection of the Constitution Act, 1867 and amendments will show him that the Senate can veto any bill whatsoever, and can amend any bill whatsoever, though it cannot increase the amount in a money bill.
>
> It can also delay any bill whatsoever for as long as it sees fit; till

Doomsday if it chooses. The six months limit applies not to bills but to resolutions for constitutional amendments; and even then the House of Commons must re-pass the resolutions to give them any effect (Constitution Act, 1982, section 47).

I wonder who has been feeding Mr Blenkarn these fairytales. Presumably some unfortunate who is unable to read.

During the 1980s the Senate became much more assertive in exercising the delaying powers described by Forsey, because the Progessive Conservatives captured an overwhelming majority in the House of Commons and had to face a hostile Senate dominated by members appointed during the long hegemony of the Liberal party. Notable clashes occurred as the Mulroney Conservative government, deploying its majority in the House of Commons, sought approval for such controversial legislation as the Drug Patents bill in 1987, the Free Trade measure of 1988, and the equally controversial bill to introduce the Goods and Services Tax in 1989. In this last instance, the normally sedate Senate witnessed a chaotic scene of filibuster, division bell-ringing, whistle-blowing, and general mayhem which became the occasion not only for much editorial tut-tutting but also for renewed calls for fundamental reform.

Forsey's defence of the Senate's delaying actions with respect to the drug patent bill was but one of several letters he felt obliged to write when the Mulroney government sought approval for this measure, as well as the free trade legislation and the introduction of the GST. His most complete exposition of the Senate's role was in a letter to the *Globe* on 7 November 1987, headed 'Senate within Its Rights over Bill C-22 Revisions.'

Your editorial Subordinate Senators (Oct.26) says, 'In rejecting the Government's perfectly acceptable drug patent bill, the Senate is flouting constitutional convention.'

The Senate is not rejecting the bill. It is proposing amendments. Surely you are not denying its right to do that?

Would the amendments be fatal to the bill?

Do they take away the multinationals' proposed 10-year

monopoly? They do not. Do they prevent or discourage the companies' proposed investments? They do not.

What do they do?

They strengthen the bill by doing four things:

First, they strike out the retroactive feature.

Second, they make the companies' promises of investments part of the law; make them legally binding.

Third, they provide for withdrawing benefits to the companies that don't live up to what they promised.

Fourth, they strengthen the safeguards against excessive price increases ...

What's so wrong with all that?

You call the bill 'perfectly acceptable.' 'Perfectly' means 'completely.' It is certainly acceptable to the multinationals, to the Government, to you, and to various people and organizations. But it is manifestly unacceptable to the generic drug companies, to the Consumers' Association of Canada, to the Opposition parties in the House of Commons, and to the Senate. Completely acceptable?

As to the alleged constitutional convention, you quote Professor Peter Hogg: that the Senate 'as an appointed body, has no political mandate to obstruct the elected House of Commons. It is accepted by opposition as well as government senators that the appointive nature of the Senate must necessarily make its rule subordinate to the elective House.' Subordinate, yes; but how far? ...

Certainly the Senate would never throw out a bill for which the electorate had given the House of Commons a clear mandate. But was this drug patent bill part of the election platform or promises of any party at the last election?

Is there any convention that says the Senate is bound to pass a bill on which the electors have never been consulted, and which might be passed by the Commons only in its dying moments? Is there any convention that says the Senate must pass a bill to which the majority of the provinces object? After all, the Senate was created partly to protect the interests of the provinces in matters under federal jurisdiction. Is there any convention that says the Senate cannot, in a matter it considers sufficiently grave, insist that the Government submit that matter to the test of a general election? It did precisely that with Borden's Naval Aid Bill in 1913; and it passed the first Old Age Pension bill only after the government that proposed it had been returned in the general election of 1926.

Sir John A. Macdonald summed it up: 'It is only valuable as being a regulatory body, calmly considering the legislation initiated by the popular branch, and preventing any hasty or ill-considered legislation which may come from that body, but it will never set itself against the deliberate and understood wishes of the people.'

The Fathers of Confederation wanted the Senate to bring 'sober second thought' to bear on radical legislation passed by the House of Commons. What they feared was radical legislation of the left. But why should the principle not apply equally to radical legislation of the right? ...

The Senate's balking at the GST bill drew a defence from Forsey which does not seem to have been published but with which we may appropriately close this section since it demonstrates Forsey's ability to apply history to current developments and draw out the lessons to be learned.[2]

In the chorus of denunciations of the Senate for blocking the GST Bill one factor seems to have been overlooked.

Till 1913, it was possible for an Opposition in the House of Commons to force a Government to go to the people in a general election. Every member could speak as long as he liked (there were no women in those days), and in Committee of the Whole, as long as he liked and as often as he liked on every single clause of a bill.

This meant that if a great new issue of public policy arose, to which there was strong and widespread objection across the country, we were not, like the Americans, stuck with a particular Administration for a solid four years. This was one of the marked superiorities of our Constitution over theirs.

There were no time limits on speeches. There was no closure. There was no time allocation for the successive stages of a bill.

So an Opposition in the Commons could, by obstruction, by filibustering, preserve the right of the people to decide on a new issue of crucial importance.

It was a formidable power; not, as the Anglican Prayer Book says of matrimony, 'by any to be entered upon, nor taken in hand, unadvisedly, lightly or wantonly, but reverently, discreetly, advisedly, soberly.' ...

The Conservatives so exercised it in 1911, on Reciprocity.

But it is a power the Opposition in the House of Commons has now lost. The last vestige disappeared with the adoption of the rule that prohibits the long bell-ringing the Conservatives used so effectively against the Trudeau Government, forcing it to divide a huge omnibus bill into component parts.

Now, therefore, if there is a great new issue of public policy on which the voters have not been consulted, only the Senate can protect their right to be consulted. Only the Senate can force a general election, as it did on Free Trade. Then, of course, it accepts the verdict of the electors, as it did with the Free Trade Bill. Again, of course, it is a power to be exercised only on rare occasions, on issues of first-class magnitude, on which the electors have not been consulted.

Is the GST Bill a great new issue of public policy? Was it before the electors in the last general election? Is it of first-class magnitude? Is there strong opposition across the country?

These are the questions that have to be answered. Clichés about the Senate 'frustrating the people's will' are beside the point. The will of the House is not necessarily the people's will. It wasn't in 1911. But then the Opposition in the House of Commons could insist on getting the people's will, in a general election. Now it can't.

The theory that once a government has won a general election it can do pretty much what it pleases for the next four or five years is not consonant with democracy. There are some rights that are not, and cannot be, covered by the Charter of Rights and Freedoms.

This assessment of the performance of the Senate in the late 1980s suggests that Forsey had come to the conclusion that the Senate had essentially taken over the role of official opposition. Unfortunately, he left us no letters that addressed the implications of this development for the system of parliamentary democracy he held dear. That system presumably relies on the capacity of Her Majesty's Loyal Opposition, located primarily in the elected House of Commons, to hold the government to account. Could any Senate reform, however sweeping, provide a substitute for a properly functioning loyal opposition in the elected chamber?

We are left to ponder Forsey's possible reply to this question but do have his final words on the subject of Senate reforms and Senate reformers. This comes in his reply to a request from Dennis Anderson, chairman of the Alberta legislature's committee on Senate reform, who had asked for Forsey's views on the Triple-E Senate proposal. He opened his response (26 October 1984): 'I am sorry to say that I have no idea at all of what the Triple-E Movement is proposing. I never heard of it till the night before last. So I am rather at a loss to comment on that part of your letter.' He then went on to issue his usual warnings about the very rigid constitution which faced any would-be reformers. In a letter to Professor MacKinnon on 29 November 1984, enclosing his reply to Dennis Anderson's inquiry, he took this parting shot: 'I am getting thoroughly fed up with all the people who waste their time (and mine) with wholly impracticable, and usually noxious, vapourings on Senate reform. I wish there were a "Gold Cure" for it!'

CHAPTER EIGHT

The Judiciary and the Rule of Law

Forsey had enormous respect for the third branch of government, the judiciary. Its traditional role as independent guardian of the people's rights against abuse of power by other agents of the state, subsumed under the concept of the rule of law, was regarded by Forsey as one of the basic inheritances from Britain. It was particularly fitting, therefore, that perhaps the major focus of Forsey's career as a senator was as co-chairman of the Joint Parliamentary Committee on Statutory Instruments – a watchdog committee to ensure that the discretionary powers conferred by statute on ministers of the Crown and exercised by their officials were not allowed to get out of hand.

In addition to this primary role as guardian of the rule of law, the federal form of government in Canada imposes on the judiciary the equally important task of adjudicating the jurisdictions assigned respectively to the Dominion and the provinces. In legal parlance, it is a question of determining whether acts of the respective governments are within the powers assigned to them, *intra vires* or *ultra vires*, constitutional or unconstitutional.

With the adoption of a Charter of Rights and Freedoms in the Canada Constitution Act of 1982, extra dimensions were added to the role of the judiciary in interpreting the constitution.[1]

Judicial Independence

The essential prerequisite for the judiciary to enable it to perform both as guardian of the rule of law and final interpreter of the constitution, including basic human rights, is that its members be independent of the other branches of government, politically neutralized, above the partisan fray. Forsey had firm views on this matter, which were tested in the late 1970s when reforms in the method of appointing members of the judiciary, particularly of the Supreme Court, were being proposed.

On 25 July 1977 he had this admonition to the *Globe and Mail*:

> An article (Federal Government Plans New Initiatives on Constitutional Reform – July 12), says: 'In general terms, Ottawa seems ready to consider' giving the provinces 'a larger role in Supreme Court appointments.'
>
> What 'larger role'? ...
>
> Any proposal to give the provinces power to appoint Supreme Court judges would be appalling. It would amount to an admission of the theory that judges are creatures of the executive, that a judge appointed by the Central Government will be biased in favour of the Central Government; that this bias must be offset, balanced, by having other judges appointed by provincial Governments, who, on the same theory, would be biased in favour of provincial Governments.
>
> Anything more subversive of the independence of the Supreme Court is scarcely conceivable.
>
> Incidentally, it does not seem to have occurred to proponents of this theory that it also involves the consequence that all judges, being appointed by Governments, are bound to be biased in favor of Governments and against the citizen; which is transparent nonsense.

As the proposals for provincial involvement in the appointment process gathered momentum, sponsored by such semi-official views as those expressed in the report of the Ontario Advisory Committee on Confederation, Forsey was compelled to extend his critique, as in this letter to the *Globe* on 13 February 1978, which took on an editorial of 6 January, 'Canada among Canadians.' In part, his letter read:

> Judges are not appointed to represent 'interests.' They are appointed to interpret and apply the law, to the best of their ability, in the light of the language of statutes (including, in Quebec, the Civil Code), the principles of the Common Law (for the civil law of the provinces other than Quebec, and for the public law of the whole country), and previous decisions by the highest court.
>
> The notion that the judges should represent 'interests' is of a piece with the notion that they are, or should be, delegates of the Government which appoints them. Either of these notions is subversive of our whole system of justice, of the rule of law, and of the individual rights which, without the protection of that system and the rule of law which it embodies, are left naked to their enemies.

On 2 May 1978 Forsey returned to the charge, stirred by the recommendation from the Ontario Advisory Committee that 'the judges of the courts of each province should be appointed by the Lieutenant-Governor-in-Council of the province' and 'should be removed only for cause by the Lieutenant-Governor-in-Council.'

> The part about appointment is bad enough. It could well be the first step on the slippery path toward the American pattern of two judicial systems, which I think few Canadian practicing lawyers would favor.
>
> But the part about removal is appalling. It would mean that the judges of the Supreme Courts of the provinces could be dismissed by the respective provincial governments.
>
> The committee would no doubt plead that it says 'only for cause.' But that is no protection ... 'For cause' is ... no substitute at all for the present provision that all judges of the provincial superior courts can be removed only after an address by both Houses of Parliament. (How effective this protection is can be seen from the fact that only one judge in the United Kingdom has ever been so dismissed, and none at all in Canada.)
>
> Judges of the district and county courts do not enjoy the same

> protection. But, under ... the Judges Act, they can be removed only after an inquiry and recommendation by the Judicial Council, consisting of the Chief Justice of Canada and Associate Chief Justices of the Supreme Courts (Trial and Appellate) of the provinces.
>
> The Advisory Committee's proposal for removal of judges, therefore, simply pours the independence of the judiciary down the drain, and with it the basic protection of our liberties. Nothing could be more subversive, more destructive of everything we ought to cherish.

Under the heading 'Umpire Is Out,' Forsey contributed this parting shot to the *Globe* on 11 November 1978:

> Geoffrey Stevens, in his column Distrust of the Court (Nov.2), quotes the British Columbia Government's constitutional proposals, which speak of the Supreme Court of Canada's 'role as impartial umpire of the federal system.' The Alberta proposals also use the same words 'umpire' and 'arbiter.'
>
> It is time provincial warlords stopped mouthing this nonsense about 'umpires' and 'arbiters.' The Supreme Court is not an umpire or an arbiter. It is a court of law, with the duty of interpreting the law, including the Constitution, let the chips fall where they may.

Forsey's insistance that the judiciary be untainted by 'interests' carried with it the requirement that judges should not publicly commit themselves to partisan causes. A particularly noteworthy case arose in 1982 when then Mr Justice Thomas Berger publicly proclaimed his criticisms of portions of the newly patriated Canada Constitution Act. On 18 May 1982 Forsey registered his strong objections to the judge's actions in a letter to the *Globe* that was highlighted with the heading 'Mum's the Word for Some Ranks, Forsey Insists':

> There may be widespread agreement with Mr Justice Thomas Berger's criticisms of the new additions to our Constitution (Probe of Berger 'Witch Hunt' – May 7). But his right to criticize is

> another matter. Many people do not seem to realize that acceptance of certain positions carries with it, and must carry with it, acceptance of certain limitations on the right of free expression.
>
> Anyone who accepts office in a Cabinet loses his (her) right to differ publicly from Cabinet policy. Anyone who accepts the position of deputy minister loses his (her) rights to differ from Government policy. Anyone who accepts the position of Governor-General or Lieutenant-Governor loses his (her) right to attack his (her) Government's policy, or to make speeches, give interviews or write articles on controverted issues of public policy.
>
> ... Anyone who accepts a judgeship also loses the right to speak or write on controverted issues of public policy. If he (she) were allowed such right, then, inevitably, the impartiality of the bench would be called into question. A judge who publicly attacks a particular law ... [or] a judge who engages in public controversy on the merits or demerits of a proposed law may find himself (herself) called upon to interpret or apply the new law, which he (she) has attacked, or the old law which he (she) has disparaged, and people who dislike the decision may, not implausibly, allege prejudice ... The danger is no way lessened if the subject of controversy is changes in the Constitution.
>
> A judge who wants to free himself (herself) from these limitations, self-imposed by acceptance of the judgeship, should free himself (herself) from the office.
>
> I prize very highly my individual right to express my opinion on any public question whatsoever; neither have I been backward in doing so. (Indeed, some might call me Canada's leading chatterbox.) But had I ever accepted any of the offices I have mentioned, I'd have been mum as an oyster, and should not have had the slightest ground for complaint.

Forsey's views were very much those of the legal establishment, as expressed through the reprimand to Judge Berger by the Judicial Council that heard the complaints against him. There were those in the public and the press, amongst them columnist Michael Valpy of the *Globe*, who deigned to disagree. Mr Justice Berger had been chairman of a highly visible royal commission on the Mackenzie Valley Pipeline, where questions of native rights had loomed large. It was the neglect of such rights in those parts of the agreement which were to become the Charter of Rights, when subsequently incorporated into the new Canada Constitution Act, that had drawn Berger's criticisms. In his column on 4 September 1982 Michael Valpy defended Berger's stand, leading Forsey promptly to take issue on 11 September. As usual, we shall allow him the final word(s):

> Michael Valpy (A Rare Case – Sept.4), defending Mr Justice Thomas Berger's 'speaking out against the constitutional accord of November, 1981,' says, 'Those of us who defended him agreed that there are some moral issues in society which transcend normal rules of conduct.'
>
> Of course there are. Ask any conscientious objector to military service ... Ask the ghosts of the English non-conformists who went to jail for refusing to pay taxes under the Education Act of 1902 ... Ask any member of the 'noble army of martyrs' of the Christian churches ...
>
> But has a judge the right, in any circumstances, to disobey the 'normal rule' that judges should not engage in active political controversy? Any judge who wants to do that should resign, just as any Cabinet minister who wants to differ publicly with government policy should resign.
>
> Your own editorial (Picking at It – Sept. 4) raises another question. You say Mr Justice Berger was 'rapped on the knuckles for venturing views on the constitution and particularly on native rights – something he had already done at great length (and with apparent respectability) in the report of a federal inquiry.'
>
> This is inaccurate in three respects. First, he was not 'rapped on the knuckles' for venturing views on the constitution, but for venturing views on particular constitutional proposals which were the subject of active political controversy. Second, he had not (to the best of my recollection) ventured any views on the constitution in his report on the Mackenzie Valley pipeline; certainly not on any aspect of the constitution which was the subject of active political controversy. Third, when, in that report, he set out his

> views on native rights, he was doing so as a Royal Commissioner expressly charged to make recommendations on policy in that very matter. The 'respectability' of his doing so is not only 'apparent' it is unchallengeable. But that is a totally different matter from speaking or writing, when the commission had ceased to exist, on a matter of active political controversy.
>
> No one questions the right of Thomas Berger, private citizen, to express his views on the constitution, native rights, or anything else, whether the subject of active political controversy or otherwise. No one questions the right of Thomas Berger, Royal Commissioner, to express his views on any subject he has been appointed to report on. The only question at issue is the right of Thomas Berger, judge, to express his views on matters of active political controversy.

Forsey would surely have said 'amen!' to the late Bora Laskin's summation: 'The Supreme Court is not a federal institution, it is a national institution and its members are under no federal allegiance merely because they are federally appointed. Just as there is no federal allegiance, there is no regional allegiance and no political allegiance.'[2]

Interpreters of the Constitution

Forsey's insistence on the independence and impartiality of the judiciary was related to his unfaltering dedication to the preservation of a strong central government upon which the judiciary's interpretations of the constitutional division of powers could have a fundamental impact. Until 1949, when the Supreme Court became the court of final resource, appeals on such matters went to the Judicial Committee of the Privy Council in England. Forsey belonged to that school of legal scholars who were critical of the Judicial Committee for handing down advisory judgments that had extended provincial powers at the expense of the Dominion – hence his declamations against 'provincial warlords' and his defence of judicial decisions that supported the exercise of the residual powers conferred on the Dominion government by the peace, order, and good government clause introducing section 91 of the Canada Constitution Act, 1867.

Many of Forsey's letters dealing with the niceties of judicial interpretation of the constitution are as densely argued as some of the decisions themselves. Forsey's dedication to 'the facts and only the facts' – even if only as a self-declared amateur – placed him in that group of constitutional commentators known as 'black letter' interpreters of the text. Typical of such readings is this extract from a long and learned discourse on the letters page of the *Globe* on 17 April 1978.

> In your editorial, Enter Mr Lougheed (March 31), you say: 'The federal emergency power to invoke the "peace, order and good government" clause of the British North America Act has to be curtailed ... For as it now stands and is interpreted by the courts, that clause empowers Ottawa to legislate wherever it sees an emergency and to see an emergency wherever it says it sees one.'
>
> That is an incorrect statement of the legal position. If Parliament decides there is an emergency, the courts will not lightly go behind that decision. But the key word is 'lightly.' 'The question of the extent to which provision for circumstances such as these,' said Lord Haldane in the Fort Frances case, 'may have to be maintained is one on which a court of law is loath to enter. ... Very clear evidence ... would be required to justify the judiciary ... in overruling the decision of the Government (he meant Parliament) that exceptional measures were still requisite.' (He was referring to continuance of certain war-time measures after hostilities had ended, but the principle is clear.) ...
>
> You are apparently willing to accept some emergency power for Parliament. How much? And how? Won't any curtailment have to be interpreted by the courts?
>
> And what would you do with the application of the 'peace, order and good government' power in matters where no question of emergency arises? That power is the basis of Parliament's jurisdiction over broadcasting, atomic energy and official languages.
>
> You are clearly dubious about Mr Lougheed's proposal that the

provinces should 'have exclusive right to the field of indirect taxation.' You could have been more so. For one thing, indirect taxation includes custom duties. Surely Mr Lougheed would not propose to hand those over to the provinces? For another, since the courts have decided that the provincial gasoline and sales taxes are 'direct,' there seems to be little in the way of indirect taxes (except customs duties) which the provinces cannot levy.

Forsey's views on the peace, order and good government clause, as its application affected civil rights, are addressed in his correspondence with Professor Donald Smiley, reproduced in the next section. As to the effect of court interpretations on the distribution of powers, the following letters he addressed to another provincial premier may be taken as a sample (*Globe*, 27 July 1965; a longer critique came on 4 October 1965):

Several newspapers reported Mr Jean Lesage as saying that Quebec 'can't recognize the authority of the Supreme Court in the matters of off-shore mineral rights.'

One can only hope that the report is incorrect, for a more scandalously subversive statement could scarcely be imagined. It is a proclamation of sheer lawlessness, of anarchy, of a principle which cuts at the very roots of civilized society. If we accept it, this country is finished.

No wonder Laurens van der Post has called nationalism 'the juvenile delinquincy of the contemporary world.'

In your editorial, Court and Constitution (Sept. 27), you take at face value Premier Jean Lesage's assurance that he did not refuse to recognize the authority of the Supreme Court of Canada in the matter of offshore mineral rights.

Why are you so sure that what he now says he meant is really any different?

If the question of who owns these rights is not a 'legal and constitutional question,' what is? And if it is, how on earth can it be settled except by a decision of the Supreme Court of Canada?

In effect, Mr Lesage is now saying that that court has no jurisdiction. If it has no jurisdiction, of course it has no authority. If it has no authority, there is nothing to recognize. So what is the difference between saying it has no authority, and saying he will not recognize its authority?

On the one basis, if the court brings down a decision, Mr Lesage says simply that there is no decision; on the other basis, he defies the decision. On either basis he behaves as if it were not there ...

It is all very well to say that this is a matter to be settled by political negotiation. But how can either side negotiate until it knows who owns the property? Theodore Roosevelt used to tell the story of a New York Irish Assemblyman, who, warned that a pet proposal was unconstitutional, replied, 'Ah! Sure, Mr Roosevelt, what's the Constitution between friends?' ...

There is also a general principle involved. Mr Lesage, it seems to me, is now saying, 'Oh! certainly I accept the decisions of the Supreme Court of Canada, provided they deal with matters on which I accept its right to make decisions.' In other words, he can, by his mere say-so, exclude from the jurisdiction of the Supreme Court of Canada any matter he sees fit. Can you imagine anything much more dangerous to the rule of law? ...

One of the most significant examples of the Supreme Court's role in interpreting the constitution occurred in 1981–2 when then Prime Minister Trudeau declared his intention of proceeding unilaterally without provincial approval to seek endorsement of the Canada Constitution Act by the Parliament of the United Kingdom.[3] This procedural question was put to the courts by the provinces and ultimately produced a Supreme Court ruling that itself required interpretation. Forsey was in his element here, instructing both the journalists at home and members of the British parliament on the fine distinctions between constitutional law and constitutional conventions.

To the *Globe* on 19 August 1981, Forsey weighed in with his first instructive letter on proper procedure.

Robert Sheppard says that if the Supreme Court of Canada rules against the eight provinces on the constitutional package, the eight premiers may 'make legal presentations to the judicial committee of the House of Lords ...'

If the eight premiers don't know any more elementary constitutional law than this, they would do better to save their breath to cool their porridge.

There is not, and never has been, a 'judicial committee of the House of Lords.' ...

The highest court for English ecclesiastical cases and for appeals (constitutional and other) from the Commonwealth (where such appeals have not been abolished) is the judicial committee of the British Privy Council. This committee was created by a United Kingdom statute of 1833. It includes judges who are members of the House of Lords, and others who are not. Several Canadian judges were members, and sat, before we abolished appeals in 1949. The judgments of this committee (which, technically, are merely 'humble advice' to the Crown, subsequently embodied in British Orders-in-Council) have at times been handed down by judges who were not peers ...

Another procedural approach suggested by Allan Fotheringham brought this withering response in the *Montreal Gazette* on 23 November 1981.

A friend has called my attention to a question and a statement in a column by Allan Fotheringham in your issue of Nov. 4.

The question is, 'If Prime Minister Pierre Trudeau insists on flying on his unilateral wings to London, in spite of the fact the Supreme Court has told him he would be acting unconstitutionally, is the Queen's denmother of the constitution, Edward Schreyer [then Governor General], then required to hold up a stop sign and yell Halt?'

The answer of course is, 'No.' It would be grossly improper for the governor-general to intervene in the matter at all.

If he did what Mr Fotheringham suggests, the government would promptly resign; the governor-general would have to call on Opposition leader Joe Clark to form a government; Mr Clark could not command a majority in the House of Commons; he would have to ask for a dissolution; and we should have an election in which the governor-general's action would be denounced as unconstitutional, and rightly so. Any suggestion that the governor-general would, or should, act in this fashion is brimstone nonsense.

The remainder of Forsey's letter to the *Gazette* was addressed to the implications of the judgment rendered by the Supreme Court on the questions posed by the provinces, and on this Forsey was well rehearsed, first in an exposition on 7 October 1981 to the *Globe* and then in *The Times* of London on 2 November, in response to a 29 October letter from some twenty members of the British parliament. Since there is much repetition in Forsey's letters to the three newspapers, the exchange in *The Times* will suffice.

From Mr Marcus Fox, MP for Shipley (Conservative), and others:

Sir, It is our understanding that the Prime Minister of Canada, Mr Pierre Trudeau, has proposed that the United Kingdom Parliament approve a number of sweeping changes to the Canadian Constitution as contained in the British North America Act 1867. These measures have proved highly contentious within Canada and are strongly opposed by eight of the 10 provincial governments whose consent is constitutionally required for amendments to the BNA Act which affect their powers.

This view was upheld by the Supreme Court of Canada which on September 28, 1981, stated that the federal request to the United Kingdom Parliament 'without such (provincial) agreement would be unconstitutional in the conventional sense.'

We do not believe that the United Kingdom Parliament should be forced to enact unconstitutional legislation pursuant to a unilateral request from the Canadian federal government. While we do sincerely wish for a settlement that will quickly place the Canadian Constitution fully into Canadian hand there is no question in our minds that until a constitutionally appropriate request is made Parliament has no choice but to continue its residual role in the constitutional affairs of Canada.

It is our fervent hope that the current series of federal provincial negotiations will produce the degree of consensus necessary to enable Parliament to act to eliminate this last trace of Canada's colonial past.

From Dr Eugene Forsey:

Sir, I have noted with interest the views expressed by Mr Marcus Fox and 20 other Conservative Members of Parliament ... in which they come to some conclusions about the meaning of the Supreme Court decision on the Canadian constitutional issue. While I have the greatest respect for their opinion, I find I must ask myself how carefully they have studied the judgment.

The court was asked to answer three main questions:

First, would the federal government's constitutional proposals 'affect federal-provincial relationships of the powers, rights or privileges granted or secured by the Constitution of Canada to the provinces, their legislatures or governments?'

To this the answer, inevitably, was Yes, and on this the Court was unanimous.

The second question was, do the amendments to the Constitution affecting federal-provincial relationships or provincial constitutional powers, rights or privileges, require by 'convention' (custom, practice, usage) the consent of the provinces?

To this, six judges answered Yes. The Chief Justice and two others answered No.

The third question was, if there is such a convention, has it crystallized into law? Is the consent of the provinces legally necessary?

To this, seven judges answered No, and two answered Yes. ...

The decision on this 1st question does not define what 'consent of the provinces' means. The six judges cited a series of precedents since 1931. All these precedents show that no amendments were adopted without the consent of all 10 provinces. But the six judges said that the consent of 10 provinces was not necessary: just the consent of 'a substantial number.' Two provinces, Ontario and New Brunswick, have given their consent to the present proposal. That, said the six judges, was not enough.

How many, between two and 10, would be enough? No answer. And which provinces? Would nine without Quebec be enough? No answer. Eight without Ontario, or Quebec, or both? No answer. The four Atlantic Provinces, with the two smallest Western Provinces? No answer.

The six judges said it would be 'inappropriate' for them to say how many, or which, provinces must consent. That was for 'the political actors' to work out. In other words, there is a binding constitutional rule that a 'substantial number' of provinces must consent, but it is still in embryo, in process of gestation by the politicians. Until that process is finished (when will that be?) no one knows how many, or which provinces must consent.

So any proposed amendment which fails to get the consent of the mysterious, undefined 'substantial number' (more than two, less than 10) risks being denounced as 'constitutionally improper,' 'immoral,' 'morally wrong.' A constitutional convention without a single precedent to support it is a house without a foundation. A constitutional convention that provides no means of finding out whether it is being obeyed or broken is empty; 'without form, and void.' But that is what the six judges say we have, and are bound by. It is a 'gulf profound in that Serbonian bog ... where armies whole have sunk.'

The Supreme Court's decision on a matter of law is final and binding. Its decision on matter of convention is not. The six judges themselves admit the conventions are 'political,' and that this one remains to be worked out by 'the principal actors.' That leaves the question open.

Once people have grasped what the court's ruling on the convention really means it is unlikely to carry much conviction. It may turn out to be, for the eight protesting provinces, no more than 'a phantom of delight ... a lovely apparition sent to be a moment's ornament.'

Upholding the Rule of Law

Turning back to the first major function of the judiciary, that of upholding the rule of law, we open a theme with which Forsey became especially involved in his capacity as co-chairman of the Joint Committee of the Senate and House of Commons on Statutory Instruments. However, years before Forsey was given this privileged position from which to stand guard over the rule of law, he had frequent occasion to come to its defence through his letters. An early and outstanding instance has already been mentioned under another theme, namely, his critique of the infamous Padlock Act passed by the Duplessis government in 1949. The following letter, published on 22 September 1954 in the *Ottawa Journal*, makes clear his view of the rule of law – a view that was subsequently sustained by a Supreme Court decision that declared the legislation an unconstitutional invasion of freedom of discussion.

> The Canadian Press despatch ... on Mr Duplessis' press conference in Quebec winds up by saying that, 'those affected by the Padlock Act have the right to appeal at law.' The Canadian Press should read the act. It would find that the tenant of padlocked premises has no appeal at all; neither has a person whose newspapers, periodicals, pamphlets, circulars, documents, or other 'writings' have been seized, confiscated and destroyed under Section 14 because, in the opinion of the Attorney-General, they 'propagate, or tend to propagate communism or bolshevism' – the definition of which reposes in the cranium of the Attorney-General.
>
> The landlord may, indeed, appeal to a judge of the Superior Court, and the judges can suspend the padlocking order if the landlord can prove he was in good faith ... and if he furnishes security that the premises will not again be used for the undefined purposes ...
>
> This is a long, long way from the Canadian Press blanket statement that 'those affected have the right to appeal at law.' Most of those affected have no such right at all, and the landlords' right depends on their ability to prove that they did not know that their property was being used for something only the Attorney-General can define. ...

The cold war atmosphere dominating the 1950s created a nervousness about potential communist spies and inadequate 'clearance' procedures for public servants that precipitated the Herbert Norman case. Forsey's letter to the *Globe and Mail* on 25 April 1957 was not addressed to the substance of the accusations in a U.S. Senate subcommittee that presumably led to Mr Norman's suicide while serving as Canadian ambassador in Cairo; rather, in typical fashion, he castigated the circumstances that had led to a denial of due process.

> The *Globe and Mail* has asked 'how on earth' the U.S. Senate subcommittee got the RCMP report of October, 1950, on Mr Norman. But there is another question which no one seems to have asked: 'why on earth did anyone in the United States get that report.' Why should security information on Canadians be made available to any agency in another country, unless there are very special and cogent reasons for it in a particular case? ...
>
> If our Government gets 'information' that one of our citizens is imperilling the security of our country, our Government should act. If the citizen in question is a Canadian Government official, our Government should investigate. If the investigation shows he is guilty, our Government should fire him. If the investigation gives him a clean bill of health, it should consign the 'information' to limbo. In either case, what business is it of the FBI, or anybody else in the United States? ...
>
> About the best that can be said for either the RCMP or the Department of External Affairs in this whole affair is that they have shown monumental incompetence. But even monumental incompetence could not have had such disastrous and tragic results if there had not been the initial indefensible policy decision to hand over to the American security 'information,' even 'unchecked and unevaluated,' on Canadian citizens.
>
> A responsible Canadian Government would do its own investigating of its own citizens, its own clearing, its own punishing. If it needed information from the Americans for this purpose, it could ask for it, if they needed information from us for dealing with their own citizens, they could ask for it, and an exchange could

take place on that basis. But the revelation that every time some gabbler in this country purveys to a credulous RCMP his suspicions of some fellow-Canadian, the tale is automatically relayed to the FBI is both humiliating and alarming.

A violation of the rule of law at the domestic rather than the international level caught Forsey's vigilant eye in 1968, as this letter of 2 October to the *Ottawa Journal* testifies.

I am dismayed that, so far as I have seen, no one has yet protested against what The Journal reports the city solicitor as having said at the Ontario Municipal Board hearing on Sept. 19.

'Backing' Mr Campeau's application to have the zoning bylaw amended for his benefit, Mr Hambling, according to your report, said: 'Why should Mr Campeau be dictated to by the federal government or even the city? He has rights too.'

How is, or was, 'the federal government' 'dictating' to Mr Campeau? That gentleman applied for a change in the bylaw. The National Capital Commission disapproved of the change, and appeared before the Ontario Municipal Board to say so. Where on earth is the 'dictation' in that? A cat can look at a king; can the National Capital Commission not appear before the board to express its disagreement with Mr Campeau.

How is, or was, the city dictating to Mr Campeau? ... The city council did what he asked, and sent its solicitor to 'back' him ... If this is the city solicitor's idea of the city 'dictating' to Mr Campeau, he had better consult a good dictionary.

Or does the city solicitor consider that the mere existence of a bylaw that gets in Mr Campeau's way consititutes 'dictation'? Should Mr Campeau not be subject to the law?

And what, pray, are the 'rights' of Mr Campeau which the city solicitor considers are being invaded? ...

Did the board deny Mr Campeau a hearing? It did not. Did it prevent him from saying anything he wanted to say? There is no indication of anything of the sort.

What other 'rights' in this matter does Mr Campeau possess? The right to prevent the NCC, or anyone else who disagrees with

> him, from being heard by the Municipal Board? The right to have that body rubberstamp any request he makes?
>
> Was the city solicitor misreported? I have not seen any suggestion that he was. If he was correctly reported, what under the sun was going on in his mind when he said what he did?

In the early 1980s, the report of the royal commission enquiring into certain activities of the RCMP and its security service provided ample opportunity for Forsey to ring the changes on violations of the rule of law. It also offered, incidentally, an opportunity for Forsey to continue his vendetta against the Department of Justice and its rulings which he had conducted throughout the previous decade as co-chairman of the Joint Committee on Statutory Instruments.

While the Royal (McDonald) Commission was still taking evidence, Forsey had this to say in a letter of 10 March 1980 in the *Montreal Gazette*:

> According to your Feb. 27 article 'Allmand OK'd illegal wire-taps,' Roger Tasse, deputy minister of justice, told the McDonald Commission that 'the law permitting interception of oral communications' (on a warrant from the solicitor-general) was interpreted to permit police inspection of written documents as well. He said the justice department 'ruled' to this effect.
>
> So the department of justice has 'ruled' that 'oral' means 'written. Of course; just as 'night' means 'day.'
>
> Evidently the department has plucked Humpty-Dumpty from the pages of *Alice in Wonderland* and made him a legal mandarin. '"When I use a word," said Humpty-Dumpty, "it means just what I choose it to mean."'
>
> Small wonder our liberties have been invaded.
>
> Perhaps the next 'ruling' will be that 'drunk' means 'sober' and 'sober' means 'drunk.' This would do away with all that tedious breathalyser business and enable the police to arrest any driver they please. We can only hope the government will not pluck Humpty-Dumpty from the department of justice and appoint him to the Supreme Court of Canada.

When the commission reported, Forsey joined a chorus of critics who denounced what were considered to be specious reasons for government inaction. To the *Globe* on 9 September 1981, Forsey wrote:

> The Government's replies to the McDonald Commission Report seem to invoke the principle of *raison d'état*: that officials, police or other, are not [*sic*] entitled to do things that ordinary citizens are forbidden to do.
>
> This is a principle unknown to English law, on which our whole public and criminal law is based. Hitherto, therefore, I had supposed that it was also unknown to Canadian law. By what authority is it now being imported to our legal system?
>
> Have ministers ever read Dicey's Law of the Constitution on *raison d'état* and its repugnance to English law? They should: read, mark, learn and inwardly digest.

Two years later, on 7 September 1983 (the mills of justice do grind exceeding slow) Forsey produced for *Globe* readers a detailed critique of 'the belated explanation of the decision not to prosecute 865 members of the Royal Canadian Mounted Police for illegal activities.'

> First, there were just too many cases; it would have involved too much work.
>
> Second, the acts happened too long ago; 'the statutory limits had expired or would soon expire.'
>
> Assuming that there are statutory limits applying to indictable offences (I should like to be referred to the applicable statute or statutes), why the delay in making the decision?
>
> The general application of these two principles of law enforcement would certainly lighten the work of the criminal courts. Let the law enforcement authorities wait long enough, and the number of cases which had piled up would be too much work to undertake, and a lot of the cases would have happened too long ago.
>
> The third explanation of the decision is that the McDonald

report gave 'no indication of any kind' that 'senior officials or ministers participated in such deception or condoned the systematic non-disclosure of information which might have tended to reveal irregularities in the force's operations.'

This seems of somewhat doubtful relevance, especially in view of the fourth explanation: that the officers 'were clearly misguided as to the application of the law, or ... were mistaken in believing that they were justified in breaching laws simply because in their view they were serving higher ends of national security or criminal law enforcement.'

Who misguided them? And since when has ignorance of the law, or belief in a higher loyalty, been a defence?

The fifth explanation is that some practices identified by the McDonald Commission went beyond the individuals involved: 'They became a problem of the system. The necessary corrections were 'primarily at the level of the institution.'

This may have been a good reason for a light sentence. But for not prosecuting?

The sixth explanation is that the officers' motives were pure: 'There was no suggestion in the commission's report or from any other source that the members were motivated by anything save a desire to effectively protect the national security or enforce criminal law.'

We have heard this one before; 'My conscience is clear.' It is scarcely a conclusive defence. Perhaps it might be another reason for a light sentence.

The seventh explanation is that, though mail openings were illegal (aren't they still?), the McDonald Commission recommended that the nation's security service should be able to open mail under certain conditions.

Acceptance of the plea that the law ought to be, or would be, changed, would, like the first two explanations, be a boon to lawbreakers. It would be hard on criminal lawyers: 'All thieves who could my fees afford,' sang the judge in Trial by Jury, looking back on his career as a barrister, 'Relied on my orations, and many a burglar I've restored to his friends and his relations.' General adaptation by the law enforcement authorities of the reasons given for failure to prosecute the Mounties would have rendered his orations needless, and reduced him to his early state of 'an impecunious party': put him out of a job, in fact!

This letter is perhaps the clearest exposition of Forsey's reasons for dropping his allegiance to the Liberal party. Since his rationale was based on his belief that the government had suborned the rule of law, one might have expected that the invoking of the War Measures Act in response to the perceived threat of violent uprising in Quebec in October 1970 would have provided an earlier occasion for Forsey to question what was then his newfound loyalty to the Liberals. This, at least, appeared to be the reasoning of the late Professor Donald Smiley when on 8 January 1975 he wrote to the *Globe and Mail* what proved to be a provocative letter that Forsey rose to like a hungry trout.

> It is gratifying to some of us that Robert Stanfield has said that the bringing into effect of the War Measure Act in October 1970 was not justified and that he now regrets that action.
>
> Yet because, with some distinguished exceptions, Mr Stanfield's party was possessed of the hysteria of the time, his action was understandable. What was and is a good deal less understandable was the support for the suspension of the normal constitutional processes by many influential Canadians not under such pressures, particularly by those in the university community. Some of these, like Senator Eugene Forsey, have set up shop under less urgent circumstances to instruct the rest of us in the intricacies of the Canadian constitutional system. None of these leaders so far as I know has been as frank as Mr Stanfield in admitting his inglorious part in the events of the fall of 1970.

Forsey's reply came on 11 January.

> Professor Donald Smiley ... reproaches me for not having been 'as frank as Mr Stanfield in admitting' my 'inglorious part in the events of the fall of 1970' in Quebec.
>
> I have no hesitation whatever in admitting my very modest

part in those events. I publicly supported the Government action. I still do.

What was at issue was not any matter of 'the intricacies of the Canadian constitutional system,' on which Professor Smiley says 'I have set up shop.' The War Measures Act explicitly provides that it may be proclaimed in a situation of 'apprehended insurrection.' Was there such a situation in Quebec in October 1970? The Government of Quebec, and the municipal administration of Montreal thought there was. So did Professor Scott and Senator Therese Casgrain, both longstanding champions of freedom generally and civil liberties in particular, and both with first-hand knowledge of the situation. I could see, and still can see, no reason to question their judgment; and I think my own knowledge of Quebec will bear comparison with Professor Smiley's.

... I am sorry to disappoint Professor Smiley by refusing to don a white sheet, or array myself in sackcloth and ashes. But I still venture to think that Professor Scott and Senator Casgrain, who have lived nearly all their lives in Quebec, and have fought valiantly there for freedom, knew more about the situation in that province in October, 1970, than (dare I say?) any of the English-speaking intellectuals in Toronto and points west who have, ex cathedra, condemned the Government's action and hurled their anathemas at those who supported it.

Professor Smiley, no stranger to the fine art of colourful retort, responded on 15 January to what he termed 'vintage Forseyana – a devastating concoction of florid vituperation and personal abuse ... [whose] inappropriate clichés debase the language for which Senator Forsey professes such respect.' Continuing with heavy-handed sarcasm of his own, Professor Smiley claimed that he was startled by Forsey's

assertion that I had neither the right nor the competence to make a judgment at variance with his. Why? Because I am 'an English-speaking intellectual living in Toronto.' I have never been quite sure what an 'intellectual' was but I am dismayed that Eugene

> Forsey, of all people, should employ it as a term of abuse. And I had understood that Canadian law and the Canadian constitution, even when the War Measures Act was in operation, permitted a citizen both to be English-speaking and to live in Toronto – and within broad limits to comment on his country's affairs.

After reciting, in true professorial style, the evidence upon which his convictions were based and citing with approval the view of his colleague, Professor McNaught, 'that the action was a "symbolic" assertion of the power and determination of the federal Government,' Smiley closed his rejoinder: 'I find repugnant the "symbolic" suspension of the normal constitutional processes in the middle of the night and on the basis of the suspension Canadian citizens who have committed no offence against the law being hauled to jail.'

As usual, Forsey was given the last word – a word that ran for nearly a column of the letters page of the *Globe* on 27 January, in which, opening with the words 'Professor Donald Smiley is letting his imagination run away with him,' he dismantled paragraph by paragraph, at least to his own satisfaction, his opponent's arguments. Let us content ourselves with his closing thoughts in a well-matched verbal tussle whose unresolved outcome reflects the divided opinions that still persist over this issue.

> Prof. Smiley says he suggested gently that I had been wrong. It seemed to me rather more than that. He appeared to be praising Mr Stanfield ... He seemed also to be reproaching me for not having been as frank as Mr Stanfield in admitting my 'inglorious part in the events of the fall of 1970.' This seemed a clear call to repentance, or, in the metaphors I used, to a white sheet or sackcloth and ashes. I am sorry that these outward signs of my Methodist upbringing are, for Prof. Smiley, 'inappropriate clichés which debase the language.' I must try henceforth to avoid Biblical metaphors (and perhaps also quotations from the Anglican Prayer Book).

Protecting Charter Rights

The role of the judiciary in upholding the rule of law was greatly expanded when, as part of the constitutional patriation process, the Charter of Rights and Freedoms was incorporated in the Canada Constitution Act, 1982. Critics opposed the move on the grounds that it imported an American feature to the constitution by conferring a new role on the judiciary to interpret constitutionally entrenched rights. Opponents viewed this as an erosion of the power of Parliament, a possible substitution of 'judge-made law' for defining and protecting rights. As a concession to such concerns, a so-called notwithstanding clause was added to preserve the principle of parliamentary supremacy by permitting a legislative override of a judicial decision.

Given Forsey's loyalty to British traditions and his inherent anti-Americanism, one might have expected him to have opposed this new venture. His letters reveal initial scepticism, coupled with a grudging wait-and-see attitude that may also have been attributable to his earlier suspicion of court bias in dealing with the rights of organized labour during the years he was director of research for the Canadian Congress of Labour.

Heavily engaged in the debate over the proposal to establish a 'Labor Court' in 1950, Forsey had written a response to Senator Farris who had sponsored such a move in the Senate. His letter must have been sent to Wilfrid Eggleston, columnist for *Saturday Night*, who quoted it extensively in his Capital Comment column on 24 October 1950. To Senator Farris's suggestion that 'an outstanding lawyer' should be chosen to be chairman of the proposed court, Forsey had objected: '"Experienced lawyers," you observe, "are trained in procedure, in the powers of analysis, and in getting the viewpoints of others." But they are not trained in industrial relations, or in statistics, and their capacity to "get the viewpoints of others" in industrial disputes is not always evident to us.' Then Eggleston quoted the part of the letter which subsequently forced Forsey into angst-ridden damage control: '"My answer to your proposal," Dr Forsey sums up, "is to ask you [Senator Farris] to look back at what I have said about the report of the two very experienced and brilliant lawyers. After our experience with this pair, we can hardly be expected to be much impressed by your proposal to deliver us bound hand and foot into the hands of more of the same kind."' Forsey's reference was to Mr Justice Wilson and T.R. Meighen, members of a conciliation board that had dealt with a railway strike. In permitting himself this last expostulation, Forsey realized he had gone too far and his private letters to the named individuals reveal a chastened Forsey that he seldom if ever showed in public.[4]

Clearly, he had moderated his views on the possible biases of judges by the time a charter of rights was being debated for inclusion in the constitution. Nevertheless, in his longest critique of the charter ('Charter "shot full of holes" by Provinces,' *Globe and Mail*, 21 November 1981), he concluded by asserting: 'If I were still in the Senate, I should have no choice but to speak and vote against the whole package.' What Forsey seized upon as the poison in the package was the notwithstanding clause (in legal parlance, the *non obstante* clause), introduced at the insistence of the provinces. Paradoxically, this inclusion was aimed at what Forsey might have been expected to support, namely, providing the last word to Parliament when it came to defining rights. But, as his letter to the *Globe* reveals, he was highly dubious of *provincial* legislatures' capacity to protect rights on a uniform basis across the nation.

> The amended Charter of Rights and Freedoms just won't do.
>
> The provinces have shot it full of holes: great, big, gaping holes. First, what the charter rightly calls 'Fundamental Freedoms' – freedom of conscience, freedom of thought, freedom of speech, freedom of peaceful assembly, freedom of association – are put at the mercy of 10 provincial legislatures, which can override them at will.
>
> The same applies to 'Legal Rights' – such as the right to *habeus corpus*, the right to public trial, the right to counsel, the right to be secure against unreasonable search and seizure, the right not to be arbitrarily detained or imprisoned.
>
> The same applies to 'Equality Rights' – the right to equal pro-

tection and equal benefit of the law, prohibiting discrimination on grounds of race, national or ethnic origin, color, religion, sex, age or mental or physical disability.

Bang goes all the charter's protection for fundamental freedoms and basic legal rights. Bang goes the ban against discrimination.

One of the prime objects of the charter was supposed to be national unity: equal rights for all Canadians from sea to sea. But now the rights will vary from province to province, in a legal crazy quilt. This is a shattering blow to national unity.

Five years after the approval of the Constitution Act, 1982, which included the charter, Forsey had this more measured assessment, contributed to *Saturday Night* in June 1987.

Of the letters on the Charter of Rights and Freedoms (March), it seems to me that two hit the essential points: the looseness of the drafting (Professor Howard McConnell's 'the vague and amorphous rights'), and Professor Bruce P. Archibald's 'It is too early to tell whether the courts will strike the right balance and avoid ... an American-style tyranny of the courts.'

I have no title to pronounce on the draftsmanship. But the late Elmer Dreidger, Q.C., former deputy minister of justice, who most certainly had, described it to me as 'abominable.'

There can be little doubt that it is still too early to tell just what the courts will make of the document. When it was adopted, I said, naively, to a very eminent constitutional lawyer, 'I suppose it will take two or three years for us to find out just what it means.' He replied: 'A dozen.' Two years ago, a veteran British Columbia lawyer to whom I repeated this said: 'Fifty.'

Kellogg Wilson's assertion that 'the political theory basic to the U.S. Constitution is rooted in the British and French political philosophies of the period of the Enlightenment' is, of course, true. But it does not follow that 'That, and the American colonial experience with the British institutions, make this thinking part of the Canadian heritage as well.' The U.S. Constitution is a republican version of the English constitution of the early eighteenth century.

The Fathers of Confederation turned their backs on that constitution and the 'American colonial experience' which flowed from it. They turned their backs also on the abstract principles of the Enlightenment beloved of the French and American revolutionaries. This does not prove that the Charter was a mistake. But American, and eighteenth-century French, rather than British (except in an antiquarian sense), it most certainly is.

That a Bill of Rights 'does not permit the judiciary to legislate but only to review acts of the legislature' is, of course, formally correct. But the whole history of the U.S. Supreme Court is proof that 'reviewing' can in fact become 'legislating,' and on a massive scale, and in fundamental matters. How successful courts will be in avoiding this sea change remains to be seen.

CHAPTER NINE

Quebec

The enduring debate over the place of Quebec in Canada raises cultural, political, economic, and legal issues to which, over the years, a significant proportion of Forsey's letters to the press were addressed.[1]

The Language Question

On the cultural front, the status of the French language was at issue, particularly with the advent of the Quiet Revolution in the 1960s, with its accompanying concern to protect the existing constitutional status of French throughout the nation and to expand its use within Quebec itself. Although a staunch supporter and practitioner of bilingualism, Forsey was compelled to correct misunderstandings of its constitutional position, as this early exchange with Guy Favreau reveals (*Globe and Mail*, 11 February 1964):

> Mr Guy Favreau asks English Canadians, in effect, to imagine how we'd feel if Ontario was an 'English' island in 'French North America. He is right. This would be a salutary exercise for us, an immense contribution to solving the problems of bilingualism and biculturalism. We should perhaps begin to understand and sympathize with the frustrations French Canadians feel, and to

> realize the necessity for a wide expansion of bilingualism in Dominion public business.
>
> But when Mr Favreau says that it was agreed in 1867 that French 'was to be recognized and applied at all federal levels on the same footing as' English, and suggests that for 'over 50 or 60 years' (that is, since about 1904 or 1914), it has not been, he implies bad faith or breach of promise on our part, and I think we are entitled to ask for evidence.
>
> First, what does 'at all levels' mean. The British North America Act puts the two languages on the same footing for the Dominion Parliament and Dominion courts. That is all.
>
> Second, what is the evidence for the suggestion that the agreements (whatever they were) were, on the whole, kept down to about 1904 or about 1914, and then broken? ...
>
> It seems odd that if the agreement of 1867 was as sweeping as Mr Favreau implies, Cartier and Langevin and Chapais, who must certainly have been parties to it, should have tamely submitted to a breach.
>
> I am not suggesting that what was good enough for Cartier and Langevin and Chapais, or French Canadians generally in 1867, is good enough now. On the contrary, I think there is ample ground for widening very considerably the degree of bilingualism the Fathers of Confederation appear to have contemplated and practiced. But if English Canadians are to be accused, by implication, of breaking the 1867 agreement ... I think we are entitled to ask precisely what the original agreement was, and what the practice was over the last 50 or 60 years ... It is one thing to be told that we are not doing enough. It is quite another to be told that we have broken our promises. Charges of that kind, unless supported by evidence, can only needlessly embitter the whole discussion of bilingualism and biculturalism.

'Doing something about bilingualism' was the purpose of the Official Languages bill which followed upon recommendations of the Royal Commission on Bilingualism and Biculturalism in the late 1960s. When the constitutionality of the bill, at the suggestion of the prairie premiers, was queried, supported by the learned opinion of J.T. Thorson (former president of the Exchequer Court of Canada), Forsey did not hesitate to enter the fray with his own 'brief,' submitted in the form of a letter to the *Globe and Mail* on 8 February 1969. As an example of one of Forsey's finest 'illegal legal opinions,' it has no equal, but it is too finely honed and too enmeshed in lengthy technical detail to be edited down for inclusion here. Suffice to say, Forsey's defence of the constitutional propriety of the measure prevailed.

Forsey often found it necessary to correct misconceptions about the applicability of bilingualism in provinces other than Quebec. A common error was the misunderstanding surrounding the use of French in Manitoba, an issue which arose in 1977 when a resident whose mother tongue was French contested payment of a parking ticket printed in English only. On 21 January 1977 Forsey entered the fray, in the *Globe*:

> Roger Newman says (Jan.8) that in 1890 the Legislature of Manitoba 'passed a law banning French as a language of instruction in the schools' (Parking Ticket in English Keeps Language Row Going).
>
> This is a pure fairy tale, as Mr Newman can easily satisfy himself by looking at the Manitoba Schools Act and Department of Education Act of 1890. Neither contains one syllable about the language of instruction, which continued to be decided by elected local school trustees. Under the acts of 1890 teaching in French in the public schools continued on the same footing as English. The other controversial act of 1890, making English the sole official language in the Legislature and the courts, did not even mention education or schools in any shape or form. (It is this latter act whose validity is now, in my judgment very properly, being challenged in the court by M. George Forest.)
>
> It is a pity that discussion of the Manitoba school question has been so often muddled by the failure of those who discuss it (and this, alas, includes even some academics) to get their facts straight.

In the same year, one such academic, Dr Camille Laurin, was

ticked off by Forsey in the *Montreal Gazette* on 16 June 1977 for the same offence when he claimed that 'Manitoba in 1890 abolished with the stroke of the pen the French school system.' But Dr Laurin had gone further:

> In the same article, Dr Laurin says: 'The rest of Canada has become unilingually English.'
>
> Newfoundland, Nova Scotia, Prince Edward Island and British Columbia never were bilingual. They started out unilingually English and have remained so. Newfoundland, under Joey Smallwood, undertook to become bilingual, but has done little or nothing to carry out the policy. New Brunswick started out unilingually English and has now made itself bilingual.
>
> Ontario started out unilingually English. In the last few years, Ontario has been making itself more bilingual by the provision of more and more services in French to Franco-Ontarians.
>
> There seems to be an impression in some quarters in Quebec that there was an agreement at Confederation that the provinces, as well as the Dominion, were to be officially bilingual.
>
> This is not so. There is not one shred of evidence that the Fathers of Confederation ever contemplated a bilingual Newfoundland (etc) ...
>
> There was little reason why they should. Their French-speaking people then made up no more than a tiny fraction of the population.
>
> What is necessary and sensible now in relation to bilingualism would have been absurd in 1867.

Forsey returned frequently to the issue raised by the closing observation in the above letter, as this testy paragraph from another letter in the *Globe* on 9 December reveals:

> I am getting very tired of this harping on the wrong done to the French-speaking minorities 60, 70, 80 years ago, with not a word about what has been done in the last decade or so to right them. It does not seem to me to be the best way to win further rights for Franco-Ontarians or Franco-Manitobans, or other French-

> speaking minorities. 'Look what your (or someone else's) blankety-blank grandfather did to us! Never mind what you've done to set it right!' How to win friends and influence people?

Just as Forsey felt duty bound to correct the misunderstandings about the state of bilingualism in the provinces other than Quebec, he also found occasion to criticize the laws enacted by Quebec that were designed to enhance the use of French as opposed to English. The enactment of Bill 22 by the Liberal Bourassa government, which dealt with the language of work, drew protestations from Forsey in the *Ottawa Journal* (6 August 1974) and the *Globe* (18 October 1974), of which an extract from the letter to the *Journal* will suffice:

> Messrs. Brian Hutton and Jean Regnier (Journal, July 23) say that 'If the Franco-Ontarians or the Franco-Manitobans ... were faced with a language act similar to Bill 22 ... whereby they, as a minority group, would be given the same privileges as given to the Anglo-Quebecois, they would be more than happy.'
>
> I wonder if Messrs. Hutton and Regnier have read the bill.
>
> Under its provisions, it would appear that McGill, Sir George Williams, and Bishops Universities will be compelled to communicate with all their staff in French; with the government of Canada and provincial governments in French; with other corporate personalities in Quebec in French.
>
> It appears also that these English-language universities will have to use French in meetings of the boards of governors, senates, faculties and departments; draw up all their contracts in French; use French in lectures, tutorials, student-faculty consultations, memoranda and letters ... (etc) ...
>
> I wonder if, for example, the College St. Boniface would be happy with a law which subjected it to the same requirements, just turned upside down? I wonder if Ontario's two bilingual universities would be happy with law which subjected them to the same requirements just turned upside down? ...

Forsey's proclivity to draw the worst possible scenario from a literal reading of the law is nicely illustrated by his comments on his reading of Bill 22. That same attention to 'black letter' reading of the constitution could equally well be applied to clarification (as opposed to 'scarification'), as revealed by this final selection dealing with Bill 101, referred to as the Lévesque government's 'Charter of the French Language.' When the Charter of Rights and Freedoms was incorporated into the Canada Constitution Act, 1982, there was much confusion over the applicability of the original provisions for bilingualism found in section 133 of the British North America Act of 1867 (and still in force) and the new charter protections for language. In the process of seeking to clarify the situation through a letter to the *Globe* on 1 January 1985, Forsey himself revealed that he was as fallible as other mortals in getting the facts wrong. Judging from the subsequent silence in the letters page, the error remained undetected by Forsey or others who might have been able for once to say, 'Gotcha!'[2]

> Pierre-Marc Johnson, Quebec Minister of Intergovernmental Affairs (letter – Dec. 5), says that the judgment of the Supreme Court of Canada that section 23 of the Constitution Act, 1982, 'over-rules Bill 101' of Quebec 'means that if Quebec ever feels it must significantly modify its linguistic laws (especially in matters of education), it might have to persuade the federal Goverment and six other provinces to modify the Constitution.'
>
> Is he quite sure?
>
> Section 41 (c) of the Constitution Act, 1982, says that 'subject to section 32,' an amendment 'in relation to ... the use of the English or the French language' requires the assent of all the provincial legislatures.
>
> But section 32 says that an amendment 'in relation to any provisions that applies to one or more, but not all, provinces' requires the assent only of the Senate and the House of Commons 'and of the legislative assembly of each province to which the amendment applies.' It specifically adds that such include 'any amendment to any provision that relates to the use of the English or the French language within a province.'

> Section 133 of the Constitution Act, 1867, says that either English or French may be used in the legislature of Quebec; that both these languages shall be used in the records and journals of that legislature or in any pleading or process in or issuing from any of the courts of Quebec; and that the acts of the Quebec legislature shall be published in both English and French. The section does not mention any other province, and that is all it says about the two languages in any province ...
>
> With respect, it seems that this means those provisions of the Constitution come under section 43 of the Act of 1982, not section 38 (the seven-provinces formula) or section 41 (the all-provinces formula); and that they could therefore be amended by the Senate and the House of Commons and the National Assembly of Quebec. The same would seem to hold for the use of the two languages in Manitoba and New Brunswick ...
>
> An amendment to section 23 of the Constitution Act, 1982, Minority Language Education Rights, which applies to all provinces, would clearly have to have the assent of the legislatures of seven provinces whose total population amounted to at least 50 per cent of the population of the 10 provinces. It would come under section 38 ...

In the event, when both the Quebec Superior Court and the Supreme Court of Canada found against certain elements of Bill 101, the route taken was not through constitutional amendment but by invoking the 'escape' clause – the notwithstanding provision in the Constitution Act, 1982. Arguably, it was Quebec's use of this mechanism in 1989 that gave Manitoba and New Brunswick reason for rejecting the Meech Lake Accord, against which (as will later appear) Forsey was to do battle.

Quebec in Canada: The Words That Framed the Debate

The debate over the place of Quebec within the Canadian federation has swirled around competing conceptions of the meaning to be attached to four terms: Two nations–deux nations; distinct society; special status; sovereignty association/associate state. Like the house that Jack built, one's views on the last three terms follow from one's interpretation of the two nations concept.[3]

Forsey was quick to make public his antagonism to the key term, two nations. The letters he subsequently wrote on 14 September 1967 to the *Globe and Mail* and on 26 September to the *Ottawa Journal* lamenting the adoption of a two nations resolution at the convention of the Progressive Conservative party, reveal not only why he opposed the particular definition given the term but also how that definition lent support to the three other terms so threatening to the kind of united Canada he endorsed. The letter from the *Globe*, headed 'Deux Nations,' is presented here.

> Lewis Seale (A Dividing Line on Unity – Sept. 11) says 'all indications' from the Conservative convention 'were that sooner or later the concept' ('deux nations') 'would be enshrined as a firm principle of Conservatism.'
>
> Principle, perhaps: but I venture to predict that the party will find it about as firm as a buttered eel.
>
> The 'hand outstretched to Quebec,' the 'extension of the rights of French Canadians all across Canada'; these are fine. But the 'deux nations' resolution is another matter altogether. The crucial point in it is those two words, 'deux nations,' inserted in brackets in the English text, immediately after 'two founding peoples.' What do those two words mean, and why are they there?
>
> They are not a translation. The French phrase completely ignores 'founding.' Nor is this without significance. 'Two founding peoples' is a statement of fact about the past. 'Deux nations' is a theory about the present and the future. The statement of fact is contestable. The theory is highly disputable.
>
> At this point I shall probably be told that the French word 'nation' means merely a 'cultural and sociological group'; that it has no legal, constitutional significance whatsoever. So when General de Gaulle told Lester Pearson on January 16, 1964, that his wish for Canada was that it should remain 'une nation forte et unie' (Le Devoir, Jan. 13. 1964), he meant that he wanted Canada

to remain 'a strong and unified cultural and sociological group'? Or perhaps General de Gaulle doesn't understand French?

Daniel Johnson, on page 2 of his brief to the Dominion-Provincial Conference a year ago said ... 'We believe that there exists in Canada, in the sociological sense of the term, a nation of French language.' But on page 3: ... 'The new Government of Quebec has set itself a fundamental task: that of getting recognized juridically and politically the French-Canadian nation ... by the elaboration of a new Constitution which would recognize ... equal collective rights for Canadians of English speech and Canadians of French speech, and which would give Quebec all the powers necessary for the safeguarding of the Quebec identity.' And M. Johnson, only a week or so ago, in Paris-Match, made plain what he means by 'juridical and political recognition' of the 'French-Canadian nation': 'political sovereignty for Quebec while remaining linked to the rest of Canada by a sort of common market.'

This illustrates perfectly the awesome ambiguity of the French word 'nation,' when used, as in the policy committee resolution, without the clarifying explanations and qualifications ... The English text of the resolution, without the two French words in brackets, contains no implication of two separate or nearly separate states. The French phrase 'deux nations' is, to say the least, wide open to such an implication.

Anyone who ... has watched the use of the words 'deux nations' in the French-language press of Quebec for the last six years, knows that in that province the phrase carries with it unmistakably, and almost invariably, the demand for independence, or for Associate States, or at the very least for a 'special status' with a massive transfer of power from the Government and Parliament of Canada to the Government and Legislature of Quebec.

Manifestly, an independent Quebec, or a Quebec Associate State, would mean two political nations. Even Claude Ryan says only: ... 'We believe that it is possible and desirable, at least for one or two generations, to maintain in Canada a federal system, on the condition, however, that this system consecrate in law and in fact the distinct position of Quebec, in the form of a "special status"' ... So even for this relatively mild advocate of a relatively

> mild form of 'Special status,' it might be only the pause that refreshes, on the road to independence; and it might satisfy Quebec for only one or two generations.
>
> ... Unless we can get into our fat 'English' heads an understanding of the fatal ambiguity of the unqualified phrase 'deux nations,' and the ease with which a skilled performer can use it to mean, at his convenience, either cultural and sociological 'nations' like Scotland, Wales, England, French Canada (and perhaps Brittany?); or political 'nations' like the United Kingdom, France and Canada, we shall be sitting ducks for every separatist, or hemi-demi-semi-separatist, in the country.

A decade later, with René Lévesque's Parti Québécois having captured power in Quebec on a sovereignist/separatist platform, Forsey was calling all the more urgently for clarification of special status, a subject which he had raised in his 1967 letters and which he was to elaborate ten years later in the *Ottawa Journal* in two article-length letters triggered by columnist Richard Gwyn's treatment of the term. The first, and longest, appeared on 3 June 1977:

> The 'two little words' (special status) which Richard Gwyn (Journal, May 26) says 'Trudeau can't utter' are in fact very big words, at any rate as they were used in Quebec a few years ago. They involved a massive transfer of powers from the Parliament of Canada to the Legislature of Quebec. Most of the list of powers to be transferred were pretty breathtaking, and they usually added that the list was a 'minimum' or 'far from exhaustive.'
>
> Further, though the proposals would have left the Parliament and the Government of Canada for most purposes the Parliament and the government of the nine provinces only, the Quebec members of the House of Commons, the Quebec senators, the Quebec ministers would all have remained at Ottawa. Over the transferred subjects, the Quebec Legislature and government would, of course, have been sovereign. No federal member or minister could have uttered so much as a squeak. But, on the same subjects, for the nine provinces, the Quebec members and ministers at

Ottawa would have had the same power as if no transfer had taken place. They could have forced on the nine legislation the majority of members from the nine did not want. They could have toppled the government the majority of members from the nine did want.

... Mr Gwyn says that 'Since 1867,Quebec has in fact enjoyed official special status – its own civil law; its own educational system. Quebec today exercises unofficial special status in everything from its own pension plan to its own tax collection.'

Mr Gwyn is mistaken. Every province has complete control over its civil law. Every province has complete control over its own educational system (subject to certain guarantees for Protestant and Roman Catholic, or, in Newfoundland, denominational rights). Every province, under section 94A of the BNA Act, could have its own pension plan. Every province could do the collection of its own provincial taxes. Under section 94 of the BNA Act, Quebec alone could not surrender the control of its civil law to the Parliament of Canada, as all the other provinces could. But that section is a dead letter ...

Mr Trudeau's 'concept of dual sovereignty' is not Mr Trudeau's at all, but a received doctrine of the present Canadian Constitution ... The present Constitution, therefore, 'enables ... Quebec to be sovereign in certain areas'; no 'special status' is required for that ...

Special status, with a massive expansion of the scope of Quebec's sovereignty, but leaving Quebec members and ministers with decisive powers over what would then be the purely domestic affairs of the nine provinces, is ... nothing less than neocolonial domination of the nine by Quebec.

Mr Lévesque's 'sovereignty-association' is also very different from special status. In his proposals, Quebec and Canada would be two separate nation states ... The two separate, sovereign nation-states could, however, have a common tariff and a common monetary policy, perhaps a common trancontinental transportation policy.

This sounds lovely. But how would these common policies be settled and operated?

> Would Canada and Quebec have equal power? If so, each would have a veto over matters which the other considered vital ...
>
> On the other hand, Canada, as the larger, more populous, economically stronger state might insist on having the deciding voice in the common tariff, the common monetary policy, or any other common policy. How long would a sovereign Quebec put up with that?
>
> Mr Gwyn says that to 'close the gaps' between special status and sovereignty-association 'all that's needed is for everyone to shut their eyes while signing on the dotted line.' The 'gaps' are, in fact, an impassable gulf between two impossibilities. People who shut their eyes on the edge of a chasm are not likely to live to sign anything.

In an adjoining editorial, commenting on this lengthy submission, the *Journal* suggested that while 'Mr Forsey has never been a master of understatement' and that he may have been subject to 'a somewhat overdrawn worry,' nevertheless he had 'performed another good service in sharing his concerns on perhaps the most delicate and central issue of the day.' He was to return to such concerns again and again throughout the remainder of the 1970s and on into the constitutional contestations of the 1980s.

On 18 November 1977 Forsey tackled Richard Gwyn once again in the columns of the *Journal*, feeling it necessary to repeat much of what he wrote in his 3 June letter but opening with this exegesis on the terminology:

> Richard Gwyn (Journal, Nov. 10) calls 'two nations' and 'special status' part of 'our original political vocabulary.' I should be interested to see the evidence for this. I never heard of 'two nations' till it popped up at the NDP Founding Convention of 1961, nor of 'special status' till even later.
>
> Mr Gwyn's quotation from Sir John A. Macdonald is taken completely out of context. I defy anyone to produce one syllable from Sir John even hinting at the two political nations the Quebec

nationalists and their English-speaking 'tail' chatter about. His whole life from 1864 on is eloquent testimony to the contrary.

No one questions the cultural concept of three nations in Britain or three or four in France. But, as Mr Trudeau said years ago: 'Don't kid yourselves. What these people want is two states.'

It is not 'Trudeau's overkill' or 'Stanfield's twin defeats' which have made the political concepts of two nations and special status into 'political ideas that English-speaking Canadians now may never accept.' It is the inherent nature of the ideas and their inescapably destructive political effect.

Forsey's concern over the manipulation of political terms by separatist-sovereignists and the apparent willingness of journalists to accept such terms unquestioningly was heightened by what he conceived to be similar misconceptions perpetrated by the Pépin–Robarts Task Force on Canadian Unity as it began hearings in late 1977. In the *Globe* on 5 December 1977 he expostulated:

The Task Force on Canadian Unity looks more and more like a Trojan horse.

First we have Jean-Luc Pépin ... saying 'Poor Stanfield was right' about 'two nations.'

Now, we have Reed Scowen, executive director of the Task Force ... saying that that body 'will likely propose a combination of three solutions – decentralization, special status and provincialism.'

All this before the Task Force has finished its 'hearings.' It looks as if it may not bother to listen; as if its model may be the legendary Irish magistrate who said he never listened to the defence: he found it confused him.

And these gentry are being paid, from funds provided by the taxpayers of Canada, to perform a 'task' labelled 'national unity.' It begins to look as if the label were a case of misleading advertising.

Misrepresentation of his own views on Quebec separation,

when testifying before the task force, also necessitated corrective letters, as this on 4 March 1978 to the *Ottawa Journal* reveals:

> Your issue of March 2 reported, accurately enough, what I had said to the Task Force on National Unity. But the headline, which appeared in quotation marks, was 'Quebec's not worth keeping for a weakened federal government.'
>
> I made no such statement, nor anything resembling it. What I said (and I read from a text) was: 'Canada without Quebec would be tragically impoverished, materially, intellectually, spiritually. It would be an amputee. But Canada with Quebec, but with a central Parliament whose jurisdiction had been gutted, a central government whose organs had been paralyzed ... would be a paraplegic. If I have to choose, which God forbid, I should choose the amputee.'
>
> That very clearly does not suggest that Quebec is not worth keeping; quite the contrary. And a 'gutted Parliament' and a 'paralyzed government,' are quite different from a 'weakened' federal government. I am 'weakened' in comparison with what I was 20 years ago; but I am far from 'gutted' or 'paralyzed.'

While Forsey had honed his critique of the separatists' claims by focusing on Richard Gwyn's columns in the *Journal*, Norman Webster of the *Globe* was also subjected to his instructive corrections. In his column of 28 February 1978, Webster acknowledged receipt of a letter which Forsey had tendered in response to a January column. In that column, as Webster reported, 'I had written airily that all three political party leaders in Ontario "agree that provinces should be able to have special and different arrangements with Ottawa – with all that implies for some sort of special status for Quebec."' Then, in an unusual salute to a letter-writer, Webster reproduced in full Forsey's response. Since most of the letter repeated Forsey's already well-rehearsed views expressed in his letters to Gwyn, only the first part makes a fresh point.

> I don't think 'special and different arrangements' do necessarily

> imply 'some sort of special status for Quebec.' What the people who want special status for Quebec have always been asking is special constitutional powers. All kinds of 'special arrangements' for particular provinces are possible under the existing Constitution ... The Parliament of Canada cannot transfer to a provincial legislature any of its legislative jurisdiction. But there is nothing in the world to prevent it from entrusting to a provincial authority the actual administration of any of its powers; just as there is nothing to prevent a provincial legislature from entrusting to a Dominion agency the administration of any of its powers.
>
> The Parliament of Canada has entrusted to the various Public Utility Boards the exercise of its power to regulate inter-provincial and international highway traffic; and it could just as easily have done this for one single province. It has done the same with its power over inter-provincial and international marketing of agricultural products.
>
> The difference between special arrangements of this sort and constitutional special status is very great and very important. If, by amendment to the Constitution, you hand to a particular province the legislative jurisdiction over a broad field and the thing works out badly, you can't modify or revoke what has been done except by constitutional amendment, which may be hard to get. You are boxed in.
>
> Of course, there is an even more fundamental objection to any massive transfer of legislative power from the Parliament of Canada to the legislature of a particular province. [The letter continues with reiteration of the observations contained in critique of Gwyn.]

Webster closed his column: 'Perhaps I should have stuck with my own earlier formulation which I attributed to Premier William Davis in November: "He stands foursquare for the third option, which probably means special status (although not, heaven forfend, Special Status). All clear?"'

When the demand for special status was raised a significant notch by a call for *separate* status, Forsey was quick to suggest the implications. In the 1960s, when early proponents of separatism, such as Pierre Bourgault, listed Quebec grievances against Canada in the *Globe*, Forsey's chapter-and-verse rebuttal (27 July 1964) closed:

> Mr Bourgault says also, 'We have fought and fought for nothing, nothing but a bilingual cheque.' Quite apart from anything else has Mr Bourgault ever heard of the Port of Montreal? Where would the Port of Montreal be without the traffic from the rest of Canada?
>
> Mr Bourgault says that 'English-speaking Canadians may like living in a glorified banana republic, but French-speaking Canadians are determined to win economic and political independence.' This is interesting. A banana republic, without bananas, is precisely what French Canada would risk becoming if it took Mr Bourgault's advice.

With the stakes becoming higher after the electoral success in 1976 of the Parti Québécois and the prospect of a referendum on separation, the legal question of Quebec's right to determine this vital constitutional question without reference to the rest of Canada, in short a unilateral declaration of independence (UDI), became a lively issue. In a speech to the Ottawa Rotary Club, Forsey took his stand, as reported in the *Journal* of 16 August 1977, under the banner 'Gov't Could Impose Sanctions If Quebec Separates.' Two years later, on 17 December 1979, he made even clearer his views on a Quebec UDI:

> If W.A. Wilson (Journal Dec. 8) is correct that the Parti Québécois referendum white paper means 'that independence would be the first step, with efforts to form an association with the remnants of Canada to follow later,' then we are faced with something altogether new.
>
> For in plain terms, this means UDI, a unilateral declaration of independence, like Rhodesia's in 1965. It means a 'yes' vote would produce a rebel government in Quebec. Has the Parti Québécois ever said this before? Not that I know of.
>
> If Mr Wilson is right, it follows also that the Parti Québécois

assumed that the government of Canada would recognize this rebel state. Where did the Parti Québécois get this idea?

Has the Parti Québécois asked itself what UDI would do not only to equalization payments but to the unemployment insurance, old age security and family allowance cheques that now go to Quebec residents? Does it imagine that they would continue to go to residents of a rebel state?

More crisply, Forsey had already pointed out to the separatists in the *Globe* of 24 November 1978 the folly of their policy: 'So the Parti Québécois is considering dual citizenship and a common passport for Canadians and citizens of an independent Quebec. As Florence Nightingale said when they presented her with the Order of Merit, "Too kind! Too kind!"'

Forsey reinforced these views in another letter to the *Journal* on 11 February 1980, as the referendum vote in Quebec drew near:

René Lévésque (Journal, Feb.5) says a strong 'yes' vote in his referendum would force the rest of Canada to negotiate 'an economic association with Quebec.' He gives two reasons, or what he evidently considers reasons.

First, without such association, Alberta would lose the market for half its beef: 'Alberta would be stuck with its beef.'

Second, 'the Maritime provinces would be afraid of being cut off from the rest of Canada.'

Both these assertions imply that if the rest of Canada refused the association, Quebec would simply declare its independence, without negotiating anything, close its borders, shut out Alberta beef (and other Canadian products), and cut off the Maritimes from the rest of Canada.

The note of threat is new, and unmistakable. We are being told, 'Either you accept a common tariff and a common monetary policy, or we refuse to buy your products and cut your country in two.'

The bland, contemptuous assumption that we would meekly cave in and give Mr Lévesque a strangle-hold on our whole economy is breathtaking in its insolence. Scarcely less so is the assumption that we would allow an independent Quebec to 'cut off' the Maritimes from Ontario and the West and North.

But perhaps we are not such mindless jellyfish, as Mr Lévesque takes us for.

Forsey was probably not as militant as this last letter might suggest, for on 18 January 1978, he had felt obliged to admonish the *Globe* and its reporter for unduly escalating the debate over the potential separation of Quebec:

Your editorial, Insensitive and Dangerous (Jan. 9), reproaches Pierre Trudeau for having said that if a Quebec Government 'attempted to take Quebec out of Confederation by breaking the law ... stopping the mails, or blowing up trains, ... or raiding arsenals,' he would be prepared to use force to stop it.

What on earth would you expect any Government of Canada to do in such circumstances? Simply raise its eyebrows? Say, 'Dear me! Fancy that!'?

Use the police? But the kind of thing Bruce Phillips' hypothetical question, and Mr Trudeau's answer, envisaged was hardly something that could be dealt with by the police, by 'the normal application of the law.' And what police? The provincial police directly, and the municipal police indirectly, are under the control of the province. A provincial Government trying to take the province out of Confederation by force could scarcely be expected to use its own police to stop itself. The RCMP? That force may always get its man; but could it get a provincial Government bent on revolution?

Mr Trudeau did indeed 'establish the context for the use of force that would be greater than the force used in the normal application of the law.' He did it in reply to persistent poking and jabbing by Mr Phillips. If anyone 'invited the sort of escalation of talk that can invite escalation of action,' it was Mr Phillips. Perhaps Mr Trudeau should simply have refused to answer the hypothetical question (after all, as he pointed out, the Parti Québécois has never proposed or advocated anything illegal or revolutionary). But if he had, he would promptly have been accused of evasion, or worse.

The implications that separatism has for the territorial integrity of Canada, still an issue of major importance, were addressed by several Forsey letters, of which two will suffice. The first, to the *Globe and Mail* on 16 May 1978, concerns the question of ownership of the St Lawrence River, passing through Quebec, to connect the Maritime provinces with the rest of Canada. The second, also to the *Globe*, on 28 January 1977, deals with the question of the integrity of Quebec's territory should Quebec separate.

In your issue of May 19, Claude Morin, Quebec Minister for Intergovernmental Affairs, says that an independent Quebec would decide how that section of the St Lawrence River that lies within the province would be used. He is reported to have added: 'After all, we own it.'

This statement is highly questionable.

'Canals, with lands and water power connected therewith' are the property of the Dominion of Canada. So are 'public harbors,' 'lighthouses and piers,' and 'rivers and lake improvements' (British North America Act, 1867, Third Schedule).

Any property rights of the Province of Quebec in the river belong to the Crown in right of Quebec. The Province of Quebec was created by the British North America Act, 1867, Section 5. If Quebec ceases to be a province of Canada and becomes a foreign country, will that foreign country have any legal title to the property of the former Canadian province, unless the constitutional amendment providing for the secession of Quebec makes explicit provision to that effect?

Your editorial, United Canadian Loyalists (Jan. 22) says: 'There is nothing in the constitution to allow for a judicial separation' of part of Quebec from Quebec.

Actually the British North America Act, 1871, Section 3, empowers the Parliament of Canada to 'diminish or otherwise alter the limits' of any province 'upon such terms and conditions as may be agreed to by the Legislature' of the province concerned. Section 4 empowers Parliament to 'make provision for the administration, peace, order and good government of any territory not for the time being included in any province.' Section 2 empowers Parliament to 'establish new provinces in any territories forming for the time being part of the Dominion of Canada, but not included in any province thereof.'

So the Parliament of Canada could take any part of Quebec out of Quebec, make it a Territory, and then make a new province, provided the Legislature of Quebec consented.

That proviso would appear, at first glance, to be an insuperable obstacle to Dr William Shaw's plan for a part of Quebec to separate itself from Quebec if Quebec separates itself from Canada. But Quebec cannot legally separate itself from Canada except with the consent of the Parliament of Canada.

So it is not inconceivable that, if René Lévesque gets a majority for independence in his plebiscite, and negotiations follow, one condition for Canada's consent for Quebec to get out of Canada might be Quebec's consent for part of Quebec to go out of Quebec.

I devoutly hope that we may never have to get into any such negotiations. But, if we do, this matter might be one of the many thorny questions which would arise in the very tough bargaining which would undoubtedly take place.

The tough bargaining which Forsey anticipated was also a process that required clarification, as the debate heated up in advance of the 1980 Quebec referendum on separation. In the *Ottawa Journal* of 20 February 1980, under the heading 'Negotiate What?,' he wrote:

Gilbert Paquette, member of the Quebec Assembly ... is recorded as saying that 'a recent York University survey indicated that about 60 per cent of business, union and political leaders said Canada should negotiate' with Quebec.

Negotiate what? Constitutional change? We've been doing that for many years. Quebec Independence? If Quebec really votes for that, yes, of course, (though the negotiations would be tough).

Sovereignty-association, giving Quebec an absolute veto over tariff and monetary policy? Anyone who thinks any Canadian government would negotiate that needs his head examined.

A month later, on 16 April in the *Globe and Mail*, Forsey became even more assertive:

Gerard Pelletier (Pelletier: a prisoner of his ties with Trudeau – April 9) is reported as 'maintaining that, more than anything else, Quebec Premier René Lévesque and Intergovernmental Affairs Minister Claude Morin want a renewed mandate to negotiate,' and that this is what the referendum is all about.

This is nonsense. The referendum asks for a mandate to negotiate what? 'Sovereignty-association'; that is, independence, plus an economic association that is as impossible as sour sugar, boiling ice or stationary motion.

Neither the Quebec Government nor any other provincial Government needs any mandate to negotiate for constitutional change. They have been at it for years, and the door remains wide open.

Forsey was to take a prominent part in the negotiations surroundng the Meech Lake Accord, as the letters in the next section demonstrate.

CHAPTER TEN

Forsey's Last Stand: The Meech Lake Accord and Its Aftermath, 1987–1991

Forsey's final engagement in his lifelong battle over the Canadian state and its constitution commenced in 1987 with the formulation of the Meech Lake Accord, a series of proposals designed to meet Quebec's objections to the Canada Constitution Act, 1982, and thereby to bring the province back into the federated family.[1]

His first reaction to the accord was presented in a lengthy article, rather than a letter, in the *Globe and Mail* on 17 March 1987. Expressing cautious approval, Forsey systematically dissected the ten categories of proposed amendments to the constitution, assessing their varying likelihood of success, in the light of the constitutional requirements in each case for approval.

As the debate on the accord heated up, criticism mounted, as did Forsey's initial reservations. On 16 May 1987, Professor Michael Bliss produced a succinct, root-and-branch denunciation in the *Globe* that is worth reproducing, not least because Forsey was listed as one of the soft-headed supporters of the accord.

> The Meech Lake accord implies the following:
>
> 1. Special status for Quebec, as a 'distinct society.'
> 2. The transfer of Quebec-Canada relations from the realm of democratic politics to that of judicial interpretation.
> 3. Political units as small as the Government of 130,000 people of Prince Edward Island will have veto power over changes in the political institutions of 26 million Canadians.

> 4. Opting-out provisions will further hinder the establishment of national social and economic programs, with grave consequences for mobility, equality and social justice in what the Fathers of Confederation believed was one country.
>
> These are potentially far more significant changes in the fabric of our nation than anything contained in the constitutional reform of 1982. It is surprising that normally sober experts ranging from Eugene Forsey to the *Globe*'s editorial board have chosen to act as cheerleaders for Meech Lake instead of thoughtful, constructive critics.
>
> Eleven power-hungry politicians have reached a hastily drafted agreement which may in fact be an agenda for dismemberment of our country. Are we going to accept Meech Lake and its consequences without serious debate? Does anyone care about trying to speak for Canada?[2]

Professor Bliss might not have included Forsey in his lament had he seen the two lengthy articles in the *Montreal Gazette* on 12 and 13 May, in which Forsey had analysed critically and in detail the key elements of the accord, bearing on the distinct society, the federal spending power, the proposals on immigration, on Senate reform, and the amendment process. In any event, Forsey promptly responded (*Globe and Mail*, 26 May 1987) to Professor Bliss's challenge:

> I am grateful to Professor Michael Bliss (letter – 16 May) for describing me as a 'normally sober expert' on constitutional matters. But my initial support for the Meech Lake Accord was qualified. I said I was 'encouraged by what had emerged' and 'hoped that when we got the final product I should feel the same way.' I said also that 'the definition of Quebec as a "distinct society" remained a question mark' and that 'I'd want to look very carefully at whatever formula was finally produced on that subject.'
>
> I have since looked very carefully at what the accord says on a variety of subjects, and have very serious misgivings not only on the distinct society but on the federal spending power, immigration and the Supreme Court of Canada. On all these, there are

> obscurities and ambiguities, some of them very dangerous, which need to be cleared up.

A day later, Forsey's growing doubts were reinforced by the intervention of an even doughtier critic, Pierre Trudeau. Erupting out of retirement, the former prime minister's views were carried in the *Toronto Star* under the heading 'Say Goodbye to the Dream of One Canada' (a version in French was simultaneously carried in Montreal's *La Presse*). The critical tone thus set was enlarged by Forsey several months later on 12 November, when, expressing serious misgivings about obscurities in the accord, he opened a continuing series of letters aimed at what he considered to be the misplaced endorsement of the accord by the *Globe and Mail*.

> Your editorial Design for Our Future (Oct. 27) contains a number of statements about the Meech Lake accord that cannot be allowed to pass without challenge.
>
> First, that 'it reaffirms the Confederation bargain of 1867 in modern times.' It would be more accurate to say that it may turn out to mean a reversal of the Confederation bargain of 1867. That bargain set up a highly centralized federalism ... It may prove highly decentralizing. It is such a cornucopia of ambiguities that we cannot be sure until the Supreme Court of Canada has given its decision on what they mean.
>
> Second, you say 'Meech Lake also explicitly strengthens federal authority ... by permitting provincial participation in selection of Supreme Court judges.' How you arrive at that conclusion is one of the mysteries that are really quite insoluble ...
>
> Third, you say the accord commits the country to Senate reform. It does not. All it does is commit the first ministers' conferences to consider Senate reform; and it gives every province an absolute veto on any proposal [for change] ...
>
> Fourth, you say that 'all significant federal powers remain in place.' This is highly questionable. We cannot know the answer until the Supreme Court of Canada decides what linguistic duality and the distinct society really mean, and what effect these two

new principles will have on the Constitution and the Charter of Rights and Freedoms. For they are expressly declared to apply to everything in both except multiculturalism and the aborigines ...

... This is the 'design for our future' which you think will enable Canada to 'continue with the process of constitutional reform.' It is, in fact, a design which could bring that process to a full stop.

Forsey continued to plug away at the substantive issues raised in the debate over the Meech Lake Accord, focusing on its potential impact on language rights, on the Charter of Rights and Freedoms, and on constitutionl amendment procedures. The impact of the accord on the constitutional protection of minority language rights, for example, was highlighted in a letter to the *Globe* on 23 August 1989.

Before you wrote your editorial attacking New Brunswick Premier Frank McKenna for Misreading the Accord, you should have taken a hard look at what Meech Lake actually says on linguistic minorities (Aug. 14).

Parliament and the provincial legislatures are to 'preserve' precisely what? 'The existence of French-speaking Canadians outside Quebec,' and 'the existence of English-speaking Canadians in Quebec.' Not rights, just 'existence.'

The existing Constitution does give linguistic minorities certain rights. Meech Lake gives them nothing except an undertaking to preserve their 'existence.'

... The Supreme Court of Canada might, of course, interpret 'existence' as carrying with it some rights beyond bare physical survival. But what? Any member of either linguistic minority may be forgiven for wondering.

The impact on the charter was conveyed in this letter to the *Globe* on 14 September 1987.

In A Strong Accord (Aug. 29), you say: 'Meech Lake still leaves Quebec under the authority of the Charter of Rights and Freedoms.'

But does it? That is just the point.

> Section 1 of the accord says the Constitution 'shall be interpreted in a manner consistent with the recognition of Quebec as a distinct society.' Section 16 says nothing in Section 1 'affects' multiculturalism or aborigines.
>
> Plainly, therefore, Section 1 does affect everything else in the Charter (and in the Constitution). Plainly, the courts could decide that Section 16 empowers Quebec to take itself out from under everything in the Charter except provisions on multiculturalism and the aborigines.

Forsey expanded on this theme on 4 January 1989, prophesying an even gloomier scenario of never-ending concessions that mocked the very notion of a firm constitutional foundation.

> Benoit Aubin says Quebec Premier Robert Bourassa's use of the notwithstanding clause shows his vision of a distinct Quebec (Bourassa's Use of Charter Clauses Shows His Vision of Distinct Quebec – Dec. 22).
>
> It does, indeed, and the light it shines on the distinct society clause in the Meech Lake accord is made still more revealing by Mr Bourassa's suggestion (reported in your Dec. 19 issue) that invoking the notwithstanding clause was necessary because the Meech Lake constitutional accord, which gives Quebec extra powers to protect its French language and culture, has not been ratified.
>
> Precisely. If Meech Lake goes through, Mr Bourassa, or any other Quebec premier, could do exactly what he pleased in this matter (and various others, too) without having to bother with the notwithstanding clause. The sky would be the limit, unless the Supreme Court of Canada decided that the distinct society clause does not mean what Mr Bourassa says it means.
>
> And if that happens, we shall be asked to accept a further constitutional amendment giving Mr Bourassa what he thought he had and found he hadn't.
>
> Fantasy?
>
> Ontario New Democratic Party leader Bob Rae warned us that, 'if the Meech Lake compromise is allowed to unravel completely

... an accommodation with Quebec must be found that also allows for constitutional change' (The Quebec Crisis: A Search for Compromise – Dec. 22).

Compromise?

Compromise implies that each side in a contest gives up something. In Meech Lake, the national government certainly gave up plenty. What did the provinces give up? Compromise with Quebec? Mr Bourassa has said that he got more than he asked for.

'Further constitutional change' to achieve 'an accommodation with Quebec ?' What further concessions would Mr Rae offer?

Mr Rae is only the leader of a provincial opposition. But read what Prime Minister Brian Mulroney said in the July issue of The Parliamentarian (the journal of the parliaments of the Commonwealth):

'The accord ... will help transform our constitution ... into a more federalist document ... Ratification will allow us to move forward with the knowledge that we are entering a new era in the history of our country. We shall have the opportunity to refine further our constitutional process. For the Constitutional Accord of 1987 is not an ending. It is a beginning. It will set Canada's constitutional process on the road again.'

In other words, if the accord goes through, we can expect from its authors further dismantling of the national government – with, no doubt, the supporters of Meech Lake singing new psalms in praise of the new 'compromises,' the new gifts to the provincial warlords, the new inducements to Quebec to 'rejoin the national family' of a nation that will be disintegrating before our eyes.

One of the 'obscurities' requiring clarification concerned the procedure to be used for adoption of the accord. Early on in the debate, Forsey staked out a position on this issue (in the *Globe* 8 July 1987) that was to prove prophetic of the forces that brought about the defeat of the accord in June 1990.

Now that the Legislative Assembly of Quebec has approved the Meech Lake accord, I notice a tendency in some quarters to say that this settles the whole question: that the approval of Parlia-

> ment and of the other provincial legislatures is hardly more than a formality; that to ask for changes is futile, an exercise in frustration. Quebec has spoken: let all the rest of Canada keep silent.
>
> To accept this is simply to relegate all the citizens of Canada outside Quebec to the status of yes-men, yes-women, nodders, second-class citizens.
>
> The Meech Lake accord does not simply give Quebec certain new powers. It gives new powers to all the provinces. Are the legislatures and the people of those provinces, and their representatives in Parliament, to be restricted to marginal comments and murmurs of humble acquiescence? The Meech Lake accord might drive a coach-and-four through almost every provision of the Charter of Rights and Freedoms. Are the citizens of nine provinces to sit mute while their fundamental rights are put at risk? ...
>
> The verdict of the Quebec Legislature is of the highest importance. But the Constitution requires the consent not simply of that Legislature, but of all the legislatures and of Parliament. Is that requirement of the Constitution mere words and breath? All the provinces are supposed to be equal. Is one more equal than others?
>
> The Constitution belongs to all of us. It is not the property of any one province, to be disposed of as the Legislature of that province sees fit.

Towards the close of the debate, Forsey was obliged to make his point more succinctly. In the *Globe* on 8 December 1889 he wrote: 'Robert Sheppard, on Meech Lake, says: "Most of the deal, including the distinct-society provisions, could be entrenched via a simple bilateral arrangement between Ottawa and Quebec City, legal scholars have noted" (The Provinces – Nov. 30). Who are these "legal scholars" and on what do they base their opinion?'

Confusion over procedure for approval of the accord was accompanied by confusion over how alterations in its terms should be handled. Forsey had this clarification in the *Globe* 25 June 1988:

> The Prime Minister says that by the Meech Lake accord 'we have

gained the ability to move on to the next stage of constitutional reform' (Meech Lake Bolsters Charter, PM Tells House – June 15). The other party leaders talk of amendments at some later date and there has been a chorus about a 'second round.'

But all the defenders of the accord say it can't be changed now by so much as one jot or tittle. It is a 'seamless garment.' Touch one thread and the whole thing unravels.

This perplexes me.

If it is impossible to make any change before the accord is approved, why will it be possible the day after? Won't the garment still be seamless.

Seven months later, in the *Globe* of 3 February 1989, Forsey continued to question the prospect of a 'parallel accord':

Thomas Walkom says that on the Meech Lake accord, '(Ontario Premier David) Peterson favors some kind of parallel accord (Tackling a Slippery Slope – Jan. 23). This could address Senate reform. But it would not have constitutional or legal force, being instead a statement of intent.'

Anyone who really wants Senate reform had better insist on getting something more than a statement of intent. The only 'parallel accord' that would be worth anything would be one spelling out the whole scheme, with every 'i' dotted, every 't' crossed, every figure stated, and coming into effect on the same date as the Meech Lake accord.

Any Senate reform the West will accept will have to give the four western provinces a substantial increase in the proportion of Senate seats. Once Meech Lake is approved by all the provincial legislatures, any change in the number of seats for any province will have to have unanimous consent. Any substantial increase in the proportion of western seats means a substantial decrease in Ontario and Quebec seats. Alberta's 'triple E' proposal, for example, would give every province six seats, bringing Ontario and Quebec down from 23 per cent each to less than 10 per cent each. The 'distinct society' might not like that.

If this, or anything like it, is what the West wants, it had better

> get it signed, sealed and delivered, down to the last syllable of fine print, before Meech Lake comes into force. For once that has happened, just one premier saying he has changed his mind, or that he has misunderstood, will send the whole thing down the drain.

Several months later, in the *Globe* of 13 November 1989, Forsey reinforced his reservations about a parallel accord.

> I see Quebec Intergovernmental Affairs Minister Gil Remillard says he is 'ready to consider' a 'parallel accord' to Meech Lake once Meech Lake has been approved by all 10 provincial legislatures (Carstairs Asks Peterson to Back Meech Talks – Oct. 27).
>
> Of course he is. Why wouldn't he be? Entrenched behind the barbed wire entanglements of the 'distinct society' clause and the unanimity requirements, he is perfectly safe in 'considering' anything under the blue dome of Heaven; and the result will be precisely nothing.
>
> In effect, he is saying: 'Give us everything we want, a veto on Senate reform, a veto even on any discussion, in the first ministers' conferences, of anything except Senate reform or fisheries, and we'll graciously listen to anything you please. Our ears will be wide open. But our minds, our fists, tight shut.'
>
> Surely in vain this net is spread in the sight of the governments of Manitoba and Newfoundland.

Discussion of a parallel accord got caught up in another proposal to unbundle the various elements of the Meech Lake Accord. Possibly because the complex amending formulas contained in the Constitution Act, 1982 had had little time to be tested, the government decided to treat the accord as a single package and to apply to all elements the requirement of endorsement by all provinces within the three-year deadline. Realization dawned late that the most rigorous amending formula had been chosen to apply to the package when, in fact, several of the amendments dealt with matters that required less than unanimity. Indeed, only for such amendments was the three-year rule applicable; where unanimity was required, no deadline for approval was involved. This point was clearly made in a lengthy technical article by Gordon Robertson, a former senior adviser on constitutional matters, as secretary to the cabinet, in the *Globe* on 19 June 1989.

Forsey did not enter this debate, for reasons best expressed in his personal letter of 22 June to Gordon Robertson, which read in part:

> You have made fools of us all ...
>
> But you may have set the cat among a flock of pigeons.
>
> Clearly, some provisions of the Accord could go into effect now, if they stood by themselves ...
>
> But of course they don't stand by themselves. What the eight provinces have approved is the whole Accord. To bring the provisions the deadline applies to they would have to start all over again; or so it seems to me; and that would mean a fresh three years Mr Bourassa might have to wait to get even that ...
>
> The first reaction to your article is likely to be relief among the supporters of Meech Lake, and consternation among its opponents. The second reaction may be just the opposite.
>
> I'm afraid we're in for a very sad time of it ...
>
> I must end by saying that I think your article has done an immense public service. Its conclusions must have come home, gradually, to more and more people, while irritation, frustration and a sense of having been 'had' mounted; and the situation could have developed more and more bitterness, more and more sense of betrayal, more and more backlash, English and French. Now we shall have to face the thing at once, and all at once, and try to find some solution that won't break up the country ...
>
> I have often said that I belong, spiritually and intellectually, to the generation of Sir Robert Borden: I should have been born fifty years sooner, and died long ago. I'd have been happier, and probably more useful. The modern world disgusts me more and more, and frightens me more and more.
>
> However, I wasn't born in 1854; I am still here, a very minor, almost extinct volcano, and the fire within me still sends off occa-

sional puffs of steam. As my health seems to be getting better, the puffs may continue for some time yet![3]

Forsey's fatalistic, elegaic mood persisted as efforts to produce a parallel accord were mounted by a special parliamentary committee, chaired by Jean Charest. Most of the terms for such an add-on accord were produced late in 1989 by this committee, in the process, causing one of its members, Lucien Bouchard, to break with the Mulroney government and ultimately head the separatist federal Bloc Québécois party which became the official opposition in a subsequent election.

Forsey continued right up to the deadline of 23 June to warn against the foolishness of entertaining second thoughts in a parallel accord. His final expostulation was recorded in the *Globe* on 2 June 1990.

> We are now being offered a series of 'clarifications' of the Meech Lake accord. Either these go into the accord itself, or they do not. If they do, they become amendments and become part of the written Constitution, binding in law. If they do not go into the accord, they do not become part of the written Constitution, they are not binding in law and they mean precisely nothing.

However, Forsey's prophetic comments to Gordon Robertson were about to be realized in a final 'roll the dice' session, described by one of its participants as 'this dinner has seven days,' during which the supplementary accord was agonizingly hammered out.[4] Forsey was one of the advisers in attendance on behalf of the province of Newfoundland and Premier Wells, whom Forsey had championed as the one participant most likely to support his conception of Canada. But Forsey survived only two days before leaving the delegation, after penning the following note:

> There is no point in my remaining on the delegation.
>
> I am completely in the dark and I have neither appetite nor aptitude for debates on how many angels can dance on the

> point of a needle, especially when there are no angels, and no needle.
>
> All these 'undertakings' to 'consider' to 'negotiate' in a 'second round'; all the 'clarifications,' all the 'companion resolutions' (to come into effect *after* Meech Lake has been ratified) are worth precisely *nothing* ...
>
> I am, accordingly, resigning from the delegation, and shall feel free to make any comments I see fit when the decisions are made public.[5]

True to his promise, on 12 June Forsey issued his own two-page press release on 'The 1990 Constitutional Agreement,' which opened: 'This document is almost totally worthless,' and went on to repeat with embellishments his previously declared objections. (Appended to his copy of the release is the delighted notation: 'Pierre told Charles Caccia, "It made my day."')

In the event, Forsey's concerns became irrelevant, since presentation of this subsidiary agreement was to be contingent on unanimous approval of the Meech Lake Accord. Such approval was in the end denied by the objections of MLA Elijah Harper, a status Indian in the Manitoba legislature and the adjournment of the debate in the Newfoundland Assembly before a vote could be taken.

Throughout the Meech Lake debate, proponents had argued that failure to adopt the accord would foreclose future discussion of some of the key concerns which had presumably been successfully addressed in the accord. Forsey found this stance open to serious doubt, as revealed by this reminder to the *Globe* on 17 May 1989:

> William Thorsell says that 'If Meech Lake dies, Quebec will surely restore its boycott, and no federal prime minister will proceed with much else on the constitutional agenda ... not reform of the Senate. Not broad constitutional entrenchment of aboriginal self-government' (Missing the Boat – May 6).
>
> If Meech Lake survives, on Senate reform the West will unques-

> tionably demand an appreciable reduction in Quebec's proportion of Senate seats.
>
> Does Mr Thorsell believe the 'distinct society' would accept that? But, under Meech Lake, Quebec would have a veto.
>
> If Meech Lake survives, 'broad constitutional entrenchment of aboriginal self-government' could not even be discussed at the annual constitutional conference of first ministers except by unanimous consent of the provincial premiers.
>
> Senate reform and fisheries must be discussed. Anything else can get on the agenda only if 'agreed upon.' Any one premier could stop the thing cold.

Globe and Mail columnist Jeffrey Simpson received a similar reminder a few months later, on 22 May 1990, when he claimed that 'Entrenchment of native self-government will have to wait, perhaps for a long time if Meech Lake fails.' Forsey's reply, 'What makes him think it will not have to wait a long time if Meech Lake is ratified?' was supported by the same evidence provided in his response to William Thorsell.

Even after the defeat of the accord, Forsey found it necessary to admonish Jeffrey Simpson at least twice with reference to the fate of native people's rights. His letter of 4 August 1990 to the *Globe* read:

> Jeffrey Simpson (Just When You Think Things Can't Get Any Worse, They Can Get Worse – June 29) echoed Quebec Intergovernmental Affairs Minister Gil Remillard's warning that if Meech Lake failed the native peoples would lose 'a precious ally' because of Quebec's absence from the constitutional bargaining table.
>
> He might have asked the Crees of northern Quebec what the 'precious ally' had done to them with James Bay One and what it was proposing to do to them with James Bay Two. He might have asked other Quebec Indians for their experience. And now, he might ask the Mohawk's [*sic*: see his correction of 16 August] at Oka.

> Mr Simpson's belief that if Meech Lake had been ratified, and Quebec had come back to the table, it would have done the Indians and Inuit a bit of good looks like what Dr Samuel Johnson called 'the triumph of hope over experience.'

A few weeks later, on 8 September, Forsey targeted Jeffrey Simpson once more:

> So Jeffrey Simpson thinks that if the Meech Lake accord had been approved the Indians would have had a 'forum' in the first ministers' conferences (A Royal Commission Could Help All Canadians Grapple with Native Issues – Aug. 30).
>
> He should take a look at clause 13 of the accord, sub-clause (2) ... the [first ministers'] conferences must discuss Senate reform and the fisheries. But they cannot even raise any other matter except by unanimous consent. Every single premier would have had an absolute veto even on the discussion of native rights.
>
> But of course they all would have consented!
>
> They would? Mr Simpson himself says ' Four first ministers' conferences on aboriginal rights came to nothing.'

In the aftermath of the aborted Meech Lake Accord, Forsey joined the voices of those who were demanding some better procedure for amending Canada's constitution. The general complaint was that the process, as exemplified during the Meech Lake debate, was far too secretive and relied too heavily on negotiations amongst a tiny clique consisting of the prime minister, provincial premiers, and their assorted expert advisers. Even the added involvement of elected legislators was deemed to leave out 'the people.' The federal government's response was to create a representative task force – known as the Spicer Commission – to conduct forums and generally take soundings of 'the people's views.' The raw material obtained in this way and also from counterpart provincial committees was to form the basis for the second comprehensive attempt to secure a package of constitutional amendment proposals, this time to be submitted directly to the people. This process led to the formulation of the Charlottetown Accord and its defeat in a referendum in 1992.

Forsey's death in February 1991 prevented him from participating in that referendum, but there can be no doubt that he would have opposed the Charlottetown agreement as vigorously as he had its Meech Lake predecessor. His opposition was signalled by his criticisms of the Spicer task force, voiced in nearly his last letter to the *Globe*, on 17 November 1990:

> So the Spicer commission is not to consider aboriginal concerns, or Senate reform, or the constitutional amending process.
>
> Senator Lowell Murray says the royal commission the government offered in June, and again in September, has been 'postponed' (no doubt because the natives are so delighted with what has happened, and is still happening, at Oka and Kahnawake that they no longer have any problems). A discussion paper on Senate reform has been 'simply abandoned.' The 'public search for new methods of amending the Constitution has been put off for the near future.'
>
> So what is the Spicer commission going to do?
>
> Keith Spicer has made it crystal clear. It is to give us Meech Lake, Act 3.
>
> It is to soften us up to accept whatever Quebec Premier Robert Bourassa's commission proposes.
>
> 'We will create,' says Mr Spicer, 'a receptive climate for the Belanger-Campeau recommendations, especially if they are radical.'
>
> And what if, in spite of Mr Spicer's efforts, the climate proves unreceptive? The natives may feel that 'postponement' is not good enough. The provinces that want Senate reform may be disconcerted to find that even a 'discussion paper' on this subject 'has been abandoned.' Those who want a new constitutional amending formula giving the people, not the politicians, the power to say what goes out, and what goes in, may be disappointed.
>
> But what does all that matter if the Quebec nationalists get what they want?

> They keep saying they want us to say what we want. I hope we shall tell them. Perhaps they will prepare 'a receptive climate' for what we may say, 'especially if it is radical.'

Surprisingly, for all the despairing scepticism reflected in this letter about the processes surrounding continuing efforts to achieve constitutional reform, at the end Forsey expressed his confidence in letting the people decide. His lifelong devotion to the concept of parliamentary supremacy, one might have thought, would have led him to oppose the use of a referendum. Apparently this was the view of a political scientist colleague, Peyton Lyon, to whose letter Forsey felt obliged to write this correction, in the *Montreal Gazette* of 19 August, 1985:

> Professor Peyton Lyon (Dialogue, Aug. 8) says, 'Authorities as illustrious as Eugene Forsey dismiss referendums as un-Canadian or as inconsistent with the responsible government we inherited from Mother Britain.'
>
> I am grateful, if more than a little surprised, to be described as 'illustrious.' But to the best of my recollection and belief, I have never made, in speech or writing, any such statements as Professor Lyon attributes to me.
>
> Indeed, I cannot remember ever holding any such opinions. On the contrary, I have repeatedly supported the Australian method of constitutional amendment, which has no place for the state governments or parliaments, but requires every amendment to have the approval, by referendum, of a majority of the electors in the whole Commonwealth, and a majority of the electors in a majority of the states.
>
> I publicly regretted the disappearance of the referendum provisions of former prime minister Pierre Trudeau's original patriation proposals. [A reference to the proposals of 1981 which led to the Canada Constitution Act of 1982.]
>
> The reason no party is proposing a referendum on the free-trade agreement is that there is no legal provision for holding one. It would require an Act of Parliament. A referendum on the Meech Lake accord could require a constitutional amendment.

Only a few weeks ago, Patrick Boyer, MP, introduced in the House of Commons a bill to provide for referenda and plebiscites, and I appeared with him at a press conference to support it.

It is clear that Forsey's support of the referendum focused on use of that procedure for constitutional amendment and not for day-to-day matters. His preference for the Australian system was amplified in a lengthy article for the *Montreal Gazette* on 28 November 1989, 'Let the People Decide on Meech Lake' and again, in the *Globe and Mail* of 5 July 1990, after the failure of Meech Lake. Under the heading 'Time to Let the People of Canada Decide the Constitution,' Forsey had this to say:

> Everyone is now saying we must have a different process for amending our Constitution. Many are saying that the Constitution belongs to the people, not the politicians.
>
> So it does, and it is time we gave it to the people. To do that, we need a process modelled on the Australian.
>
> In Australia, the state governments and the state parliaments have no part in the process. A proposed amendment begins in the federal Parliament. If it passes both Houses (both elected), it goes to the electorate in a referendum. If it gets a majority of the electors in the whole country, and a majority of the electors in a majority of the states, it goes into effect. If it does not get these majorities, it dies. The electors say what goes into the Constitution and what stays out.
>
> We cannot just copy the Australian system, for one simple, and cogent reason: Australia has no Quebec; we have.
>
> So an Australian process here would have to provide special safeguards for Quebec's special institutions and special needs. The French language is already constitutionally guaranteed in the Quebec Legislature and courts. The Quebec Civil Law is already constitutionally guaranteed ... Quebec can already opt out of any transfer of power from its Legislature to the Parliament of Canada. Quebec is already constitutionally guaranteed one-third of the judges of the Supreme Court of Canada. It could be guaranteed a minimum proportion of the total number of seats in the Senate.

> There might be other matters where it should be given a veto; that would be a matter for negotiation; real negotiation, not dictation.
>
> The French language is already constitutionally guaranteed in the federal Parliament and courts, and in the New Brunswick Legislature and courts; and the English language is already constitutionally guaranteed in the Quebec Legislature and courts.
>
> But under the present Constitution, it is the legislature of each province (usually controlled by the provincial government) that has the veto. It ought to be the electorate of each province. The people of each province should decide on all the proposed changes, what goes in, what goes out.
>
> The decision should not be left with provincial jacks-in-office who may have been elected years before, on wholly different issues, and sometimes without a popular majority.
>
> This does not, of course, settle by any means all constitutional questions, notably the rights of the native peoples (which Elijah Harper has certainly put on the front burner), or the educational rights of minorities. But giving the Constitution to the people would at least mean we would never have a repetition of Meech Lake. No more cliff-hangers.
>
> The present amending process puts things hindside foremost. If ratification of amendments is left with the legislatures, the jacks-in-office, hungry for powers for themselves, could still frustrate the wishes of the people.
>
> If there is any frustrating to be done, it is the people who should frustrate the politicians. If things need changing, it is the people, not the politicians, who should change them ...
>
> Everyone now says we must have mandatory public hearings. Yes. But that is not enough. Democracy means the rule of the people. Let's make sure it does, in this most vital of all matters political. Give the Constitution to the people.

Was this late enthusiasm for referendums – for letting the people decide – attributable to their tendency to conserve rather than approve drastic change? Forsey had made this point more than a decade before the defeat of the Meech Lake Accord in a piece solicited by the *Ottawa Citizen* on 30 August 1977. In the wake of the Quebec government's white paper on a proposed referendum on the question of independence, Forsey was asked to explain the difference between plebiscites and referendums. To the query, 'What do you want to accomplish by referendums?' and would they accomplish it?, Forsey replied:

> The answer, judging by Australian and Swiss experience, seems to be that if you want important changes in legislation or the constitution, you had better fight shy of referendums, because the people usually vote 'no.' But, if you want to block change, referendums may be just what the doctor ordered. Plebiscites are a different matter. They can be most useful for getting a party off a hook.

The closest approximation to meeting Forsey's clarion call for letting the people decide occurred in 1992, after Forsey's death, with the referendum on the Charlottetown Agreement. Its defeat validated Forsey's earlier analysis. Knowing Forsey's preference for conserving the tried and true, particularly when it came to constitutional change, it is not unjust to suggest that there may have been more than a hint of Machiavellian intent behind Forsey's last call for 'letting the people decide.' Might he himself, had he still been alive, written a letter that would have concluded with the inversion of one of his favourite expressions, that the defeat of the Charlottetown referendum marked the triumph of experience over ill-conceived hopes for constitutional change.

CHAPTER ELEVEN

True Patriot Love

As an unabashed monarchist and dedicated believer in political institutions inherited from Britain, Forsey fought strenuously to preserve what he considered to be the symbolic hallmarks of a True North strong and free, attached to, but independent of, the British Crown. His lifelong conviction that Canada must preserve a strong central presence against the fragmenting pressures from 'provincial warlords' was accompanied by his fear of 'creeping republicanism.' Such fear often emerged as nationalistic barbs directed at our powerful, republican southern neighbour.

O! Canada: The Demise of 'Dominion'

Forsey's most famous campaign over symbols was his battle to preserve the official title, Dominion of Canada, in association with heraldic connections with the British Crown found in such terms as 'Royal Mail.' In the 1950s he lost an initial skirmish when a home-grown governor general was selected. His struggle to protect 'Dominion' from 'the conspirators' extended over three decades and was fought on several fronts. Despite progressive erosion that left 'Dominion' much like the fading smile on the Cheshire Cat, Forsey never conceded defeat. Loyal supporters, long after his voice has been silenced, still invoke his spirited protestations, almost a ritual performance around the first of July of each year.[1]

The attacks on 'Dominion' had begun in the 1940s with an aborted effort to substitute Canada Day for Dominion Day in the Holidays Act. In 1951 the St Laurent government undertook a frontal assault in a bill to transform the Dominion Elections Act. Forsey's anguished rebuttal took the form of two very long letters, that of 26 November 1951 in the *Globe and Mail* (copied three days later in the *Ottawa Journal*), and a second, appearing first in the *Journal* on 6 December and reproduced in the *Globe* on 11 December, comprising a point-by-point response to the prime minister's own lengthy defence of his government's actions. Forsey was bucking the policy not only of his political foes but also of his CCF colleagues, as he revealed in a letter to Arthur Meighen to whom he had sent a draft of his submission to the *Globe*. 'I may get into trouble with my political friends over this,' he wrote. '[M.J.] Coldwell and [Angus] MacInnis both spoke, I think, in favour of substituting "Canada" for "Dominion" ... However, I have no patience with such nonsense, no matter where it comes from, and shall stand up to them if they remonstrate with me.'[2]

Since Forsey was to have frequent occasion to repeat, with little variation, his early arguments for retaining 'Dominion,' it seems appropriate to make liberal use of his 26 November 1951 effusion to the *Globe and Mail*, headed 'Depriving Canada of Its History':

> I see the Government's merry game of depriving us of our history goes on apace. First, it was the time-honored heading, 'Dominion Government' disappearing from the local telephone book. Then it was the 'Royal Mail' becoming 'obsolete' and making way for 'euphonious' and dignified 'Canada Post.' ... and we are told that it is official policy to eliminate 'Dominion' and substitute 'Canada' or 'Canadian' whenever the opportunity occurs.
>
> All this raises two questions. First, why? Second, where is it going to stop? Why is 'Royal Mail' 'obsolete'? (Incidentally, I notice it still appears on postal trucks in Toronto. Has Toronto become a separate state? Or has the Government just run short of paint there? ...) Is this country still a monarchy? If so, the mail is

still 'Royal.' If the mail is no longer 'Royal,' what about the navy, the air force, the mint, the King's Regulations? Unless we are committed to proclaiming a republic, this jiggery-pokery is wholly indefensible. If we are committed to a republic, when was this change submitted to, let alone sanctioned by, the Canadian people?

There might be a serious reason (though, in my judgment, a bad one) for jettisoning 'Royal.' For replacing 'Dominion' by 'Canadian' there is no reason that is worth the breath to utter it. The clatter about 'Dominion' implying subordination to some other country is just rubbish. It is a fine old word, with a long and honorable history. The official French translation is the equally fine old word, 'Puissance' ('Power'), which by no stretch of the imagination can be taken to imply subordination. 'Dominion' was good enough for Macdonald, for the rest of the Fathers of Confederation ... and I think even Mr King. It was highly convenient for distinguishing between the central authority and its institutions and property, and the provinces and theirs. 'Canadian' has a much broader, and for these purposes, less precise, meaning: much the same is true of 'national,' and 'federal' is an importation.

The abolition of 'Dominion' is going to have some ridiculous by-products. 'CBS' will mean either 'Canadian Bureau of Statistics' or 'Columbia Broadcasting System.' ...

On the face of it, the whole business is childish. What lies behind it? Is it an attempt to root out, little by little, familiar and distinctive terms which bind us to our past? If so, we should be told so, frankly; given the reasons, if any; and allowed to say whether we want it done or not. The most objectionable feature of the performance is its surreptitiousness. Apparently the Government hopes that if it is quiet and cautious enough, no one will notice what is happening until it is too late.

Where is it all going to stop? Are we going to wake up some morning and find ourselves citizens of the Republic of Canada? It looks like it. But I think there are a lot of people who don't want it ... They object most of all to having this sort of thing thrust upon them, without even a pretense of consultation or consent. Some have already protested. I hope more will. I am convinced that

> what has been done so far is mainly the result of propaganda by a few noisy chatterboxes. Perhaps if the rest of us can make enough noise the thing will stop.

Forsey sustained his attack with a detailed rebuttal of the seven reasons for declaring 'Dominion' obsolete, offered in the House of Commons by the prime minister on 8 November 1951. Published in the *Globe* on 11 December, Forsey's letter closed on this note:

> The simple fact is that we are citizens of a Dominion, just as Americans are citizens of a republic and Englishmen citizens of a kingdom. The British North America Act says twice that we are a Dominion, and the Government has not yet even proposed an amendment to strike out the word. That would be the logical conclusion of its present policy: to strike out 'Dominion' and leave a blank, for it could hardly make the act read 'One Canada under the name of Canada,' and it has not suggested anything else. That, presumably would be the real 'culmination' of the 'progression.' That would be the real equality. That would enhance our status. Then, at last, we should achieve our destiny: neither kingdom nor republic, nor anything else known to political terminology, but just a nameless Something, a sublime Blank!

Forsey's intervention, as with subsequent ones on the same theme, drew a flurry of comments from other readers. Following the policy of encouraging a good verbal sparring match, the *Globe* accepted a number of correspondents prepared to joust with Forsey. No stranger to such encounters, Forsey gave as good as he got, usually being given the last crack at the subject, as this round-up Forsey response to his critics reveals (*Globe*, 18 December 1951):

> Mr Down says he can't find that our stamps ever carried the words 'Royal,' or 'Dominion.' Who said they did? He also wants to know whether I 'would change the CBC to DBC,' and so forth. Nobody except the Government has proposed to change anything.

> Mr Bruce settles the whole question by proclaiming, ex cathedra, that 'Dominion means, at best, a top-drawer colony,' and pronounces an anathema against those who disagree with him. Then, having elevated the Saturday Evening Post to the rank of a constitutional authority, he wants to know how I would 'square' with its statements my 'argument ... that we are a sovereign country and ... that it is shameful to drop "Dominion."' The answer is simple: we are a sovereign country, and a Dominion, and the Saturday Evening Post doesn't know what it's talking about.
>
> Mr Bruce says 'Royal' 'also has colonial connotations.' Royal Navy, Royal Mint, Royal Society, Astronomer Royal. ... Poor old England! All this time a colony without knowing it!
>
> Mr Knight says I would 'like to see Canada a colony rather than a nation.' This is wholly false. He says I 'criticize others who dare to talk about a Canadian flag or anthem.' I said nothing about either, and neither has anything to do with the question at issue. Even a province can have a flag of its own. Two have: Nova Scotia and Quebec. Even a colony can have an anthem of its own: Newfoundland did, half a century and more ago. Then, 'Canadian people have earned the right to full nationhood, and, in my opinion this nationhood is going to be achieved sooner or later.' This is Rip Van Winkle nonsense. We achieved full nationhood long ago; on the Prime Minister's showing, at least twenty years ago.

Ever on the alert, Forsey returned to the defence in yet another lengthy letter, which the *Globe* published on 8 July 1952 under the heading: 'Back to the Old, Stealthy Methods.' The letter opened: 'The sapping and mining against "Dominion" have started again.' Incensed to find that *Saturday Night* had taken up the cause, after a private member had withdrawn his bill to change the name of Dominion Day, Forsey castigated its 14 June editorial as having 'all the characteristic beauties of "Liberal" "Nationalist" propaganda.' There followed an eight-point rebuttal that concluded: 'Saturday Night some months ago explained that we had to drop "Dominion" because "some foreigners" didn't understand what it meant. Now it says we can't call our national holiday "Confederation Day" because the Americans mightn't like it! (How many of them care a button what we call it?) And this cringing and crawling calls itself "nationalism"!'

Three years later, in the *Globe* of 7 September 1954, it was the turn of the Department of External Affairs to receive Forsey's scornful tongue-lashing:

> The Department of External Affairs explains that its use of the term 'Canada Day' for 'Dominion Day' is for external consumption only, for 'convenience,' because the poor foreigners wouldn't know what 'Dominion Day' meant: 'it means very little abroad.' ...
>
> The principle seems to be that if foreigners don't understand any of our own legal terms for our own institutions, we don't explain what they mean; we change the names. Perhaps this accounts for the Canada Year Book's funny work with 'Ministry' and 'House of Commons' and 'Parliament.' Henceforth, our 'Parliament' can be 'National Assembly' when we're talking to Frenchmen, and 'Congress' when we're talking to Americans ... and 'Supreme Soviet' when we're talking to Russians. And, of course, the foreigners would understand better if we called our Secretary of State for External Affairs' 'Foreign Minister,' [he lost that one, too!] and our 'provinces' 'states.' ...
>
> This is not the first time the Government has been caught at this sort of game; and, as usual, it has produced a whole series of far more indefensible 'explanations' and excuses. ...
>
> If, as your editorial suggests, it is civil servants who are doing this sort of thing on their own, it is high time they were reminded that they are not entitled to repeal Acts of Parliament ... We need in Canada more of the spirit of the Englishman who, whenever he writes a letter to a civil servant, ends with: 'You have the honor to be, Sir, my obedient servant.'

The Canadian Broadcasting Corporation also had to be reminded of its legal trespass in a letter to the *Globe* on 4 July 1957:

> The CBC Times for this week is studded with references to July 1 as 'Canada Day.'
>
> But the Dominion Day Act ... says 'Throughout Canada, in each

> and every year, the first day of July, not being a Sunday, shall be a legal holiday, and shall be kept and observed as such, under the name of Dominion Day.'
>
> By what authority does the CBC undertake to set aside an act of Parliament? ...
>
> The Bill of Rights, which is part of our constitution, declares that the Crown has no power to suspend the laws without consent of Parliament. Can a mere agent of the Crown do what the Crown itself, these 268 years, has been forbidden to do?

When, in 1982, a private member's bill to replace Dominion Day with Canada Day slipped through Parliament with scarcely a murmur of dissent, Forsey made his final ironic pronouncement, signing his letter to the *Globe*, on 16 July, with a flourish: 'Member, National Council of the Royal Commonwealth Society.'

> The House of Commons has now passed the bill changing Dominion Day to Canada Day.
>
> This comes at a very odd moment. The Constitution Act, 1867 (formerly the British North America Act, 1867, and still, by virtue of the Constitution Act, 1982, part of the Constitution of Canada) says twice, in section 3, that Canada is to 'form and be one Dominion.' Moreover, that section has just been entrenched by the Constitution Act, 1982, section 38 (1). It cannot be changed except with the consent of the legislatures of seven provinces with at least half the population of the 10.
>
> So Dominion remains the official, constitutional title of our country, and will so remain till it is changed by formal constitutional amendment.
>
> ... The title Dominion was chosen by the Fathers of Confederation (when they could not get their first choice, Kingdom) 'as a tribute to the Monarchical principle which they earnestly desire to uphold.' So Lord Carnarvon officially told Queen Victoria.
>
> The Constitution Act, 1982, has just entrenched the monarchical principle. Section 41 (1) provides that the monarchy cannot be touched except with the consent of the Legislatures of all 10 provinces.

Yet this is the moment the House of Commons chooses to delete the 'tribute to the Monarchical principle' from the name of our national holiday.

The excuses proffered for this performance ... [are] just rubbish. [The letter then rehearses arguments made in previous communiqués.]

Creeping Republicanism

Forsey's battle to preserve 'Dominion' merged with his battle against 'creeping republicanism,' as he lamented the erosion of 'the monarchical principle' embedded in the constitution. In a nationally broadcast radio address, reproduced in whole in the *Ottawa Journal* on 18 January 1955, he rehearsed his criticisms of the government's policy of deleting 'Dominion' and 'Royal Mail,' but saved his choicest invective for those who would undermine the monarchy by attacking such symbols. 'What I am afraid of,' he complained, 'is the "creeping republicanism" which "slinks unbreath'd" from any encounter; which shuns discussion like the plague; which substitutes for Act of Parliament and will of the people act of Minister and will of the bureaucrat; which defies the law and the constitution; whose strategy is the fait accompli.' Excoriating the government, he raged on: 'I just wish I had time to recite to you the bad history, the bad law, bad logic, the insults, the crass ignorance, the distortions of the dictionary, with which the Government and its hangers-on have tried to defend the indefensible. They are almost beyond belief.' He concluded: 'They would never have got as far as they have if more of us had realized what the monarchy meant and why it was worth preserving. But that's another story: the melancholy story of how, for nearly 30 years, our people have been steadily and systematically miseducated about our constitution, and particularly about the role of the Crown as the guardian of that constitution, the protector of Parliament and the people against cabinet dictatorship.'

More than a decade later, carried by both the *Globe and Mail* and the *Ottawa Journal* on 19 October 1966, Forsey felt obliged to reprise his views, opening his letter with his outraged cry: 'So the creeping republicans are at it again!' Taking off from an official announcement that 'the royal coat of arms on post office trucks and mailbags is to be replaced by a maple leaf,' Forsey proceeded to sketch the worst-possible scenario:

> The Postmaster-General says that the maple leaf is 'an emblem which will represent a truly Canadian post office and which will give a real interpretation to the Post Office Act.' What on earth does this mumbo-jumbo mean? What kind of post office have we had hitherto? German? French? English? Russian? The very first Post Office Act, in 1867, the same one that asserted firmly that our mails were 'Her Majesty's' called our post office 'the Canada Post Office' and 'Her Majesty's Canada Post Office.' As for the real interpretation: since what is being taken off the trucks and mail bags is the coat-of-arms of Canada, what is being ditched is not merely the symbol of our historic monarchy, the monarchy which the Fathers of Confederation unanimously, deliberately, chose to preserve, but a historical symbol of Canada itself, embodying (as no merely vegetable emblem can) our historic past, French and English.
>
> Perhaps, then, its removal means that we are being softened up not only for sly, gumshoe, undercover change to a republic ... but also for an equally sly, gumshoe, undercover change to Associate States, or to a counterfeit Canada à la Daniel Johnson, in which Quebec would have made itself for most purposes a foreign country ... If so, I can suggest a more appropriate emblem than the maple leaf to put on the trucks, the mail bags, and anything else the Government contemplates defacing: two jackasses eating leaves off one maple tree.

This effusion was greeted on 21 October with a lead editorial in the *Globe*, 'Let the Argument Be Public,' in which it was observed that the leader of the opposition, John Diefenbaker, in the House of Commons the previous day (inspired perhaps by Forsey's letter?) had accused the prime minister's office of 'mounting a silent underground movement to remove the monarchy from Canada.' Following Forsey, the *Globe* recited the 'powerful arguments for retaining the monarchy,' and asserted that 'no one would want to silence the abolitionists,' but if change is sought 'it should be openly advocated rather than stealthily pursued.'

A flurry of letters, in late October, most of them siding with Forsey, appeared in response to the *Globe*'s challenge. Nearly all the writers, and particularly the thoughtful critics, discussed the broad issue of retention of the monarchy. The respondents in the *Ottawa Journal* included more critics, most of these focusing on the displacement of the 'Royal Mail.' The issue of 22 October contained one particularly sour critic who signed 'W.J.K.' and who invited Forsey to 'go back to good old England where he belongs and can see all the royalty he wants.' The closing line, beginning 'It is sickening to listen to these limeys,' not unexpectedly drew an exasperated reply from Forsey on 29 October:

> Mr W.J.K. (who seems as furtive as the people he is supporting) suggests ... that if I do not 'like the removal of "Royal Mail" from the mail trucks,' I should 'catch the next boat or plane back to good old England, where, says Mr K., 'he belongs.'
>
> This would involve a journey that is rather beyond me. I was born in Canada; the most recent of my ancestors to reach this country arrived more than 125 years ago; and the rest of my forebears settled in Nova Scotia and Newfoundland between 1760 and 1783. To go 'back to England,' I should not need a 'boat or plane' but a time-machine.
>
> But, whether or no: what right has any Canadian, new or old, to tell other Canadians who wish to preserve the historic character and constitution of this country that they should go elsewhere? ... By what title does Mr K. undertake to banish everyone who has the misfortune to disagree with him, or even with the government of the day?
>
> Apparently he feels that anyone who objects to any Government action does not 'live and think like a Canadian-born citizen,' and that the only right such people have is to emigrate. The impli-

> cation is that to ask to have public policy settled by Parliament and the people is treasonous.
>
> Is this part of what Mr K. calls 'our Canadian way'?

Proffering a more light-hearted closure to the over-heated debate over symbols and exorcising the surliness of the 'limey' reference, came this anonymous letter to the *Journal*, dated 26 October:

> Guvnor: – Me an' me mates read Mr Forsey's letter about taking the coat of arms off the mail bags. We have been working with mail bags for many years and we share his views, although none of the long-sentence boys in this pen can remember any con named Forsey working on the mail bags. Maybe he was doing an alias when he wrote to the papers.
>
> Anyhow we wish him luck and we took up a collection to help him to get back to dear old Blighty where they have abolished the death penalty and French men are treated like foreigners.
>
> Since we are guests of Her Majesty we cannot join him in return to civilization where bookies and pools are legal and if a bloke cops it he can feel secure that the mail bags in Dartmoor will still have the coat of arms ...
>
> The two-bob (shillings) enclosed is all that is left of the collection. Give it to Mr Forsey if he is still on the outside.
>
> 103790.
>
> *Editors' Note: The two bob arrived safely and has been sent to him via Her Majesty's Mail.*

Undoubtedly, the build-up to the celebration of Canada's centenary in 1967 accounted for the government's efforts to introduce modifications in terms and symbols thought to be more emblematic of a sovereign state, fully emancipated from its colonial past. It was these efforts that Forsey castigated as signs of 'creeping republicanism.' Even with the much-debated adoption of a positive symbol of Canadian nationhood, an official flag, Forsey remained unrepentantly opposed, apparently not so much because it meant the abandonment of the Union Jack, yet another emblem of the monarchical tradition, but for aesthetic reasons. As we have observed with his views on sculpture in public spaces, Forsey did not bow to the views of any man (including 'the so-called intelligentsia') when it came to such matters. Here is his pronouncement on the new flag in the *Ottawa Journal* 13 June 1964:

> The most surprising thing about Mr Pearson's new flag is something that no one seems to have noticed. The Government is firmly committed to 'the basically bicultural character of our country,' yet it proposes a flag which contains not the slightest reference to any culture whatever, even agriculture. (The maple tree grows wild.)
>
> If the country is 'basically bicultural,' then the flag should be 'basically bicultural' too. It should contain something to remind us of 'our mighty heritage,' both French and British. Mr Pearson's flag can remind us of nothing except the sea, east and west, and the earth between. Everything human, every vestige of our history, everything 'distinctively Canadian' except a piece of vegetation, has been carefully excluded.
>
> Voltaire is said to have described Canada as 'some acres of snow.' Mr Pearson's flag may be an adequate symbol of that conception of Canada. But surely the Canada that commands our allegiance is something more: a Canada with a history, French and British; a Canada of countless other peoples; a Canada which is more than the sum of all of these. Finding an adequate symbol for this real, flesh-and-blood Canada is not easy, but at least a Government conscious of its responsibilities might try, instead of being content with a least common denominator.
>
> We have been promised a flag. Are we to be fobbed off with a dish towel from Woolworth's?

In nearly the last of his offerings to the *Ottawa Citizen*, on 3 January 1990, Forsey revealed that his views on the inadequacy of the flag as symbolic reference had hardened with the passing years. Commenting on an exhibition celebrating the twenty-fifth anniversary of the adoption of the flag, Forsey used the occasion to voice one final time his fear of 'creeping republicanism,' this time couched in anti-American terms.

> The Museum of Civilization announces a special exhibition, 'The Maple Leaf Forever,' to 'relive the post-Confederation struggle for independence.' What 'post-Confederation struggle?'
>
> This is a travesty of Canadian history. It goes even beyond what Donald Creighton used to call 'the Authorized, or Grit Version.' ...
>
> This brazen attempt to rewrite our history to make it look more like the United States model may sit well with the Free-Trade Agreement, and with the government's approval of the American invasion of Panama (which provides an object lesson of what membership in the Organization of American States may mean). But it is likely to give viewers a curiously biased impression of what really happened.
>
> The Americans won their freedom by force. Our freedom 'slowly broadened down. From precedent to precedent.' ...
>
> Is the Museum going to provide Sir John A. Macdonald with a cherry tree and a hatchet, and a Saint John Tea Party ...
>
> 'O say can you see?' I can't.

It is not likely that Forsey was won over by the placating explanations of the guest curator, published in the *Citizen* on 10 January, which concluded: '"The Maple Leaf Forever New" does not tamper with Canada's history. It simply outlines a captivating portion of the country's evolution toward maturity.'

Forsey's fears of close encounters with our southern neighbour received their fullest expression in a seminal letter to the *Globe* on 23 December 1963, headed 'Shall We Join the United States?' His letter was triggered by a survey reported in the 13 December issue of the *Globe* in which annexationist sentiment was found to be widespread. Deploring the incompleteness of the survey (and 'random survey' techniques in general), Forsey attributed such annexationist sentiment as there was to two failings which he had been hammering at since the 1940s:

> One is the evident failure of our educational system to teach our

people what kind of a country this is and how it is governed and how radically different it is in both respects from the United States ... The other main cause ... is surely the campaign to persuade us that there is no Canadian nation and, rather oddly, that this Nondescript should have a distinctive flag and anthem, both, presumably, carefully un-national ...

If a large number of Canadians do in fact feel we should join the United States, and if we are not to be governed by mere feeling ... then it is high time our leaders started giving the populace some instructions on the differences between the two countries.

One of the fundamental differences is that the United States is a country of one language and one culture, Canada a country of two languages and two cultures ... If we could all get it firmly into our heads that both the British and the French traditions are basic in the Canadian tradition, and that to remove either is to destroy ourselves, we might at least have some better notion of what we should lose or gain by annexation.

A second fundamental difference is in our systems of government. They are both forms of democracy, but otherwise as different as chalk is from cheese. The Americans have a presidential-congressional democracy, modelled on the early Eighteenth Century British Constitution. It is a proof of their genius that they manage somehow to manoeuvre this political sedan chair through Twentieth Century traffic with astonishing success. We have monarchical-parliamentary responsible government democracy modelled on the late Nineteenth Century British Constitution, and steadily modernized to meet new problems. Joining the United States would be, politically, reactionary, in the proper sense of that word. It would be going back, not, indeed, 'to Methuselah,' but to a system of government which the British peoples outgrew nearly two centuries ago. We should have to adjust ourselves to a whole series of quaint practices, fraught with meaning for Americans, because rooted deep in American history, but a veritable obstacle race to anyone else ...

If these fundmental differences between Canada and the United States seem high-falutin' and academic, there are others, less fundamental, but important, which are not open to that

> reproach. We have family allowances; the Americans have not. We have non-contributory old age pensions; the Americans have not. We have hospital insurance; the Americans have not. We have a national system of unemployment insurance; the Americans have not. We have Workmen's Compensation; the Americans have nothing like it. Perhaps some of the people ... interviewed might not have been so glibly annexationist if they had realized the solid benefits they would lose by union. My old Scots tutor at Oxford used to say that there were two ways of wanting a thing: Really and un-really. If you really want it, you are willing to pay the price; if you are not willing to pay the price, then you only un-really want it. I suspect that a good many Canadians who say they want union with the United States only un-really want it.

One close encounter with the United States, membership in the Organization of American States, was debated over many years and vigorously opposed by Forsey in at least half a dozen letters, but finally consumated by the Canadian government shortly before his death. His campaign began with a letter to the *Globe* on 17 March 1969, in which he wrote: 'I am dismayed by the indications that the Government is seriously considering applying for membership ... I should have thought that by this time it was crystal clear that this would be a prize example of how to win enemies and not influence people.' Again, on 10 February 1976, he exclaimed, 'Why any Canadian with anything better than a cabbage perched on the top of his neck wants us to join the Organization of American States is beyond me ... It is time people stopped trying to give this old bird wooden wings and make it fly again.' When the *Globe and Mail* editorially endorsed membership in the OAS on 2 September 1989, Forsey invoked a memory of his old CCF colleague, M.J. Coldwell, in his rebuttal on 23 September. '[He] told me that he had formerly favored joining the OAS. What cured him was an experience as a delegate to the Economic and Social Council of the United Nations. A Latin American delegate made a proposal Mr Coldwell thought good. He held up his hand to vote for it. The U.S.

delegate frowned fiercely at him and motioned him vigorously to put his hand down.'

Such interference with our capacity to have our own views Forsey always found objectionable, as this 15 May 1982 missive to the *Globe* reveals:

> Re Canada Overspends on Social Services: U.S. Envoy (May 12):
>
> So the American Ambassador thinks we are spending 'too much on social services' and wants us to spend more on defence.
>
> This gentlemen should be firmly told to mind his own business and if he repeats this kind of impudence, the Government of Canada should ask the Government of the United States to take him home and put him on ice.

The period of the Reagan presidency provided ample opportunity for expression of Forsey's anti-American sentiments. On 15 February 1985, for example, this cryptic piece of advice, under the heading, 'And Don't Slurp' was offered the prime minister: 'If Sir John A. Macdonald was alive now, I think he might warn Brian Mulroney that he who sups with an American government must have a long spoon.'

President Reagan's military build-up was greeted with this 30 May 1985 offering to the *Globe*:

> U.S. President Ronald Reagan seems to see the world as a combination of wild-west movie (with himself as sheriff) and science-fiction novel. This would be pathetic, or ludicrous, if he were a private citizen or a moving picture actor. But as he is President of the richest and most powerful nation on earth, it is blood-curdling.
>
> His Star Wars plans, in the opinion of many experts of very differing views on other matters, are an appalling danger to the whole world. In my opinion, we ought not allow ourselves to be sucked into his fantasies, or made accomplices to what may well be an annihilating cosmic folly.

Year's end, 14 December 1985, found Forsey seeking desperate humour in the prospect:

> You wonder why U.S. President Ronald Reagan 'needs to reach to outer space for a compelling reason to get human beings to curb their mutual aggression' (Look Up, Look Way Up – editorial, Dec. 6).
>
> Perhaps he is looking for the UFO vote for his party and his successor. A more charitable interpretation might be that the Great Communicator has become a poet, his 'eye, in a fine frenzy rolling,/ Glances from earth to heaven, from heaven to earth ... and gives to airy nothing/ A local habitation and a name.'

On a decidedly more serious note, Forsey questioned the *Globe*'s editorial 'Striking at Libya' (16 April 1986) where 'the moral rightness' of the U.S. 'resolve' to 'retaliate for terrorist attacks on the lives and property of its citizens' was said to be 'clear.' 'Is it?' asked Forsey, continuing:

> Where does international law come into the question? You yourself call the action 'Sheriff Ronald Reagan' turning 'his six-shooters on the Tripoli Kid.' What international authority made him sheriff, or gave him any authority to take this action? You say that 'because the Europeans have made collective economic sanctions impossible, they have made universal military ones inevitable.' What we have is not universal military sanctions, but the military sanctions of a single nation (with the passive aid of Britain).
>
> Almost half of your editorial says, in effect, that the single U.S. military sanction probably won't work. You note that even Mr Reagan has 'no illusions that the U.S. air raid would bring down the curtain on Libyan terrorism.' ... In short, you virtually admit that the U.S. policy won't work. It won't stop terrorism, it may make it worse ... Even if it did, have you considered the price? What would be left of the world after the policy had wrought its will?

The build-up to the free trade agreement brought added expressions of Forsey's fear of further close encounters. Nine months of negotiation over an agreement on controlling acid rain produced this Forsey warning of worse things to come (*Globe*, 25 January 1986).

> So now we have the report of the special envoys on acid rain ... They recognize that there is a problem. They recognize that it crosses the international boundary.
>
> This is like the lady who told Thomas Carlyle that she 'respected the universe.' Carlyle's comment was: 'Gad! She'd better!'
>
> What else does the report say?
>
> It recommends that the United States spend $2.5 billion over a period of years on finding cheaper technology for reducing poisonous emissions. It recommends that the industries concerned spend the same amount.
>
> Will Ronald Reagan accept the first recommendation? Slim chance. Even if he does, will the Congress, which has just passed a drastic act to eliminate the deficit, pass the necessary legislation? Slimmer chance. Will the industries accept the second recommendation? It's a chance so slim that only an electronic microscope could detect it.
>
> Is this a foretaste of what we may expect from the free trade negotiations?

Another dispute over the exchange rate on the Canadian dollar provided Forsey with added reasons for resisting the free trade option (*Globe and Mail*, 7 June 1986):

> Your editorial The Dollar Plot (May 26) deals faithfully with the ludicrous side of the accusation of U.S. Treasury Secretary James Baker that Canada has adopted a deliberate policy of keeping its dollar down.
>
> But there is a serious side. Can anyone doubt that if we get into free trade with the United States, that country will insist on controlling our monetary policy so that U.S. industries will not be subjected to 'unfair' competition of Canadian firms 'subsidized' by a depreciated Canadian dollar? Can anyone doubt that our interest rates would be completely at the mercy of Mr Baker and his successors?
>
> At present, he can complain that he pipes unto us but we will not dance. Under free trade, we should have no alternative.

In 1911, U.S. President William Howard Taft wrote to former President Theodore Roosevelt that if the Reciprocity Agreement went through, 'Canada will become an adjunct of the United States.'
Is Mr Baker telling us the same thing?

Forsey had this parting shot on the question of trade negotiations with the United States in the *Globe* on 13 January 1987: 'The attitude of the Americans in trade matters as revealed by the "softwood" lumber agreement, reminds me of the attitude of an acquaintance of mine to his dog: "I give him absolute freedom. But I demand total obedience."'

Long Live the Monarchy

Forsey's fear of creeping republicanism was the negative side of his positive belief in the monarchical principle. He remained ever alert to counter-proposals for abolition or even suggestions that the days of monarchy were numbered.

In 1965 (*Globe and Mail*, 13 January), he had this advice for the Ontario University Liberals:

> The Ontario University Liberals are reported to favor 'abolition of the Queen as Canada's sovereign and retention of the Governor General as head of state.'
>
> Nowadays, queer proposals for constitutional change fall 'thick as autumnal leaves in Vallombrosa' but this is the queerest yet. If it were carried out, what would this country be? Not a monarchy, for the head of state would not be a king, queen, emperor or empress. Not a republic, for the head of state would not be a president. Presumably 'governor-generalship,' or, in French, 'gouvernment-general,' the title borne by the Nazi-occupied part of Poland during the last war; hardly, one would have thought, an inspiring example, especially for Liberals.
>
> This weird creation is perhaps intended as a compromise between monarchy and republic. But how long does anyone suppose it would last?

> ... So the 'gouvernment-general' could be no more than the briefest prelude to the republic. That is the destination to which the Ontario University Liberals are urging us.
>
> Why? The only reason I can think of is that they have heard the suggestions now advanced in some quarters that a republic would help solve the problems arising out of French Canada's position in Confederation.
>
> Surely it is time someone asked, 'How?' Would a republic automatically mean more bilingualism in the central administration and public service ... in the courts? Would it automatically mean more top jobs for French Canadians in public administration or private business? Would it automatically mean wider taxing powers, or more revenue, or wider legislative jurisdiction, for Quebec? ... Would it even, automatically, smooth the path to the 'associate state' or outright independence for Quebec?
>
> Until we are given some kind of rational answer to questions like these, why should we even consider giving up a system of constitutional monarchy which most English-speaking Canadians, at any rate, think is serving us as well as any republic could, or better, and to which many of us are deeply attached.

The depth of Forsey's attachment to the monarchy was revealed in 1978, when Prime Minister Trudeau introduced a far-reaching Constitutional Amendment Bill (C-60) that was intended to resuscitate the hardy perennial of Canadian debate, after the abandonment in 1971 of the proposals for constitutional reform enshrined in the Victoria Charter. The *Globe and Mail* turned over its Op Ed. page to Forsey's detailed critique of the bill on 7 July 1978. Amongst the many issues raised, Forsey called attention to the lack of constitutional protection for the monarchy, as contrasted with the safeguards proposed in the aborted Victoria Charter. 'Under Bill C-60, a Government with a majority in the House of Commons could, within two months, make us into a republic,' he declared. He concluded this part of his analysis by asking: 'Should such changes be within the sole power of a House of Commons whose majority had never represented a majority of the popular vote, and had never got a mandate for any such measures?'

Apparently Forsey set out to confirm his reservations about the adequacy of the protections provided for the monarchical principle by commissioning a special study of the question, the results of which he distributed to the provincial premiers. In an editorial, 'Mr Forsey and His Fears of All-Powerful PMs,' the *Globe* on 21 July quoted extensively from the report whose tone, they wrote, 'is one of alarm.' Reflecting Forsey's proclivity for investing an accumulation of the minutest of facts with the most grandiose consequences, the report embellished in the finest technical detail Forsey's already expressed concerns about the monarchy. These were altogether too complex to lend themselves to the usual letter format; the *Globe*'s editorial reference was to a report 'painstakingly analysing the bill clause by clause and often word by word, extracting from often obscure verbiage the underlying implications, tracing the patterns in which it finds these implications linked ... [marshalling] evidence for its view of the sort of Canada to which the bill would lead.'

Interviews with Forsey, reported widely by journalists of several newspapers, conveyed both the main point of Forsey's attack but also the typically colourful language with which he dressed his opposition. The *Ottawa Citizen* of 24 July reported Forsey as describing the draft proposals for constitutional reform as a 'nightmare'; a 'weird concoction.' 'If it goes through it will be a licence to print money for the lawyers.' The *Ottawa Journal*'s account on 27 July was headed: 'Constitution bill "a dog's breakfast": Forsey predicts public row if monarchy is "phased out."'

'I'll filibuster it as long as possible. Even if I stand alone in the Senate I'll fight it ... at every step if the government brings it before us in its present form.'

The particular proposal that induced this Horatio-at-the-bridge rhetoric was clause 42, creating a governor general 'who *shall*, not *may*, exercise the functions of the Queen. And since the one function left to the Queen is that of appointing Governors-General, that means that a Governor-General is appointed by the Governor-General before him, on the instructions of the Government of the day.' Further interpretation of the bill produced the

6 June 1979. Reprinted with permission from the *Globe and Mail*

conclusion that 'there would not seem to be any impediment ... to a Prime Minister securing his own appointment as Governor-General.' In short, the Queen was 'reduced to an empty symbol, having no factual or legal role in the governance of Canada.'

In his strident attack on certain parts of the constitutional amendment bill, Forsey was prepared to attribute the defects to bad drafting, doubting that 'Prime Minister Trudeau really wants to convert Canada into a republic.' There were others, during this same debate, who seemed to feel that the days of monarchy were numbered, and to these, Forsey had this to say in the *Globe* on 9 September 1978:

> Geoffrey Stevens says the disappearance of the monarchy is 'inevitable' (Aug. 31). René Lévesque says the independence of Quebec

is 'inevitable.' Marx and his followers say the revolution is 'inevitable.' Those who oppose these several prophets no doubt should give up the fight and slink away abashed. But, as Cromwell said to some predestinationists of his day, 'I beseech you, think it possible that you may be mistaken.'

Marcel Pépin says (Aug. 30) that in 1964, when 'several "experts" maintained that Canada was ready to lay to rest the Union Jack,' Lester Pearson 'overrode those fears.' It was the House of Commons, not Mr Pearson, which did the 'overriding.'

Mr Pépin's contempt for democracy leaps to the eye in the next sentence: 'Some day, one of his (Pearson's) successors will certainly have to exhibit the same courage to force this country to become adult.' So, if Mr Pépin has his way, we shall some day have a Prime Minister forcing us to abolish the monarchy whether we will or no. No mention of Parliament, no mention of the will of the people; one individual will do it all, regardless ...

Both Mr Stevens and Mr Pépin had better make up their minds to the fact that 'Ere the Queen's crown goes down, There are crowns to be broke,' minds to be convinced, Parliament, still the Queen's Parliament, still the people's Parliament, to be reckoned with.[3]

In the event, the final constitutional package that comprised the patriated Canada Constitution Act, 1982, to Forsey's satisfaction, asserted the monarchical principle and encircled it with stringent amending procedural protections, thereby confirming his belief in the monarchical principle which he had extolled in doggerel verse in the *Ottawa Journal* on 5 January 1966:

Because our monarch is not resident,
Some people want to have a president.
They feel we should be much more up-to-date
If we were to elect our Head of State.
Republic's what they want; perhaps banana,
Perhaps akin to Kenya or to Ghana?
Perhaps South Africa would be the model?
It's really hard to know what's in their noddle.

An adaptation of the scheme Iraqi
Might seem to some of them a trifle wacky.
Perhaps to fit our country's dual souls,
What we need's two republics, both de Gaulle's?

... Again, there is, iwis,
The ancient federation of the Swiss.
And if we can't have something gay from Bali,
Perhaps we could adopt the ways of Mali?
They've a republic down in Mexico,
I think expropriated Texaco:
A model for us, against the Yanks,
If branch plants here indulge in any pranks?
Perhaps the thing we're looking for may lurk
Among the followers of Ataturk?
The possibilities are infinite.
Enough to cause the strongest head to split.
The simple citizen with hollow groan,
Says 'Why can't they leave well enough alone?'

CHAPTER TWELVE

Keeping the Faith

'In every generation Canadians have had to rework the miracle of their political existence. Canada has been created because there has existed within the hearts of its people a determination to build for themselves an enduring home. Canada is a supreme act of faith.'

These are the moving and luminous reflections of the great Canadian historian, Arthur Lower.[1] Eugene Forsey, through his personal life and published works, must surely qualify as one of the most distinguished and dedicated tenders of the flame of that faith.

Keeping the faith, constantly 'reworking the miracle,' involved Forsey in a perpetual series of constitutional crises. In Canada, it may be said that such crises come in two forms. The first type derives from the difficulties of having to operate within a constitution that, though essentially written, is driven by a parliamentary–cabinet system of government inherited from Britain. That system relies on custom, practice, and precedent, as much as the words written in the formal constitution, to determine the relationships between the various instruments of government. Forsey's command of history, phenomenal memory, and emphasis on 'the facts,' ideally fitted him to be a formidable exponent of the constitutional proprieties surrounding the operation of governments in Canada. Through his letters to the press, perhaps best revealed in the selection brought together under the theme 'The Governor General and the Reserve

Power,' Forsey never hesitated to bring the ill-informed and the biased to account before his stern court of judgment. No one was immune from the caustic pen. Governors general, prime ministers, civil servants, editors, journalists, lay readers, and academic colleagues with the highest credentials – all were equally subjected to his acerbic admonishments, his instructive history lessons, or his crushing factual corrections.

The second type of constitutional crisis relates essentially to the maintenance and preservation of the state itself. Such crises, of course, invoke the legal/factual, custom/convention concerns which surface with the first category and which are especially suited to Forsey's mode of thought and analytical approach. However, the second category of crisis challenges the very social fabric of a country and evokes issues that are driven more by emotion and subjective judgments. Thus, for example, the technical problem of how one amends the constitution becomes entangled in emotive questions, such as what constitutes a 'nation,' whether, in the case of Canada, there are 'two nations,' how the legal concept of sovereignty may be affected by such sociological issues, and how it is to be applied in a federally organized state whose constituent provinces operate within constitutionally determined boundaries laid down much more than a century ago.

Many of the letters in the preceding sections show that Forsey was deeply engaged in both types of constitutional crisis. However, Forsey's logical, fact-driven approach was clearly more appropriate for addressing the 'objective' technical constitutional issues rather than the issues which went to the roots of Canada's existence. The latter, particularly as revealed by the letters in the section on Quebec, carry a heavy baggage of terms which are less open to a resolution of the debate by a mere invoking of the facts, as such facts bear on history, attitudes and, above all, on accelerated rates of change that profoundly alter the power balances between Canada and its provincial components or, indeed, between both and the changing face of international forces.

How will we remember Forsey's responses to all these forces through his letters to the press? Will it be as a twentieth-century

King Canute: a lone figure relying doggedly on due process and what he liked to call, in deference to Arthur Meighen, 'the commonplace quality of common sense' to settle differences and preserve the established order in seemly fashion?

Whatever the verdict – and it is likely to gyrate widely around a person with such aggressive views on such an eclectic range of interests – surely no one could dispute the impact of Forsey's letters to the press. They reveal him as the civic censor, the proverbial social gadfly, as concerned with preserving the aesthetic integrity of public spaces as he is with maintaining the accuracy and purity of the language with which civil discourse is conducted.

On the broader community plane, where constitutional crises touch on both technical and state-preserving issues, Forsey's letters have surely acquired a status as virtually legendary components of the public discourse. They assert and reassert, usually by way of correction, the faith that inspired the Founding Fathers. He is revealed in his letters as schoolmaster to the nation, instructing us on the niceties of proper practices in operating a complex federal system by means of parliamentary–cabinet government, housed under the 'monarchical principle.' Above all, at the end as at the beginning of his life, he is revealed as the indefatigable defender of the kind of Canada which he believed to have been willed into existence by its founders but of whose continued existence he had come to despair.

The forces he conceived to be eroding 'his' Canada are summarized in his two satirical versions of Canada's national anthem. The first version, voiced (sung?) as part of a speech at the University of Western Ontario and reproduced in the *Ottawa Journal* on 26 October 1966, was obviously aimed at the mounting separatist threat to Canada's existence.

O Canada! We don't know what you are.
Nation, we thought, but that Quebec doth bar.
And a colony you have ceased to be,
So we know what you are not;
And we stand on guard,

Though it's rather hard,
When we're not quite sure for what;
Oh Canada! Great Undefined!
O Canada! Can't you make up your mind?
O Canada! Can't you some status find?

The second version appeared in the *Globe and Mail* on 10 February 1977, as dramatic conclusion to his opposition to proposals for regional decentralization.

> The article, Cost of Decentralizing Canada Could Be High (Jan. 29), by Arthur Donner and Fred Lazar raises a number of questions.
>
> How could regional equalization goals be 'administered regionally,' in this hypothetical twentieth-century North American version of the Holy Roman Empire?
>
> We have at present a single Canadian trade area and monetary union. Have the authors made any estimate of the sheer dislocation costs of breaking this into 10 separate tariff units and 10 separate monetary units?
>
> How could the poorer provinces, deprived of the equalization grants and other Dominion funds they now receive, maintain anything like their present standards of public services, education, and social security? Handing over tax powers to the rich provinces, which have plenty of tax, is one thing. Handing over the same powers to the poor provinces is very different.
>
> The authors say the 'central government would still have to act as a referee to prevent regional competition in such things as tariffs, exchange rates, and monetary policies from having an aggregate negative effect on the Canadian economy.'
>
> How precisely? The Bank of Canada, it is clear, would become a sort of miniature Bank of International Settlements. But how would the (gossamer) 'central government' act as a 'referee' on the provincial tariffs? And how much 'Canadian economy' would be left to suffer any 'aggregative effect,' negative or positive? Why bother to retain a cobweb, which would be of little use to the rich mini-nations, and probably none to the poor ones?

How many would leap to their feet to sing:
O Canada! Beloved Referee!
Of customs dues and banking policy!
With glowing hearts we've seen arise
Ten Norths, nor strong nor free,
But we'll stand on guard, O Canada,
To keep our Referee!
O Canada! Pale, shadowy!
O Canada! Be still our Referee!
O Canada! Long live our Referee!

But of course the Referee could still have a distinctive flag, which would surely stir the blood of every citizen of the 10 mini-states: 10 jackasses eating their leaves off a single maple tree.

Forsey was to repeat this attack, in early 1980, when Claude Ryan, on behalf of the Quebec Liberal party, issued a report proposing a radically decentralized Canada. Inveighing against this 'ten-headed monstrosity,' Forsey's reaction appeared in his letter to the *Globe* on 24 January 1980:

> Reed Scowen, Liberal member of the Quebec Legislative Assembly, in an ecstatic article on the Ryan Report ... has stripped the veil from its proposals.
>
> It is, he says, 'asking all Canadians ... to understand that each of us should henceforth see ourselves as members of two sovereign nations, our own province and Canada, united in one state.'
>
> So we must forswear the single Canadian nation and replace it with a 10-headed monstrosity, a miniature United Nations, in which the 10 provincial 'nations' will have 'the primary responsibility for re-defining what they want the central government to do in future, what powers it is to have.'
>
> The eleventh, puppet, government, on which Mr Scowen would confer the ludicrous title of 'Canadian nation,' might, moreover, be only a (far from) 'lovely apparition sent, To a moment's ornament.' For, says Mr Scowen, 'Quebec' (and hence every other provincial 'nation') 'would have the right to leave the federation if it wishes.' This last does not, I think, appear in the

report itself. If Mr Scowen is correct in thinking it is implied, then Quebec (and Ontario) would hold a sword of Damocles over the whole country, and could at any moment bring the paralytic 'new federation' to an abrupt end.

But even if the Ryan proposals do not imply a right of secession, why should any Canadian be expected to give up a real country, capable of doing real things for real people, and accept in its stead this thing of shreds and patches, this wretched tatterdemalion remnant of the nation which Cartier and Macdonald, Langevin and Brown, Chapais and Tupper, Taché and Tilley, Galt and McGee created, and which Laurier, Lapointe and St Laurent helped bring to maturity and power? Why should we sell our splendid birthright for this mess of potage?

Forsey's final defence of the Canada he loved, though written just a few days before he died, carries the same dogged faith he had always expressed in preserving a Canada that was something more than a sum of its parts. Once again, the occasion was provided by yet another report from the Quebec Liberal party, the so-called Allaire Report, prepared as a contribution to the debate surrounding the Meech Lake Accord. The posthumous publication of these final words from Forsey, appearing in both the Sunday issues of the *Calgary Herald* and the *Toronto Star* on 24 February 1991, was introduced by the *Star*: 'Before he died last Wednesday at age 86, an ailing Eugene Forsey – considered Canada's foremost constitutional expert – was asked by friends to help convince Canadians that Quebec sovereignty meant partition and fatal weakness for Canada. Under the defiant title No Surrender, the retired senator assailed the premises of the Quebec Liberal party's Allaire report. He finished the essay Feb. 7, explaining in a letter that "it seems to be all I can do: because of health problems."' On a subject with which his letters were deeply engaged for so many years, we may surely allow Forsey the luxury of some repetition in this 'last will and testimony' to his faith as Canada's keeper.

The report of the Quebec Liberal party's constitutional committee is the latest, and most explicit, version of 'sovereignty-association.' It is presented as our 'last chance' of keeping Quebec within the boundaries of Canada; as the 'knife at our throats' which alone will extort from us concessions that will prevent separation. [Forsey was referring to Professor Leon Dion's challenging remark in testimony, as Quebec's constitutional adviser, to the Belanger-Campeau commission on Quebec's constitutional future, testimony he had challenged in a letter to the *Vancouver Sun*, 25 January 1991.]

Of course it sets out how Quebec will be governed. But with brazen insolence it also sets out how the rest of us, the nine provinces, will be governed.

First and foremost, there will be a new 'Quebec-Canada structure' (note the name; note which comes first), 'to establish a new political Constitution,' with one clause giving every member (which presumably means every province) the right to secede, and another giving Quebec a veto on all amendments.

The central government of 'Quebec-Canada' would have power over 'defence and security of territory, customs and excise, the management of the public debt, and currency equalization' (whatever that means) ...

The new 'central state' would have a new court, 'to ensure respect for the new Constitution' and 'the application of the laws of the central state.' It would also have a 'common Parliament,' elected by universal suffrage, 'from sea to sea.' The Senate would be abolished.

What powers would the 'common Parliament' have?

First, what would it not have?

Within Quebec, very few. The 'National Assembly' would have total power over unemployment insurance, hospital insurance, medicare, agriculture, regional development, energy, the environment, language, research and development, public security, and 'revenue security.' Certain powers it would share with the 'common Parliament,' aboriginal affairs, revenue and taxation, immigration, financial institutions, justice, fisheries, foreign policy, the post office, and telecommunications, 'according to each jurisdiction.' 'Overlapping jurisdictions' would be 'eliminated.' Any power not specifically mentioned in the new Constitution would belong to Quebec. The Canadian Charter of Rights and Freedoms would cease to apply in Quebec.

Over the nine provinces, the 'common Parliament' would presumably have the same powers the present parliament has. ...

The present provisions for amending the Constitution would of course have to be rewritten, because every one of them involves the Senate, which would no longer exist. (This, incidentally, disposes neatly of the whole problem of Senate reform.)

This means, among other things, a separate Quebec post office. It means that the Indians and Inuit of northern Quebec and the English-speaking minority could be at the mercy of the National Assembly. So might the banks. It means the National Assembly could restore those provisions of Bill 101 which the Supreme Court has ruled beyond its power. It means Quebec could take over an unspecified part of the field of criminal law. (The Padlock Act was thrown out by the Supreme Court of Canada because it invaded the exclusive federal power over the criminal law.)

Of course it could mean also that Quebec could get no more Canadian money for regional development, or research and development, and that if it ran into another Oka, or anything else the Quebec government considered subversive of public order, it could not call upon the Canadian army. The Quebec Provincial Police would have to handle the problem unaided.

But there could be a catch in this.

The Parliament of Canada could always say that it was for the 'peace, order and good government of Canada' that it give Quebec free gifts of money, or offer it the Canadian army to 'restore order.' After all, collapse of an important Quebec industry could have serious repercussion for one or more of the nine provinces. So could a collapse of public order in Quebec.

But would Parliament provide the money or the troops?

It very well might. The 75 Quebec members might, very probably would, hold the balance of power. They could well be in a position to throw out any government that said 'No.'

For the 'common Parliament' would not be the Parliament of

the nine provinces, elected by the people of the nine provinces, to manage the affairs of the nine provinces.

For most purposes, it would have no power over Quebec; Quebec would be out. But for the affairs of the nine provinces, Quebec would very definitely be in. Not only would the 75 Quebec members usually be able to throw out any government they didn't like, but in the vast mass of legislation which applied only to the nine provinces, the 75 Quebec members could have a decisive voice. The nine provinces would be in a neo-colonial situation, with Quebec as the Imperial Power.

There is no mention of the Supreme Court of Canada. Presumably it would still exist.

Would its jurisdiction still extend to Quebec, for whatever powers the 'common Parliament' still possessed over Quebec? Would Quebec still be guaranteed three of its nine judges?

The Quebec Liberal party's constitutional committee's proposals have an extra wrinkle: a customs and monetary union between Quebec and Canada.

Who'd decide whether tariffs went up or down? No answer. Who'd decide whether monetary policy should be restrictive or expansionary, tight or loose? No answer except that the central bank must be reformed to assure regional representation while ensuring its independence from political pressure.

These are the terms of the proposals for an 'agreement' between Quebec and Canada.

If they are not accepted, then Quebec must become an independent state, with 'an economic union with Canada, managed by institutions of a confederal nature.' 'Confederal' meaning what?

Conceivably, one of the two partners would have a majority on the Joint Boards.

It is hardly likely to be Quebec; if it's Canada, it blows an ozone hole through Quebec's independence. If the two partners have equal representation, then each has a veto, which blows a hole through both Quebec's independence and Canada's.

The truth is that sovereignty-association in any form is a horse that can't run.

If Quebec insists on becoming a foreign country, we can negotiate that. It will not be easy. It will not be pleasant. It will impoverish us all, spiritually as well as materially. It will be a tragedy. But it can be done.

But there is no way to negotiate dry water, boiling ice, sour sugar or stationary motion.

Some people think that we should be willing to swallow any kind of nonsense in order to 'preserve the unity of Canada.'

I am not interested in a Canada that would just be a splash on the map, with a six-letter word scrawled across it.

The only Canada I want to preserve is a Canada that can do something; for its own people, for the hungry two-thirds of the world, for the survival of the planet; not a phantom that can only watch helplessly as we all tumble down a steep place to destruction.

Ottawa Citizen, 24 February 1991 (Reprinted with permission from Fred Sebastian)

Notes

1: Forsey's Letters to the Editor

1 In the foreword to Jack Kapica, *Shocked and Appalled: A Hundred Years of Letters to the Globe and Mail* (Toronto: Lester and Orpen Dennys, 1985), ix.

2 Royal Commission on Newspapers (Kent Commission), *Report* (Canada: Minister of Supply and Services, 1981), 287; 245–6.

3 Letter to author, 10 June 1997; quoted with permission.

4 Letter to author, 28 June 1996; quoted with permission.

5 Letter and enclosures to author, 27 February 1997; quoted with permission.

6 Ibid. See also *Saturday Night*, June 1996: John Lorinc, 'He's in the Mail,' describes Stewart introducing himself to Andrew Coyne, who acknowledged his presence with: 'Oh, you get published more than I do.'

7 Eugene Forsey, *A Life on the Fringe: The Memoirs of Eugene Forsey* (Toronto: Oxford University Press, 1990), 66–7.

8 Dr Frank MacKinnon has shared with me a treasure trove of Forsey memorabilia, replete with t-shirt bearing Forsey's portrait, a retirement gift from 'grateful' students, and an obvious reference to reliance on Forsey's constitutional expertise for course work. Letter from 'Victorian' is quoted in *The First Cuckoo: A Selection of the Most Witty, Amusing and Memorable Letters to* The Times, *1900–1980*, 2nd ed. (London: Allen & Unwin, 1980), 27.

9 I am indebted to Helen Forsey for bringing this material to my attention. In the course of preparing a biography of her father she has shared many items pertinent to this study but falling outside the letter-to-the-editor files. The Macaulay quotation is located in the National Archives of Canada, Manuscript Division, (the papers of) Eugene Alfred Forsey, MG 30, A 25 (henceforth Forsey Papers), vol. 47, file 26.

10 Ibid., vol. 45.

11 Canada, *Debates of the Senate*, 28 January 1971, 437–9.

12 Royal Commission on Newspapers (Kent Commission), *Report*, 287; Kapica, *Shocked and Appalled*; Richard V. Ericson, Patricia M. Baranik, and Janet B.L. Chan, *Negotiating Control: A Study of News Sources* (Toronto: University of Toronto Press, 1989), especially chapter 6; Institute of Law Research and Reform, *Defamation: Fair Comment and Letters to the Editor*, Report No. 35 (Edmonton: University of Alberta, 1979).

13 Kapica, *Shocked and Appalled*, xi.

14 Ericson, et al., *Negotiating Control*, 338ff.

15 Forsey, *A Life on the Fringe*, 15: 'Grandfather Forsey gave me a bicycle in the fall of 1912 and I can still remember its number: 417263. It accompanied me to Oxford in 1926.'

16 Eugene Forsey, *Freedom and Order: Collected Essays*, with an introduction by Donald Creighton, Carleton Library 73 (Toronto: McClelland and Stewart, 1974), 17–18. The Introduction is a splendid capsulated biography of Forsey.

17 Letter to author from Donn Downey, 20 June 1996.

18 Letter from Brian Eglington to author, 1 January 1996; quoted with permission.

19 Quoted by courtesy of Helen Forsey, from her own binder of Meighen–Forsey correspondence.

20 Forsey, *A Life on the Fringe*, 61–2. See also Forsey's letter to the *Toronto Star*, 21 October 1962, on ghost writing: 'Ghost writing, in my opinion, is simply dishonest. It is the very opposite of the quality of mercy: it is twice cursed; it curseth him that gives and him that takes. Any man that cannot write his own articles or make his own speeches should go home, go to bed, pull the covers over his head, and stay there until he is ready to get up and do his own work.'

21 Forsey, *A Life on the Fringe*, 106.

22 Murray Donnelly, *Dafoe of the Free Press* (Toronto: Macmillan, 1968), 27. After a careful review of the Forsey-Dafoe engagement, Donnelly concluded: 'A war of words which he [Dafoe] could not hope to win but would never admit he had lost was not so much his Liberal partisanship but his antagonism to the Governor General as a symbol of colonialism and empire' (196–8).

23 Forsey Papers, vol. 9, file 1952–9.

24 David Hayes, *Power and Influence: The Globe and Mail and the News Revolution* (Toronto: Key Porter Books, 1992), 77. Senator Doyle confirmed his decision to drop the 'Ed. Note' in a letter to author, 10 June 1997.

25 Kapica, *Shocked and Appalled*, xi.

26 Ericson, et al., *Negotiating Control*, 344–5. Although the anonymity of the

'national' newspaper surveyed is preserved, I am reliably informed by one of those surveyed that the *Globe and Mail* was the object of this comprehensive analysis of selection practices and procedures.

27 Forsey Papers, vol. 9, file 1963–4, letters of 15 May, 9 June 1964.

28 Ibid., vol. 9, file 1952–9, 7 April 1959.

29 Ibid., 9 December 1957

30 Ibid., files 1967 and 1968.

31 Ibid., file 1942–51, 4 February 1948.

32 Ibid., vol. 54, file 1977–8, 8 April 1978.

33 Ibid., vol. 55, file 55–3, 1986–7, 12 January 1987.

34 Ibid., vol. 9, file 1942–51, 19 July 1948.

35 Ibid., vol. 9, file 1952–9, 3 April 1959.

36 Ibid., vol. 55, file 55–2, 1984–5; letter 3 April 1985, quoted with permission.

37 Ibid., vol. 59, file 49–11, 'Invitations'; letter from Grace to Forsey, 13 November 1978, quoted with permission.

38 Ibid., Kalbfleisch to Forsey, 31 May 1979; quoted with permission.

39 I am grateful to Graham Eglington for this vignette of Forsey's letter-writing practices. He was Forsey's right-hand legal adviser to the Joint Committee on Statutory Instruments, of which Forsey was co-chairman. Letter to author, 1 January 1996; quoted with permission.

40 Professor Paul Fox, who was associated with Forsey at Carleton University in the late 1940s, paints a wonderfully vivid picture of the verbal battle that occurred at the 'contradictory meeting' during which Forsey was nominated as candidate for the CCF party. Forsey's nominator denounced Drew as the premier who had tried to debauch the youth of the country by introducing cocktail bars into Ontario. Forsey added to Mr Drew's rising blood pressure and came close to precipitating a more physical rebuff by repeating the denunciation and assuring the audience that he 'had been temperance for four generations.' Letter to author, 18 October 1995; quoted with permission.

41 Forsey to Douglas Fisher, 1 April 1979; quoted with permission. Donald Creighton also quoted Forsey as saying that 'he lacked the "staying power" needed to complete a large ... work.' See Creighton's introduction to *Freedom and Order*, 10.

42 Canada, *Debates of the Senate*, 1971, 441.

43 My thanks to Jeffrey Simpson of the *Globe and Mail* who first called my attention to the extensive private correspondence with which Forsey was wont to pepper his journalist opponents after a preliminary public critique.

44 Forsey Papers, vol. 9, file 1963–4.

45 Professor Dawson's precautionary strategy with reference to anticipated

Forsey criticism was conveyed long ago to the author in Dawson's customary stentorian voice at a time when author was trying to fill Dawson's tattered gown as his temporary stand-in lecturer at the University of Toronto. Its formal confirmation by the late Professor Norman Ward is to be found in the sixth edition of Dawson's textbook, *The Government of Canada* (Toronto: University of Toronto Press, 1987).

46 Forsey Papers, vol. 55, file 55–2, 1984–5, quoted with permission.

47 Ibid., vol. 9, file 1963–4, Fournier to Forsey, 7 October 1964.

48 Ibid., exchange of letters 20 and 24 September 1955, quoted with permission.

49 Ibid., vol. 5. Hutchison letter, quoted with permission. The reference to the 'Chisholm letter' was to Brigadier Brock Chisholm, then director of Canadian Army Medical Services and Toronto's first practising psychiatrist, who had gained instant notoriety with his declamations about the harm wrought to the youth of the country by perpetuating the myth of Santa Claus.

50 Ibid.; George Drew letter cited with permission of Edward Drew, executor for George Drew Papers in National Archives.

51 Ibid., vol. 9, file 1965. The exchange with Roland Bird begins 16 July; Bird's first reply, 23 July; to which Forsey replied 30 July; occasioning Bird's final retort on 27 August.

52 Ibid., Ohearn to Forsey, 19 September 1965. Although unable to trace Mr Ohearn for permission to use his letter, it was reliably reported that he fought a life-long battle to preserve this spelling of his name as opposed to the O'Hearn designation which appeared in the files.

53 Ibid., vol. 55, file 55–3, 1986–7, 25 January 1987.

2: A Census of Forsey Letters

1 Letter to author, 10 June 1997; quoted with permission.

2 Forsey Papers, vol. 39–12, file 1923, 1943, 1949.

3 See 'Pecuniary Degrees,' *Canadian Forum*, September 1936, 15–16. (Author anonymous, but Helen Forsey confirms her father as author.) Also 'A Rose by Any Other Name,' in ibid., 20 September 1937. In *A Life on the Fringe* (61–2), Forsey describes his unmasking of his chief pseudononomous opponent in the *Montreal Gazette*. The fact that he was the chief adviser to the president of the CPR, Sir Edward Beattie, and the latter was chairman of the board of McGill University, did not faze Forsey, but it does help to explain why he was in constant hot water as lecturer and why he was finally ousted.

4 See 'Unemployment and Relief,' *Canadian Forum*, July 1939, 106.

5 Forsey, *A Life on the Fringe*, 61.

6 Forsey's experiences at McGill, as recorded in the letters cited here, are supplied courtesy of McGill University Archives, RG 2 Records of the Principal and Chancellor's Office, container 42, file #00301, Communism and socialism. Professors Forsey, Gordon and Scott and the Canadian Commonwealth Federation, 1918–1933.

7 National Archives of Canada, Cahan Papers, MG 2, III, B1, vol. 2, Cahan to Sir Edward Beattie, 11 March 1941. I am indebted to Gregory P. Marchildon for bringing this illuminating letter to my attention. He turned up this letter in the course of research for his book, *Profits and Politics: Beaverbrook and the Golden Age of Canadian Finance* (Toronto: University of Toronto Press, 1996). Forsey describes Cahan affectionately in his memoirs (p. 126) as one who, even though eschewing the label 'Progressive Conservative,' was really a 'Red Tory'; Forsey does not indicate that he knew of Cahan's generous intervention on his behalf nor of the part Cahan played in bringing Forsey and his widowed mother back from Mexico to his maternal grandfather's home in Ottawa after his father's death. As revealed in his letter to Beattie, Cahan as chief executive of the Mexican Heat and Power Company had employed Forsey's father, befriended the family, and kept a close watch on Forsey's career.

8 Forsey, *A Life on the Fringe*, 136. Recalling this episode, Forsey wrote: 'I had had a brief moment of thrilling anticipation of being called to the bar of the House to withdraw what I had written, or face imprisonment in the Carleton County jail ... The Speaker's change of heart ... robbed me of my one possible moment of glory' (p. 136).

9 During March and April 1963, the *Hamilton Spectator* carried five long articles which also appeared, under somewhat different captions, in the *Ottawa Journal*. Their subject matter is revealed in such titles as: 'A Minority Can Govern'; 'Reserve Power of the Crown'; 'What Happens When a Prime Minister Resigns.'

10 In his memoirs, Forsey recalls the events that led to his break with the newly minted NDP. See *A Life on the Fringe*, 205–7.

11 Ibid., 207.

12 Letter to author from Christopher Young, 4 September 1996. A similar experience was reported by Senator Lowell Murray in his tribute to Forsey at the time of his death: 'The last time I referred to Eugene Forsey as "Senator" Forsey in his presence, he immediately corrected me. He said, "I am no longer a senator. You do not call retired senators in this country senators. That is an Americanism."' Canada, *Debates of the Senate*, 1991, 5344.

3: En Garde! For the English Language

1 In granting permission (letter of 29 October 1998) to use his letter, Professor Oppenheimer enclosed a review by Frederic Raphael in the *Times Literary Supplement* of 16 October 1998 of several updated dictionaries. The title of the review 'Equaller, hopefully,' indicates that the battle of words is endless. Writes Raphael: 'Both the self-vaunting and the editorial policy of *The New Oxford Dictionary of English* ... [and] Collins's "Millennium edition" ... take the same low road. "Usage" is, in both cases, determined by the voters' habits and not decreed by their betters' (p. 7).
2 Unable to trace in order to seek permission.
3 Letter to author, 28 June 1996.

4: Moral Arbiter and Civic Censor

1 Forsey was wont to entertain his family with such offerings. I am indebted to Helen Forsey for the Puffers v Pushers ode, which she calculates was written circa 1958.
2 Attributed to Christopher Young by fellow journalist Tim Creery in one of several helpful letters to the author, this one dated 19 April 1996.
3 Canada, *Debates of the Senate*, 22 March 1972, 1210.
4 Quoted with permission.
5 Forsey Papers, vol. 39, file 15, 1970–3, and file 16, 1974. Letter from Forsey to Arthur, 5 January 1974.
6 Permission to quote granted by Professor Meisel.
7 Canada, *Debates of the Senate*, 1978, 322–3.

5: 'You've Got Me Wrong!'

1 I have been unable to trace Mr J.O. Wyse in order to secure permission to publish his vigorous exchange with Forsey.

6: The Governor General and the Reserve Power

1 Professor MacGregor Dawson's review of Forsey's thesis appeared in the *Canadian Journal of Political Science* 10 (1944), 88–93 and was highlighted by his prophetic closing observation: 'To argue with Professor Forsey's position in a book so loaded with debatable material is inevitable. ... The most encouraging feature about Mr Forsey's venture has been the controversies which the book has raised throughout the Dominion. Dr Forsey has ...

accomplished what everyone else thought to be impossible: he has made a constitutional issue ... a subject of intense popular interest' (p. 93).

2 Dr Frank MacKinnon shared this recollection with the author in letter dated 15 June 1995; quoted with permission.

3 Again, I am grateful to Dr MacKinnon for making this paper available to me – only one of several offerings from his own Forseyana collection.

7: The Senate

1 I am grateful to Profesor C.E.S. Franks, an authority on the Parliament of Canada, for bringing this particular change to my attention. I am also indebted to him for his observations on the capacity of Parliament to make rule changes, independent of fundamental constitutional reforms but nevertheless having significant impact on the workings of our two legislative chambers and the relations between them.

2 Again, I am indebted to Dr MacKinnon for sharing this unpublished paper conveying Forsey's late views on Senate reform; he also provided the correspondence between Forsey and Mr Dennis Anderson concerning the Triple-E Senate proposals. My final query concerning Forsey's view of the Senate's 'checking' role standing as a surrogate for the 'Loyal Opposition' in the Commons is prompted by Professor Franks's assessment of the performance of the Senate since the mid-1980s. See C.E.S. Franks, 'Not Dead Yet, But Should It Be Resurrected,' in *Senate: Bicameralism in the Contemporary World*, ed. Samuel C. Patterson and Anthony Mughan (Columbus: Ohio State University Press, 1999), 120–61.

8: The Judiciary and the Rule of Law

1 For an accessible account of the role of the judiciary, see Peter H. Russell, *The Judiciary in Canada: The Third Branch of Government* (Toronto: McGraw-Hill Ryerson, 1987).

2 Bora Laskin in a speech in March 1981, quoted in Robert Sheppard and Michael Valpy, *The National Deal: The Fight for a Canadian Constitution* (Toronto: Fleet Books, 1982), 336. On the other hand, Laskin was also reported as claiming that 'We [the Supreme Court] are the umpire of the Canadian constitutional system,' thereby invoking a metaphor Forsey found objectionable.

3 An insider account of the events surrounding the patriation of the constitution, as seen from the perspective of the provinces, is to be found in Roy Romanow, John Whyte, Howard Leeson, *Canada ... Notwithstanding: The*

Making of the Constitution, 1976–1982 (Toronto: Carswell/Methuen, 1984). Another useful account by two journalists who covered these events is to be found in Sheppard and Valpy, *The National Deal.*

4 Forsey Papers, vol. 9, Forsey to B.K.Sandwell, 20 October 1950. See also Wilfrid Eggleston, 'Second Look at Labor Court,' *Saturday Night*, 24 October 1950.

9: Quebec

1 It is difficult to select from the seemingly endless reports and books dealing with Quebec's struggle to establish a special place for itself within the federated family. An invaluable starting point is the bibliography appended to the chapter on French Canada which has become a standard reference in successive editions of Paul W. Fox's splendid assemblage of readings entitled *Politics Canada* (Toronto: McGraw-Hill Ryerson).

2 It is to the sharp eyes of Professor Peter Russell I owe the discovery of this sighting of a rare Forsey error. Observed more in sadness than glee, Professor Russell notes (letter, 1 February 1999): 'Somehow he got section 32 mixed up with section 43. Section 41 (c) which he quotes says "subject to section 43 ..." The next paragraph should begin "but section 43 says that an amendment ..." So I am now absolutely sure he meant section 43 when he referred to section 32.'

3 Forsey's own appraisal is offered in his *A Life on the Fringe*, chapter 11. Quebec Nationalism. The chapter opens with this prophetic comment: 'This subject has taken a disproportionate amount of my time and energy for most of the last thirty years' (p.202).

10: Forsey's Last Stand: The Meech Lake Accord and Its Aftermath, 1987–1991

1 A useful context-setting account by a participant in the negotiations leading to the Meech Lake accord is Patrick J. Monahan, *The Inside Story* (Toronto: University of Toronto Press, 1991). A capsule account of the events leading to the accord is found in R.L.Watts, Peter Russell, Richard Simon, et al., *Meech Lake: Setting the Record Straight* (Sponsored by Canadians for a Unifying Constitution, with the cooperation of the Friends of Meech Lake, 1990). Carrying the assessment beyond the aborted Charlottetown Agreement is Roger Gibbins, 'Constitutional Turmoil and Frustration: From Trudeau to Mulroney,"' chapter 16 in M.S. Whittington and Glen Williams, eds., *Canadian Politics in the 1990s*, 4th ed. (Toronto: Nelson Canada, 1995).

2 Quoted with permission of Michael Bliss.
3 Quoted with permission of Gordon Robertson.
4 Chapter 8 of Patrick Monahan's *Inside Story* is entitled 'This Dinner Has Seven Days.'
5 I am indebted to Deborah Coyne who, even before she became formal adviser to Premier Wells of Newfoundland, had been carrying on a running correspondence with Eugene Forsey expressing growing opposition to the accord. This file was placed at the disposal of Helen Forsey, who shared it with me. In the file is Forsey's agitated hand-written note of resignation from the final negotiating session that is quoted in the text. I am grateful for permission granted by Deborah Coyne to refer to and quote from this file, the original of which she has entrusted to the National Archives of Canada.

11: True Patriot Love

1 Foremost 'patriot' is columnist Michael Valpy of the *Globe and Mail*, whose annual appeal for restoration of the 'Dominion' frequently invokes the supportive shade of Forsey.
2 Forsey Papers, vol. 5, Forsey to Meighen, 20 November 1951.
3 I have been reminded by my colleague Professor Franks that Forsey could have made his critique of the anti-monarchists even more forceful had he deployed against them in full the words of that great Republican, Oliver Cromwell: 'I beseech you, *in the bowels of Christ*, think it possible that you may be mistaken.'

12: Keeping the Faith

1 Arthur R.M. Lower, *Colony to Nation: History of Canada* (Toronto: Longmans, Green, 1946), 567.

Index